CHURCH, STATE, AND JEW IN THE MIDDLE AGES

Edited, with

introductions and notes, by

ROBERT CHAZAN

BEHRMAN HOUSE, INC. | PUBLISHERS | NEW YORK

For Daniel, Michael, and Rachel

ACKNOWLEDGMENTS

The author and publisher thank the following for permission to reprint:

Basil Blackwell Publisher for selection from d'Entreves, *Aquinas Selected Political Writings.*

Burns and Oates for selections from Bruno James, *The Letters of St. Bernard of Clairvaux.*

Columbia University Press for selections from Otto of Freising, *The Deeds of Frederick Barbarossa,* trans. Charles Mierow, © 1953 by Columbia University Press, New York.

Commerce Clearing House for selections from *Las Siete Partidas* by Samuel P. Scott, published and copyright by Commerce Clearing House, Inc., Chicago, Illinois.

Dr. Solomon Grayzel for selections from *The Church and the Jews in the XIIIth Century,* published by Dropsie College, 1953 and Hermon Press, 1966.

Oxford University Press for "Because Winchester should not be deprived," and "Gold won the judges' favour," from John Appleby, *The Chronicle of Richard of Devizes.*

The Pontifical Institute of Medieval Studies for "The ma'amin said," and "If his faith is not perfect," from Joseph Kimhi's *The Book of the Covenant,* trans. Frank Talmadge, © Pontifical Institute of Medieval Studies, 1972.

Revue des études juives for "The Confessions of a Medieval Jewish Convert," by Solomon Grayzel, from *Historia Judaica,* XVII, © 1955.

The Union of American Hebrew Congregations for selection from Jacob Marcus, *The Jew in the Medieval World.*

Library of Congress Cataloging in Publication Data
Main entry under title:
Church, State, and Jew in the Middle Ages.
    (Library of Jewish studies)
    Includes index.
    1. Jews—History—70-1789—Sources.   2. Jews—Legal
status, laws, etc.—Sources.   I.   Chazan, Robert.
DS102.C48
ISBN 0-87441-302-8

CONTENTS

PREFACE

THE IMPORTANCE OF THE RELATIONSHIPS among Church, State, and Jews for an appreciation of Jewish life in the Middle Ages has long been recognized, and much effort has been expended by gifted historians on delineating the major facets of these relationships. While the subject of this volume is thus not new, the approach is somewhat unusual. Rather than attempting to dissect and describe the relationships among Church, State, and Jews, the volume presents in organized fashion a series of primary documents illustrating these key aspects of medieval Jewish existence in the idiom of the period itself.

While source readers for the study of history in general and Jewish history in particular now abound, certain periods present special problems. Medieval Jewish history is one such problematic epoch. The evidence for reconstructing the medieval Jewish experience is after all not copious. Moreover, the materials that have survived are often couched in an idiom foreign to modern readers. Given the extensive interest in medieval Jewish history, the effort to provide further sources in English translation is fully justified. In addition, the endeavor to present texts organized around key aspects of medieval Jewish existence seems all the more worthwhile.

The relationships among Church, State, and Jews set the stage for Jewish experience in the Middle Ages. Where these relations were wholesome and generous, Jewish life flourished; where relations were constricted and unduly limited, Jewish life was inevitably crippled and sometimes impossible. A source reader depicting aspects of these critical relationships can thus serve as a broad introduction to medieval Jewry, its limitations and achievements.

The area included in this study is termed "medieval western Christendom" or "medieval western Europe." These terms refer to the large area in which the Roman Catholic Church played a dominant role and imposed a measure of unity. More specifically, this area includes the Iberian Peninsula, southern France, Italy, England, northern France, Germany, and Poland. It is of course clear that there were great differences in the organization of Christian and Jewish existence in this large geographic expanse, but the inclusion of documents from these widely varying lands reveals fundamental aspects of Jewish life which were by and large shared throughout this vast territory.

The term "Middle Ages," when applied to Jewish history, has given rise to endless debate. There is strong disagreement over the essential characteristics of the Middle Ages of Jewish history, and over the starting point and termination of the period. Since this volume does not treat the entire Jewish world, there is no need to enter into that debate. What can be sought, rather, is some chronological period appropriate to the development of the Jewries of medieval western Christendom. While the roots of these Jewish communities are quite old, stretching back into the Roman Empire, it has been decided for the purposes of this collection to deal with the new societal structure that emerged in the wake of the Carolingian Empire and with the new forms of Jewish life which that civilization spawned. This means a starting point somewhere in the sparsely documented tenth and eleventh centuries, when a new European civilization began to emerge in the north and Christian rule began to expand on the Iberian Peninsula in the south. The bulk of the documents presented derive from the central centuries in the development of this new society, that is, from the eleventh through thirteenth centuries. Only occasional sources from later centuries are included. The emphasis on the eleventh through thirteenth centuries derives from an interest in utilizing the earliest texts available and in seeing significant aspects of Jewish life in their primitive stages of development.

In a number of instances, two or more texts relating to the same incident are presented. In most such cases, the materials are both Christian and Jewish. This combination affords an added dimension, for it discloses some of the conflicting perspectives of the Middle Ages on Jewish existence. The reader thus has the opportunity to study not only the relationships among Church, State, and Jews, but a variety of perceptions of these relationships as well. Protection of the Jews may be perceived as an unusual act of human kindness by one group or as a venal act motivated by Jewish bribery and Christian greed by another. The slaughter of Jewish youngsters by their parents during periods of crisis is to one set of observers the very highest form of martyrdom and self-sacrifice, while to another it is an act of unspeakable barbarity. An awareness of conflicting perspectives adds a significant and fascinating dimension to the study of history.

Organizing the documents for a volume such as this is no easy task. The simplest expedient, organization by geographical provenance or chronological period, is the least useful. In a volume designed to illustrate the relationships among Church, State, and Jews, the only acceptable mode of organization is to isolate key elements in these relationships and to gather data highlighting these elements. In each case, an effort has been made to identify the most useful setting for the text in question. So long as the reader remains sensitive to the varied implications of every document, he will benefit from the organizational framework of the volume without being restricted by it.

The first two parts present broad ecclesiastical and secular statements concerning the Jews and their status. The position of the Church is the more fully and carefully articulated of the two, in part because of the impressive hierarchical organization of the Roman Catholic Church. The ecclesiastical statements are taken from a variety of sources, including papal pronouncements, conciliar decrees, legal codes, and theological formulations. Expressions of the secular position toward the Jews are far more primitive. The major source utilized is the series of charters granted to Jewish communities. While these do not in fact give a broad and balanced depiction of the status of the Jews, they are the closest approximation to a comprehensive statement of State policy.

The remaining four parts focus on one or another aspect of the relationships among Church, State, and Jews. Part Three deals with efforts to provide physical security and safety—obviously a matter of utmost significance for the Jews. We first see ecclesiastical warnings against violence, followed by secular actions to obviate, suppress, or punish attacks upon the Jews. Part Four presents the interaction between Church and State in promulgating and enforcing some of the restrictions upon Jewish life which ecclesiastical leadership saw as indispensable. We observe both friction and agreement over two particularly significant campaigns of restriction, the first against blasphemy in Talmudic literature and the second against Jewish usury. Part Five illustrates the Church's ongoing effort to proselytize among the Jews, while Part Six highlights a variety of modes of governmental persecution of the Jews. These closing two parts involve a series of actions which were highly deleterious from the Jewish point of view. The movement of the last four parts is thus from protection to restriction to negation.

Individual texts will, it is hoped, lead attentive readers in many directions. Even to the modern observer, looking back over the centuries, with all the advantages that hindsight confers, there remains a sense of bewildering complexity and of ongoing historical development. It is that sense which this volume of historical sources attempts to capture and convey.

I would like to thank my colleague Professor Joseph Lynch of the Department of History at The Ohio State University for his generous and good-natured help with difficult Latin passages. I also wish to thank Neal Kozodoy for his editing of the text, and Ms. Lisa Berland and Mrs. Gerry Gould for preparing the whole for publication.

In dedicating this book to my three children, I express both paternal feeling and the hope that this volume may help answer some of the questions which they—and other young people like them—often voice about the Jewish past.

Robert Chazan
Columbus, Ohio

INTRODUCTION

THE JEWISH SITUATION in medieval western Christendom was a most difficult one. Constituting only a tiny minority of the population, the Jews were widely viewed as latecomers and interlopers. In a society that was highly homogeneous, united primarily by the Roman Catholic Church and its standards of Christian practice and belief, the Jews stood out as the major dissenting element in society, a people in fact stigmatized not only by religious dissent but by the charge of deicide as well. To the extent that feelings of national and ethnic identity developed in medieval western Europe, the Jews were isolated yet further.

Thus the basic realities of Jewish existence were isolation, circumscription, and animosity. Jews tended to reside in separate neighborhoods as a result both of their own desires and of the will of the Christian majority. They were normally quite limited in their economic outlets, plying those trades in which Christians for one reason or another were not prepared to engage. As a consequence of these economic restrictions, the Jews could never constitute a significant percentage of any urban settlement; they were constantly forced to limit their numbers in the towns. Social relations between Jews and Christians were stringently regulated, again reflecting the wishes of both majority and minority. Underlying this rigid delimitation of the Jewish position, and reinforced by the anomalous situation of the Jews, was a constant, unabating hostility. In normal times, this animosity was kept under control; in periods of stress it flared with murderous violence. Among the potential targets for mob assault in medieval western Christendom, none ranked higher than the Jews.

As Jews cast about for security in this inhospitable and dangerous environment, only two possibilities emerged: the twin pillars of authority in medieval Christian society—the Church and the State. The Jews quickly learned that although the Roman Catholic Church fostered much anti-Jewish animosity and pressed for many of the most irksome limitations on Jewish life, its basic position toward the Jews included safeguards for Jewish life and property and a recognition of the right to practice Judaism within the Christian world. As for the ruling authorities, they too could offer protection, if for different reasons. For the princes, the decisive issue was not theological tradition but pragmatism. Violation of Jewish rights threatened the political stability and the economic progress of their realms and diminished their immediate personal revenues as well. Thus, a study of Church, State, and Jews in the Middle Ages entails an analysis of the critical relationships which allowed Jews to settle and flourish in medieval western Christendom. The decline or disintegration of these relationships meant the decline or dissolution of Jewish life.

In the development of medieval western Christendom, the Church played a special role. It was the most cohesive institution in Europe and thus served as a unifying force in a badly fragmented and divided area; it had the strongest sense of historical continuity and thus bound medieval society to the great epochs of earlier Christian history; by virtue of its control of education, it was provided with the most highly trained bureaucracy available at the time. But, above all else, the Church administered the sacraments, shaped the education and culture of Christian society, and articulated the goals of that society. The vision of a truly Christian existence, both for the individual and for the group, was the province of the Church and its leadership.

The Church's establishment of priorities for Christian living derived from a careful balancing of the political, economic, social, and cultural realities of European life with the accepted legacy of Church doctrine bequeathed from antiquity. The realities of tenth-century Europe differed substantially from those of the earlier ages of Christian history, and hence the doctrines of an earlier Church faced inevitable modification. At all times, however, the Church made every effort to articulate clearly and fully the accepted norms of Christian behavior and belief as it then understood them.

In many senses the Church was highly successful in its attempts to consolidate the religious life of medieval Europe. Medieval western Christendom was remarkably homogeneous. The Christian faith dominated in a way that has rarely been duplicated. Few non-Christians made their way into medieval western Christendom, and, despite periodic outbreaks of heresy, few Christians diverged sharply from the officially sanctioned tenets of the faith. It is in the light of this homogeneity that the Jews loomed as an important factor in the eyes of the Church. As small as the Jewish community of medieval western Christendom was, it represented the only major non-Christian group in almost all the states of western Europe, and hence had to be dealt with by the Church as a special facet of European reality.

The mere presence of Jews as the major dissenting group in medieval western Christendom would have sufficed to arouse Church concern, but there were further complications as well. Coupled with the reality of Jewish presence and Jewish influence was the complex tradition of Christian-Jewish relations. From its earliest history, Christianity had sought to define its relationship to Judaism or, more specifically, to buttress its claim that it had supplanted the older faith. The Church shared the Jewish view that there could be but one true faith, and that this faith was introduced to mankind by the patriarchs, by Moses, and by the prophets. Upon breaking out of the Jewish community, the Church strongly asserted that its practices and doctrines entitled it to the title of True Israel, the genuine heir to the legacy of Abraham, Isaac, and Jacob. Such a claim had clear-cut implications for the Jews and the Judaism that continued to exist after the advent of Jesus of Nazareth. In the Christian view, Judaism had lost its vitality and viability and had degenerated into the fossilized remnant of a once eloquent vision. It was an Israel of the flesh, a pointless foil to the Israel of the spirit.

The animosity felt toward Judaism and Jews derived only partially, however, from these abstract considerations of theological truth. In the process of retelling the life of Jesus, the early Church made the failures of the Jews, as it perceived them, tangible and compelling. It cast the Jews in the role of the deniers of Jesus, responsible for the ultimate crime: his death. The concept of the Jews as deicides, and that concept's symbolic expression at major moments in the Christian calendar, served to widen immeasurably the gulf that in any case existed between mother faith and daughter faith. Artistic representations of the Jews as Christ-killers imprinted an indelible image upon the minds of even the humblest and most ignorant of Europe's Christian populace. In sum, the reality of a Jewish presence, the theological quarrel between the two faiths, and popular imagery served to keep Christian Europe conscious of Jews and Judaism.

What, then, was the basic stance of the Church toward European Jewry? In the first place, the Church proclaimed the fundamental right of Jews to live safely in a Christian society. Although much of the insecurity of Jewish life in medieval Europe stemmed from the theological claims and the evocative imagery of the Church, and although important figures in the Church often played a prominent role in inciting anti-Jewish feeling, nevertheless, ecclesiastical leadership resolutely advanced the notion of toleration. Jews were to live in physical safety; they were to be permitted to organize their own affairs within their communities; and they were to enjoy the freedom of worshiping according to their tradition and of following Jewish law.

Many factors combined to produce this stance of toleration. One was the reality of Jewish economic contribution to the developing European society. Just as the State was greatly influenced by such considerations, so too was the Church. But the Church's vision of Christian life was affected by more than contemporary realities; it was also bound by its legacy. On this issue, the early Church, upon achieving power in the Roman Empire, had announced a position of toleration of Jews and Judaism. The reasons cited for this toleration varied. For some early authorities, the Jews, by their devotion to the Old Testament, supplied proof for the truth of Christianity. Although the Jews themselves had failed to perceive that which the Church saw as the true message of Isaiah and Jeremiah, they did, by virtue of their acceptance of Isaiah and Jeremiah as divinely inspired prophets, serve to buttress the argument of Christianity to the pagan world. For others, the Jews afforded different evidence of the truth of Christianity. Their dispersal and oppressed condition was itself an indication of the veracity of the ruling faith, revealing clearly the punishment meted out to those who had failed to acknowledge Jesus. Yet another view saw the ultimate conversion of the Jews as one of the harbingers of redemption: The Jews must be preserved, for without them the drama of redemption could not begin. While none of these theories accorded much dignity to post-biblical Judaism, they did at least serve as a rationale for preserving the Jewish people and their religion.

This doctrine of basic protection of Jewish faith and lives, however, was only a part of the story. For while both reality and theory dictated preservation of the Jews, Jewish life had to be structured so that it did not detract from the effort to transform Europe into a truly Christian society. Although maintaining that it was permissible for Jews to observe Judaism, the Church viewed with horror the possible spread of the Jewish rite, and imposed a series of demands designed to obviate any detrimental Jewish impact. Thus, Jews were not to occupy any position which might afford them power and hence influence over their Christian neighbors. Jews were not to own Christian slaves, nor were Jews to serve as public officials.

Concern focused not only on the influence conferred by authority, but even over the impact of excessive contact. Increasingly, the medieval Church demanded isolation of the Jews, as the means for avoiding the spread of Judaism. The Church came to call for the legalization of the *de facto* reality of separate Jewish neighborhoods, and the removal of Jews from small towns and villages where substantial contact between Jew and Christian was inevitable. Unquestionably the most extreme form taken by this drive for isolation was the introduction, in the thirteenth century, of distinguishing garb. The special badge or cap was intended to make Jews readily identifiable at all times. In a sense, the Jewishness associated with a special residential area thus became portable; the Jew was to bear his Jewishness with him at all times. The essential purpose behind all this legislation was the same: The Jews had to be isolated in order to minimize or eliminate any potential religious influence.

In addition to the concern with limiting Jewish religious influence, various aspects of Jewish life demanded ecclesiastical attention. Given the Church's aspirations for a broad and inclusive system to govern every facet of Christian society, many activities of the Jews had to come under special scrutiny. Concerning material issues, the Church was constantly alert to the methods by which Jews made their livelihoods and to possible problems which might arise. The most striking instances of this concern are associated with moneylending, which by the twelfth century had become the mainstay of northern-European Jewish economic life. In a sense the Church itself paved the way for this Jewish specialization through its efforts to enforce traditional anti-usury prohibitions within the Christian populace. The more successful these efforts were, however, the more concerned the Church became with the development of Jewish usury, defined simply as any profit realized from the lending of funds. This concern stemmed in part from the tangible social results of Jewish usury: the impoverishment of Christians, the pressures brought to bear on those unable to repay their loans, the loss of family estates—all these excited recriminations against Jewish usury in ecclesiastical circles. At the same time, some churchmen objected to the theoretical basis for the Jews' right to take interest from Christians. In any case, powerful ecclesiastical opposition to Jewish moneylending had developed by the late twelfth and early thirteenth centuries. To this it must be added that Jewish material well-being of any kind, whether expressed in elaborate institutions or in ostentatious individual behavior, was enough to arouse Church opposition, since it was held that the secondary status of the Jews should be reflected in their mode of living. For such an inferior group to live in luxury was thought to be an affront to the faith of the majority.

The effort to restrict Jewish life went beyond the realm of material affairs. While the basic doctrine of toleration included an affirmation of the Jews' right to practice their religion, it was understood that Jewish belief and practice could not be expressed in a fashion offensive to Christianity. Any Jewish practices that might seem disparaging to the majority religion were thus forbidden. This meant, first of all, that routine Jewish behavior was occasionally subject to restriction. Jews were expected to comport themselves on Sundays and festivals in a manner appropriate to the sanctity and tranquillity of those days. Particularly sensitive was the issue of Holy Week, because of the role imputed to the Jews in the crucifixion of Jesus. Since many Christians suspected the Jews of mocking the lamentations over their fallen messiah, there was an effort to remove Jews from the public scene altogether during this strained period.

More significant yet was a concern with the possibility that Jewish religious practice might include blasphemy against the ruling faith. There were good grounds for such suspicions. In the first place, Christian liturgy was studded with pejorative references to the Jews and Judaism, and many churchmen may well have assumed that Jewish rites responded in kind. Moreover, the strong commitment of Jews to Judaism and their equally strong dislike of Christianity were made manifest in the occasional attacks against Jewry by popular forces. These demonstrations of Jewish rejection of Christianity remained in the Christian mind long after the passions generated by violence subsided, reinforcing suspicions of Jewish enmity and blasphemy. These suspicions were present during the early centuries of the Middle Ages, when churchmen in fact knew very little of post-biblical Judaism; beginning with the twelfth century and increasingly during the thirteenth century, as Christian knowledge of Talmudic tradition developed, churchmen became more fully aware of materials harshly derisive of Christianity. The result was a series of trials and condemnations of the

Talmud, followed by practical efforts either to suppress Talmudic literature in its entirety or at least to expunge harmful passages. For the Church, this was an absolutely necessary protection of the dignity and honor of the ruling faith; for the Jews, it constituted critical interference with the heart of Jewish religious literature and doctrine.

Finally, while the right of Jews to practice Judaism was recognized by the Church and while there was even a notion that Judaism must continue to exist down to the time of redemption, there nonetheless remained the strong desire to attract individual Jews into the Christian fold. The use of force in such missionizing was consistently eschewed by the Church. Conversion was seen as a decision of the heart, which could be truly made only with the fullest free will. Techniques of persuasion were developed, however, to draw Jews out of their community and into Christendom. One step in this campaign was to smooth the path of the convert materially. There were extensive efforts to ensure that the convert was not penalized by the secular authorities as a result of his opting for the Christian faith. The Church insisted, for example, that the convert was not to lose any of his hereditary rights. Beyond this, the Church itself actively provided for its converts: As a great institution of charity and social welfare the Church had ample resources with which to succor converts in need. The general principle was that, at a minimum, converts should not suffer by virtue of their decisions and, if possible, their circumstances should be improved.

Such material considerations, however, were secondary. The real struggle took place on the spiritual plane, where the fundamental challenge was to reveal the flaws of Judaism and the truths of Christianity. Here, as in so many other areas, the twelfth and thirteenth centuries brought an intensification of ecclesiastical concern and activity. Up until that point churchmen were satisfied to repeat older arguments for the veracity of Christianity, arguments based mainly on biblical texts. Such claims, which had no real impact on the Jews, served largely to reinforce the sense of superiority of Christian authors and readers. With the thirteenth century, all this began to change. In particular western Christendom became far more committed to serious missionizing. Partly, this was related to the failures of military crusading; as a sense of this failure struck more deeply into medieval western Europe, hopes for military success were replaced by plans for spiritually overwhelming the world of Islam. Intensified proselytizing also stemmed from the great intellectual advances of the period and the growing sense of the absolute rationality of Christianity. The specific effort at missionizing among the Jews was further stimulated by a group of zealous ex-Jews anxious to win over their former brethren, and by the new information which these converts brought with them. By the middle of the thirteenth century, the Church had proceeded far beyond the old arguments based on biblical verses. By this time it was relatively well-informed about rabbinic Judaism and was able to mount arguments based on accurate knowledge of contemporary Jewish practice and belief.

Two major techniques for missionizing among the Jews predominated during the latter half of the thirteenth century. The first was forced preaching: Gathered against their will, Jews were subjected to sermons—debasing Judaism and extolling Christianity—which were often delivered by devoted new converts. The second technique was the forced debate: A leader or a number of leaders in the Jewish community were assembled for an involuntary confrontation with a Christian spokesman or spokesmen, again many times drawn from the ranks of recent converts. The new stress on proselytizing, the new personnel devoted to approaching the Jews, the new information and arguments, and the new techniques of the forced sermon and the forced debate combined to produce far more effective results than earlier missionizing had.

These, then, were the major thrusts of medieval Church policy toward the Jews. It was one thing, however, to define policy concerning the Jews; it was another to implement that policy. Rarely was the Church itself in direct control of the Jews. Only when a churchman functioned as the Jews' secular overlord could ecclesiastical policies be enforced directly, and there is in fact little evidence that churchmen were particularly zealous when such opportunities presented themselves. More typically, Jews were subservient to a series of secular authorities, ranging from the emperor and the great kings down through many insignificant barons. Under these circumstances the Church could only implement its programs by winning the support of the Jews' overlords. Whether the goal was protection of the Jews, restriction of Jewish life, or missionizing, the Church normally had to seek out the assistance of the political authorities in achieving its purposes. And on the issue of the Jews, as on so many other issues, Church and State often cooperated, and often disagreed.

The role of the State in medieval western Christendom was, in theory at least, complementary to that of the Church. The secular authorities were charged with the responsibility of protecting society from all dangers, both external and internal, and of executing those Church programs for which their cooperation was needed. While this was the theory, in reality the secular rulers of medieval Europe tended inevitably to enlarge their sphere of action, often coming into conflict with the hierarchy of the Church as a result.

As noted earlier, Jews came to the attention of the Church because of both their actual presence in western Europe and the theological frictions of Christian-Jewish relations. For the medieval State, however, there were no abstract problems concerning the Jews, nor any longstanding tradition of governmental policy with which to contend. Authorities were by and large free to relate to the Jews in terms of contemporary realities. This meant, first of all, that the economic utility of the Jews was a major consideration of the State. Both for altruistic and selfish reasons, the ruling class in medieval Europe was committed to fostering economic development and growth. Particularly during the tenth, eleventh, and twelfth centuries, there was broad awareness of the need for urban development, of the lack of an indigenous urban population, and of the potential contribution which the Jews might make. As the bishop of Speyer noted in the preamble to his generous charter of 1084: "When I wished to make a city out of the village of Speyer, I, Rudiger, surnamed Huozmann, bishop of Speyer, thought that the glory of our town would be augmented a thousandfold if I were to bring Jews."

One of the most pressing problems of the maturing states of western Europe was revenue. Without revenue the activities of defense, aggrandizement, and expansion could not take place. Yet the rulers of these emerging states were severely limited in the funds at their disposal. In a society where tradition was venerated and innovation abhorred, new financial needs could hardly produce new taxes. The Christian population felt itself securely protected against such effrontery on the part of its rulers. Since the needs were so pressing, the ruling class sought new techniques for acquiring the necessary funds. One such method involved the Jews. Because of their special status, the Jews could not appeal to a tradition of protection and they were thus taxable almost at will. In this sense, Jews were a direct personal boon to the ruler under whose authority they lived. In fact, it was clearly perceived by both Christian and Jewish observers that fiscal exploitation of the Jews went one step further. Not only did the State tolerate Jewish presence in order to benefit from Jewish taxes; in many cases the authorities actively supported lucrative Jewish business, so that expanding Jewish profits could then be heavily assessed. Viewed in this way, the State and the Jews became business partners, with revenue shared between them. The Jews acted as a vehicle through which funds could be extracted from the

Christian population and directed to government coffers. This function, while making the Jews important to their overlords, made them hated among the populace.

There was yet another immediate benefit which the Jews conferred upon their overlords. As the states of western Europe slowly coalesced, the authorities had to build for themselves a base of power and support. In the never-ending struggle for power, the Jews were again particularly useful. Lacking roots in the population at large and totally dependent on the protection proffered by their overlords, the Jews were fully trusted allies of the rulers of western Europe.

The rulers of western Christendom, hardly restricted by considerations of tradition and accepted practice, were relatively free to follow the dictates of utility. This freedom, however, was far from absolute, for there were a number of constraints at work. The first, and most significant, was the pressure of the Roman Catholic Church. The Church had a fully developed and articulated program of regulations and restrictions which it called upon the Jews' overlords to introduce. While on many occasions various rulers decided to neglect Church teaching and pursue their own interests and desires, the cumulative effect of ongoing Church pressure cannot be denied. The clergy was zealous in carrying its message to the secular courts, and this tenacity was rewarded. The rulers were, willingly or unwillingly, forced to implement much of Church doctrine.

There was a second pressure brought upon the Jews' overlords— pressure related to that of the Church and yet distinct. This was the force of popular will. The masses of medieval Europe were unorganized and leaderless; their will was normally shaped and expressed by churchmen. Yet, at the same time, crude attitudes did exist, could be felt, and occasionally had an impact. Popular animosity toward the Jews was a brute fact of medieval European life. In a real sense, the rulers of medieval Europe fanned this hostility by exploiting the Jews. By aiding Jews in profiting from the masses and then by surreptitiously enjoying the fruits of those profits, the governing authorities circumvented the restrictions that bound them and left the Jews holding the bag of popular hatred. The authorities could not be oblivious to that hatred, which became yet another pressure on the State, leading often to restriction of certain Jewish activities and occasionally to persecution of the Jews as a means of currying favor with the masses.

From the interplay of all these factors, what coherent governmental positions developed? Like the Church, albeit for different reasons, the State emphasized the Jewish right to safety and security. While in the

case of the Church this emphasis was rooted in theological considerations, the State's position was again primarily pragmatic. In the first
place, an essential function of the State was to maintain internal stability
and tranquillity. All internal disturbances were dangerous, for what
began as rioting against the Jews might well end as a broad anti-establish-
ment movement. The general tendency of governments to preserve law
and order thus had specific implications for the stance of the medieval
State toward its Jews. A second consideration that prompted energetic
protection of the Jews was concern for the Jews' broad economic contribution. Disruption of Jewish life was seen as damaging to general
economic well-being. Most decisive, however, was the ruling class's
anxiety over its own immediate losses. As noted, the Jews were an
important source of governmental revenues. Assaults on the Jews meant
direct and tangible loss to their rulers. This, more than anything else,
won them the protection of their overlords.

On all these grounds, then, the Jews were normally accorded substantial protection by the secular authorities. This meant warnings
against violence when passions were inflamed, efforts to put down
violence when it did flare up, and finally, imposition of heavy penalties
when the attempts at protection failed and Jews suffered loss of life and
property. The basic thrust of governmental policy toward the Jews was
protection. When the rulers of medieval western Christendom were
strong enough to protect their Jewish subjects, the Jews lived in relative
tranquillity; when the basic policy of protection shifted or when the ruling class was too weak to enforce its will, tragedy confronted the Jews.

While both the Church and State pursued a policy of guaranteeing
Jewish safety, there was much disagreement over the conditions to be
established for Jewish existence. Given its interests, the State tended to
support favorable conditions which would stimulate Jewish settlement,
Jewish profits, and Jewish taxes. Most of the charters issued by the
rulers of medieval western Christendom reflect this position. In many
instances, the State went beyond the promulgation of favorable legislation; it actually involved itself in Jewish business affairs and afforded
specific aids to its Jews, particularly in the vexing area of collection of
outstanding obligations. This was, to be sure, not disinterested and
charitable intervention; a portion of the monies thus realized would
inevitably make its way to governmental coffers. Yet, Church leaders
often criticized such practices on two grounds. First, Jewish prosperity
in and of itself was offensive, and this prosperity was all the more galling
in that it seemed to flow from exploitation of the Christian masses.
Secondly, there was anxiety over the flaunting of specific Church prohi-

bitions. Thus the Church opposed a policy supportive of the Jews. It was in this area that the major Church-State clash over the Jews took place. The Church fought both to counteract secular support for Jewish business affairs and to lobby for implementation of its restrictive legislation. As ecclesiastical power grew, particularly in the thirteenth century, the Church was increasingly successful in winning governmental backing for its programs. With growing governmental enactment of Church-sponsored limitations on Jewish life, the fortunes of western-European Jewry inevitably suffered.

In addition to their roles as protectors of the Jews, supporters of Jewish enterprises, or circumscribers of Jewish activities, governments occasionally played the part of persecutor. Most often the motivation was simple cupidity. Pressed for funds, many rulers chose the expedient of despoiling the relatively defenseless Jews. Of course, in the process, these rulers gave up a fairly secure and stable future income. At moments of crisis, however, it was difficult to keep in mind long-range benefits; the weight of immediate needs often proved decisive. On occasion there were other motivations as well. Rulers would sometimes turn against their Jews as a means of winning favor with the masses. Anti-Jewish actions would normally raise the standing of the prince in the eyes of his Christian subjects. Finally, the secular authorities of medieval Europe sometimes persecuted their Jews out of genuine conviction of Jewish malevolence and wrongdoing. There was, of course, no reason why the higher classes should be totally immune to the virus of hatred that so widely infected the masses.

The most common form of mistreatment of the Jews was economic despoliation. Heavy fines were imposed on Jewish communities; special taxes were levied; Jews were detained or imprisoned and their goods confiscated. In some cases, Jews were physically attacked by those who normally labored to defend them from assault. The most decisive form of mistreatment was the abrogation of the formal relationship between ruler and Jew. Given the Jews' total dependence upon their overlords, annulment of the promise of protection and revocation of the right of settlement meant an end to Jewish presence in any given area.

The range of governmental positions was thus wide. The secular authorities of western Christendom normally protected the Jews living under their jurisdiction, sometimes supported their activities, sometimes restricted their activities, and occasionally turned upon them, endangering or ending their existence in the overlord's domain. For the Jews of medieval Europe, the stance of their rulers was critical. Only those rulers could enable them to overcome the broad animus that prevailed in

Christian society; without such backing, Jewish life was an impossibility. Emphasis has been laid thus far on the attitudes of Church and State toward the Jews of medieval western Christendom. It would be misleading, however, to present the Jews as wholly passive, totally at the mercy of the larger society about them. Certainly the options open to the Jews of medieval western Christendom were highly limited. Nonetheless, within circumscribed bounds, these Jews were active in attempting to influence their own destiny.

The first area in which the Jews exercised their own independence was in the decision to become a part of medieval western Christendom. While demographic data are sparse for the Middle Ages, it is widely agreed that the existing Jewish population of western Europe grew during the tenth, eleventh, and twelfth centuries. What caused the Jews already living in this region to remain, and what attracted new settlers? Jews were surely not blind to the fundamental hostilities and the pervasive dangers which we have depicted. The decision to remain or to settle seems to reflect a sense of opportunity, a sense that this was a dynamically expanding area in which Jews might carve out for themselves a useful and dignified place. Only hindsight tells us that a permanent position of dignity was not to be. The signs were promising enough to draw numbers of Jews and their families to this developing new center of civilization.

Once settled in medieval western Christendom, there was nothing that the Jews, as a tiny minority, could do to alter radically the structure of the society in which they had chosen to live. What they could do was to exploit as fully as possible the avenues open to them. Particularly important was their ability to fulfill the economic function which loomed so large in the eyes of their overlords. The fundamental physical security of the entire Jewish community rested on the economic achievements of its members. Yet Jews could hardly be blind to the dangers involved in their economic successes; they must have been aware of the ill feelings harbored by the masses. Nonetheless, there was no real alternative. The masses were hostile in any case; the key to Jewish well-being lay in the support of the ruling class; and the key to such support lay in the general and specific benefits to be gleaned from Jewish economic achievement. Little wonder, then, that Jews should have devoted themselves so assiduously to business affairs.

Beyond this basic drive toward the success which would win the backing of those whose protection they so sorely needed, the Jews had to develop their negotiating skills. This meant, first of all, an awareness of the political realities in their particular areas of settlement. Who was strong and who was weak? What was the power and influence of the Church? What was the potential impact of the masses? In addition, Jews had to learn to marshal the proper arguments for the proper audience, to balance appeals to the general economic good with tangible douceurs, to mix arguments for general societal stability with references to Christian theological doctrines promising protection for Jewish life, limb, and property. Unfortunately, little evidence of this ongoing Jewish negotiation has survived. Those sources which do remain preserve for us a sense of keen awareness and of the need to develop the skills of manipulation. For the Jews, such skills were indispensable.

Thus the Jews were not simply pawns, passively observing their fate being meted out. At the same time, it is equally clear that the range of options open to these Jews was strictly limited. The challenge of medieval Jewish life in western Christendom was to enhance influence and support, while minimizing opposition and restriction. Within the narrow bounds available to them the Jews were relatively successful, particularly during the expansive periods of the eleventh through the thirteenth centuries.

These brief observations sketch the outline of the relationships among Church, State, and Jews during the Middle Ages. The reality was far more complex. The collected documents are intended to substantiate the generalizations that have been advanced, to modify and refine them, and, most important, to introduce the reader into the historical diversity which primary sources capture and convey.

PART ONE

THE
FORMAL POSITION
OF THE CHURCH

INTRODUCTION

THE MEDIEVAL CHURCH had a strong intellectual tradition and was deeply concerned with establishing norms for both behavior and belief. It is thus not surprising that considerable effort was expended in attempting to define the status of Jewry and Judaism in both practical and theoretical terms.

In the drive to formulate Church norms, there were two decisive authorities, the received teachings of earlier ages and new pronouncements by contemporary ecclesiastical leadership. Obviously, a major task was collating this mass of diverse materials and resolving whatever discrepancies might come to light. This chapter begins with a series of citations from Gratian's *Decretum*, the great twelfth-century effort to compile earlier Church law. The impact of this code was enormous; thus the specific statements cited in regard to the Jews were destined to be widely quoted by subsequent churchmen.

A century later, with rising papal authority, Church law had expanded rapidly. A number of private collections of papal decrees were in use, but all of these were superseded by the authoritative code commissioned by Pope Gregory IX and compiled by Raymond of Penaforte. In the section devoted to the Jews, the first three canons are quoted from early authorities, but all the following are taken from twelfth- and thirteenth-century papal pronouncements. Like the *Decretum*, the *Decretales* had great impact and was widely studied; its statements relative to the Jews and Judaism were of decisive significance.

While the *Decretales* organize Church law chronologically, by citation of major papal edicts, there were also efforts made at a more systematic presentation of ecclesiastical doctrine. One such synthesis was effected by the same Raymond of Penaforte, some years prior to his compiling the *Decretales*. In this synthesis we see an effort to define the Jews and their place in western Christendom.

Church efforts at systematization included theological doctrine as well as legal norms. Deeply involved with issues of religious belief and committed to articulating the principles underlying Christian behavior, the Church had a rich tradition of theological speculation. This tradition was both challenged and enhanced during the twelfth and thirteenth centuries by newly translated works of Greek and Arabic philosophy. The result was the reformulation and systemization of Christian belief, culminating in the broad and inclusive *summae* of the thirteenth century. Like so many issues, the problem of the Jews found its place in these majestic syntheses. Here we shall see an effort to move beyond practice and to define the basic theory of Jewish existence in Christendom. Why in theory should Jews be tolerated in Christian society, or why should they not be tolerated? After the pros and cons had been examined, were they in fact to be accepted or not? What was the status of Jewish ritual? Then, given the broad definition of Jewish status, what were some of the implications for the place which Jews were to occupy in the Christian world? These are some of the questions posed by the theologians. Again the thrust is toward a clarification of the position of the Jews, with its positive and negative features. The *summa* which we shall examine, that of Alexander of Hales, exhibits the quest for order and understanding and also takes a specific position toward the Jews.

This section thus focuses on four major statements of Church doctrine concerning the Jews. Each of these formulations reveals major ecclesiastical attitudes; because of their significance, all four also contributed to the developing definition of the roles of Judaism and the Jews.

1 THE TEACHINGS OF EARLIER EPOCHS: GRATIAN'S *DECRETUM*

DURING THE ELEVENTH and twelfth centuries, as the level of civilization in western Christendom rose, there was increasing knowledge of the legacy of the past and a growing desire to codify that legacy. While a number of efforts at codification were made in the late eleventh and early twelfth centuries, it was the compilation of the Italian monk, Gratian, completed in the early 1140s, that emerged as the authoritative statement of Church law. A vast work, Gratian's Decretum drew upon a wide variety of sources and attempted to arrange these materials in a useful manner and to reconcile some of the contradictions among different sources. While never officially recognized by papal authority, Gratian's work had an enormous influence. It was extensively studied, commented upon, and utilized as a definitive statement of Church norms.

Gratian devoted no special section of his compilation to the Jews. Instead, items relating to the Jews were included at a number of points. From these discrete references, however, emerges a broad sense of the Church's view of the Jewish place in Christendom. On the one hand, Jews are to be allowed to exercise their faith and are not to be coerced into accepting Christianity. An important letter of Pope Gregory I and a canon of the Fourth Toledan Council are cited as proof texts for this principle. At the same time, Gratian introduces a number of texts designed to circumscribe the actions of the Jews. Most important, the Jews, while free to observe their religion, must not be permitted to spread their faith by influencing others. Specifically, Jews are not to marry Christians; they are not to own Christian slaves; and they are not to occupy public office. While Jews are not to be forced into the Christian fold, they are to be persuaded of Christian truth whenever possible. Gratian notes a number of provisions for testing the sincerity of potential Jewish converts and also indicates that, however converted, the new adherent must not be permitted to return to his former faith.

PART I: DISTINCTIO XLV

Canon III   Others are to be invited to the faith not by harsh means, but by gentle words.

Pope Gregory to Pascasius, bishop of Naples:

Those who sincerely wish to lead people who stand outside the Christian religion into the proper faith should strive to do so by gentle means rather than by harsh means, lest adversity alienate the mind of those whom a reasonable argument would have been able to attract. For those who do otherwise and wish to force them, under such pretext, from the customary observance of their rite are seen clearly to attend to their own affairs more intently than those of God.

Certain Jews living in Naples have beseeched us claiming that some Christians have improperly attempted to hinder them from certain observances of their festivals, so that they not be permitted to practice the observances of their festivals, as they and their ancestors have been permitted to do for a long time. If this be true, then those Christians seem to be acting in vain. For of what use is it when—although they are prohibited in defiance of long usage—there is no profit toward the conversion of faith? Why should we establish rules for the Jews as to how they should observe their ceremonies, if through such rules we are unable to afford them gain? We should therefore behave in such a way that, appealed to by reason and mildness, they wish to follow us and not to flee, so that, showing them what we learn from their books, we might, with the help of God, be able to convert them to the bosom of the Mother Church. Therefore you must, as fully as possible, with the help of God, move them to convert by admonitions without permitting them to be disturbed again concerning their observances. Rather they must have the full right of observing and celebrating all their festivals and holidays. as both they and their ancestors have had for a long time past . . .

Canon V   Jews are not to be forced into the faith, although, even if they accept it unwillingly, they must be forced to retain it.

Whence in the Fourth Toledan Council it was enacted:

Just as Jews are not to be forced into the faith, so too, once converted, they are not permitted to leave it.

Concerning the Jews the Sacred Council orders that no one henceforth force them to believe. "The Lord shows mercy as He chooses, but also makes men stubborn as He chooses." For those who are unwilling are not saved, only those who are willing, so that justice remains perfect. For just as man, heeding the serpent, perished through the exercise of his own will, so too, called by the grace of God, one should be saved in faith by the conversion of his own spirit. Thus, in order that they be converted by the free exercise of will and not by force, they are to be persuaded but not impelled. However, as for those who have already been forced into Christianity, as was done at the time of the most pious Prince Siseburt, since it is manifest that they have linked themselves with the divine sacraments and have accepted the grace of baptism and have been anointed with the oil and have been participants in the body of the Lord, it is necessary that they be forced to uphold the faith which they accepted under duress or by necessity, lest the name of the Lord be brought into disrepute and the faith which they accepted be held vile and contemptible.

PART I: DISTINCTIO LIV

Canon XIII   This then is to be observed, since a lord and his slave should be of the same faith. Moreover, if a Jew purchases a Christian slave, the slave should be set free by the authority of the judge or bishop, even if the slave himself is unwilling.

Whence Pope Gregory to Bishop Libertinus:

Christian slaves purchased by Jews should be set free. You must set free, according to the precepts of the law and without delay, Christian slaves whom a Jew happens to purchase, lest—Heaven forbid!—the Christian religion be defiled by being subject to the Jews.

Canon XIV   Public offices should not be committed to Jews.

From the Third Toledan Council:

No public office shall be accorded to the Jews, offices through which opportunity might be accorded them to inflict harm upon Christians. If any Christians are defiled by them into the Jewish rite or circumcised, they shall be set free and returned to the Christian faith, without any price paid.

Canon XV   Pope Gregory indicated to Fortunatus, bishop of Naples, what should be done concerning those who, sold as infidels, desire to enter the grace of baptism:

Slaves who proceed from infidelity to faith are to be set free.

It is necessary that you be concerned, if, in place of the servitude of the Jews, not only a Jew but also a pagan wishes to become Christian, that—after his desire is clear—there be no opportunity of selling him on some pretext or subterfuge to another Jew. Rather he who desires to be converted to the Christian faith shall be set free in all ways through your protection.

Indeed it is necessary that you protect carefully those who happen to lose their slaves, lest they perhaps consider that their well-being has been improperly harmed. Thus, if it happens that pagans, whom the Jews buy from foreign lands for the sake of trade and for whom a buyer to whom they might be sold is not found within three months, flee to the Church and say that they wish to become Christians or proclaim such a desire outside the Church, then they shall receive their price from a Christian buyer. If, however, after the aforesaid three months, any of the slaves of the Jews shall declare his will and wishes to become a Christian, then no one shall purchase him, nor shall his master under any circumstances dare to sell him. Rather he shall undoubtedly receive the gift of liberty, since it is assumed that he bought him not for commerce, but for serving him.

Canon XVI   The same to Januarius, bishop of Cagliari.

If a slave of the Jews flees to a holy place because of faith, you shall not allow him to sustain damage. Rather, whether already Christian or just now baptized, he shall by all means be set free, through the proper protection of ecclesiastical piety, without any harm to the Christian poor.

Canon XVII   Also from the Twelfth Toledan Council.

If the slaves of the Jews, not yet converted, flock to the grace of Christ, they shall be granted liberty.

Canon XVIII   From the Council of Macon.

In the present council, by the authority of God, we ordain that no Christian slave shall henceforth serve a Jew. Rather, when twelve shillings have been paid for each fit slave, any Christian shall have the right of purchasing that slave, either for release or for servitude. If a slave wishes to become a Christian and is not permitted to do so he shall do likewise, since it is abominable that a blasphemer of the Christian faith hold in chains one whom the Lord Christ redeemed by the spilling of his blood. If any Jew does not wish to agree to these things which we have enacted, so long as he postpones agreement to the set sum, that slave is permitted to live with Christians wherever he wishes.

PART II: CAUSA II, QUESTIO VII

> *Canon XXV   Heretics, Jews, and pagans may not accuse Christians.*

Pope Gaius to Bishop Felix:

Pagans or heretics or Jews may not accuse Christians or impute against them a charge of infamy.

PART II: CAUSA XXVIII, QUESTIO I

> *Canon X   It is found to the contrary in the Fourth Toledan Council.*

Unless a Jew joins the faith, he is to be separated from his Christian mate.

Jews who hold Christian girls in matrimony should be admonished by the bishop of the city that, if they wish to remain with them, they must become Christians. If, once admonished, they refuse, they are to be separated, since an infidel cannot remain in union with one who has already been brought into the Christian faith. Moreover, children who are born from such parents are to follow the faith and condition of the mother. Likewise those who are born of infidel women and Christian men are to follow the Christian faith, rather than the Jewish superstition.

> *Canon XI   Indeed this is decreed lest, while the Christian seeks the salvation of the infidel, he along with the infidel shall find the damnation of infidelity.*

Whence in the same council it was decreed concerning the children of Jews as well as others coming into the faith that they leave the society of infidels.

Christians are to be removed from the fellowship of parents, lest they become entrapped in their errors.

We order that the sons and daughters of Jews be removed from the fellowship of their parents. They are instead to be sent to monasteries or to God-fearing Christian women or men, so that through contact with them they may become acquainted with the religion of faith and, better instructed in manners and in faith, they may improve themselves.

> *Canon XII   Nothing is to be shared between Jews coming into the faith and infidels.*

In the same council:

Fellowship with the wicked can often corrupt the good, especially those inclined toward vice. There is therefore to be no contact between Jews brought into the Christian faith and those who still remain in the old rite, lest they be subverted by contact with them. Therefore henceforth any of those who have been baptized and who do not shun the company of infidels are to be turned over to Christians and those infidels are to be condemned to public flogging.

> *Canon XIII   One is not to dine with Jews, to live with Jews, nor to accept medicine from them.*

From the Sixth Toledan Council:

No one who is in sacred orders or a layman shall eat their unleavened bread nor live with them nor call any of them in illness nor accept medicine from them nor bathe with them. If anyone do so—if he is a cleric, he should be deposed; if he is a layman, he should be excommunicated.

> *Canon XIV   Clerics and laymen should avoid the friendship of Jews and should not receive them at their gatherings.*

From the Council of Agde:

All clerics and laymen should avoid the fellowship of the Jews nor should anyone receive them in fellowship. For, since they do not associate with Christians in common meals, it is improper and sacrilegious that their bread be consumed by Christians. For those foods which we eat with the Apostle's permission are judged impure by them. Thus Christians will begin to be inferior to Jews, if we use those foods which are offered by them, while they disdain foods offered by us . . .

Canon XV   Thus also Ambrosius in his Book of Patriarchs.

Christians are not to be joined in wedlock with infidels.

Beware, O Christian, of giving your daughter to a Gentile or to a Jew. Beware, it is said, of seeking for yourself a Gentile or a Jewess or a stranger, i.e., a heretic, or anyone foreign to your faith as a wife.

If the woman is Christian, it is not sufficient, unless you are both initiated by the sacrament of baptism. Likewise you are to arise at night for prayer, and God is to be beseeched in joint supplication . . .

Canon XVII   He who associates himself by conjugal bond to Jewish depravity shall be cut off.

From the Council of Auverne:

If anyone joins himself by conjugal bond to Jewish depravity, whether a Christian female is joined by carnal bond to a Jew or a Jewess to a Christian male, and is known to admit such a misdeed, he shall be excluded from Christian assembly and society and from the communion of the Church.

PART III: DE CONSECRATIONE, DISTINCTIO IV

Canon XCIII   For how many months Jews are to be held among the catechumens.

From the Council of Agde:

When Jews, whose perfidy often leads back to their vomit, wish to enter the Christian fold, they shall enter for eight months among the catechumens of the Church. If they are known to enter in pure faith, only then shall they merit the grace of baptism. However, if for any reason they incur the danger of illness during the set time and are desperate, they may be baptized.

Canon XCIV   Concerning the many Jews frequently returning to Judaism.

Converts = Jews

From the Fifth Toledan Council:

Many Jews who were formerly moved to the Christian faith, now blaspheming Christ, are known not only to observe Jewish rites, but also to commit abominable circumcision. Concerning such persons the

Sacred Council, with the advice of our most pious and religious lord, King Sisemand, decrees that such transgressors, corrected by pontifical authority, shall be brought back into the cult of Christian dignity and that clerical censure shall coerce those who are not converted by their own volition. Moreover, those whom they circumcised—if their children, they are to be separated from the company of their parents; if servants, they are to be awarded freedom because of the injury to their bodies . . .

2 CODIFICATION OF PAPAL DECREES:
RAYMOND OF PENAFORTE / THE *DECRETALES*

AS NEW PAPAL *and conciliar legislation burgeoned in the thirteenth century, a number of difficulties, all normally associated with such prolific activity, soon manifested themselves. Doubts as to the accurate version of key texts, questions as to the binding ruling in cases of conflicting opinions, and most of all the problem of clear and useful organization of a vast body of materials soon plagued both the administrators and the scholars of the thirteenth-century Church. In a highly significant step, Pope Gregory IX, in 1230, commissioned a distinguished jurist, Master Raymond of Penaforte, to compile an authoritative collection of ecclesiastical law. Completed in 1234, the* Decretales *were promulgated by Gregory IX as the recognized statement of the laws of the Church.*

The achievement of Raymond of Penaforte is an imposing one. Huge quantities of material were examined and sifted, difficult decisions of inclusion and exclusion were made, an organizational framework was provided. Toward the end of the five books of the Decretales, *Raymond of Penaforte devotes a section to the "Jews, Saracens, and Their Slaves." The nineteen chapters in this section present material from the sixth-century Council of Macon down through the same Gregory IX who had commissioned the collection, with most of the sources stemming from the late twelfth and early thirteenth centuries.*

What are the major issues addressed? By repeating Clement III's version of the Constitutio pro Judeis, *Raymond affirmed the basic notion of Jewish rights and Jewish safety in Christendom. Clearly, however, major attention is focused on the limitations to be imposed upon the Jews. A prime concern is potential Jewish influence upon Christian neighbors. Among the topics that relate to this concern are Jewish holding of Christian slaves, Jews exercising public office, Christians serving in Jewish homes, and, finally, a crucial thirteenth-century innovation, distinguishing Jewish garb. Another major concern is to ensure that Jews in no way impugn the dignity of the ruling faith, e.g., by striking a cleric or by appearing publicly and frivolously during Holy Week. In order to emphasize the relative standing of the majority and minority religions, the old prohibition against building new synagogues was included. In sum, Raymond does achieve a fairly full depiction of Church policy, although certainly not a comprehensive one.*

TITLE VI: CONCERNING JEWS, SARACENS, AND THEIR SLAVES

Chapter I   If a slave, bought by a Jew as merchandise, became or wished to become a Christian, he shall be redeemed for twelve shillings.

From the Council of Macon:

In the present council, by the authority of God, we ordain that no Christian slave shall henceforth serve a Jew. Rather, when twelve shillings have been paid for each fit slave, any Christian shall have the right of purchasing that slave, whether for release or for servitude. If a slave wishes to become a Christian and is not permitted to do so, then the same thing should be done, since it is abominable that a blasphemer of Christ hold in the chains of servitude one whom the Lord Christ has redeemed.

Chapter II   A Jew may not hold a Christian as a slave. However he may hold him as a serf.

Pope Gregory to the bishop of Lucca:

Through the reports of many we have learned that Christian slaves are held in servitude by Jews living in the city of Lucca. This matter seems to us all the more severe in the light of the effort on your part. It is indeed fitting that you, by virtue of your office and out of consideration for the Christian faith, leave no occasion for them to attract the simple to the Jewish superstition in any way, by argumentation or by the force of power. Therefore, we warn you that, according to the strict sense of the most sacred laws, no Jew is permitted to hold a Christian slave in his power. Rather if Christian slaves be found among them, they shall be given their liberty, by virtue of the protection stemming from the sanctity of the laws. By the strict meaning of the laws, those who are on the Jews' estates should also be free. However, since they have belonged to the Jews for a long time and have cultivated their lands, owing dues according to the condition of the case, they may remain and cultivate their farms, offering the customary payments to those people. They shall observe all which the laws decree concerning colonists and no extra burden shall be imposed upon them. If any of the Jews wishes to transfer any of these to a different place or to retain him for a different service, then he has revealed himself as one who, by his own temerity and the severity of the law, violates the law of slaves and the law of master. Therefore in all these matters we wish that you be devoted skillfully, etc.

Chapter III   Jews may retain old synagogues. They may not demand new ones.

Pope Gregory to the bishop of Cagliari:

The Jews of your city, coming here, complained to us as follows. Peter, who by the will of God was led from their superstition to the cult of the Christian faith, when he had gathered some rowdies, on the day following his baptism, that is on the Sunday of the festival of Passover, in grave scandal and without your assent, occupied their synagogue, which is located in Cagliari. He placed there an image of the mother of our God and Lord and the sacred crucifix and the white cloak in which, risen anew from the fountain of baptism. He had been clothed. They sent us letters attesting these things from Eupater the glorious master of the knights and from the fine and pious count and from other knights of your city. They also added that this was known to you and that the aforesaid Peter was prohibited from daring to do such a thing. Knowing this, we fully praise you, since, because reverence for the good is seemly for a priest, you wished that nothing be done which would be reprehensible. Since you involved yourself in these things which were wrongly done, you demonstrated that what was done was displeasing to you. Considering in this matter the intent of your will and your wisdom, we urge by these words that, when the venerable image and cross have been removed, with the veneration which is fitting, you ought to restore that which was violently removed. Since, just as the law does not permit the Jews to build new synagogues, so it permits them to hold their old synagogues without disturbance. Therefore, lest the aforesaid Peter or other, etc.

> *Chapter IV   On Holy Friday it is not permitted the Jews to have open doors or windows.*

Pope Alexander III:

Since, concerning those matters of which you wrote in your letter relative to the Jews, we do not have a fixed law, we inform you through the content of this letter that, when your clergy has been convoked, you may generally forbid, both by our authority and by your authority, the Jews from having open doors and windows on Good Friday. Rather they must keep them closed for the entire day. Also you shall permit no Christian slaves to live with them. Rather you shall generally order all that no Christian dare to remain in servitude to them, lest they be converted through conversation with them to the Jewish perfidy.

> *Chapter V   Christians who serve Jews or Saracens or pagans in their houses should be excommunicated. Also secular rulers who presume to deprive baptized Jews of their goods should be excommunicated.*

Pope Alexander III in the Lateran Council:

Jews and Saracens shall not be permitted to have Christian slaves in their homes, neither for the purpose of nursing their children, nor for domestic service, nor for any other purpose. Those who dare live in the homes of Jews or Saracens shall be excommunicated.

If, moreover, with God's inspiration, anyone become a convert to Christianity, he shall under no condition be deprived of his property. For converts ought to be in better circumstances than they had been before accepting the faith. If, however, any act to the contrary be found, we command the princes and the potentates in their respective places that, under pain of excommunication, they shall cause the hereditary portion and property of those converts to be restored to them intact.

> *Chapter VIII   Jews may repair old synagogues into their prior state. They may not demand synagogues anew.*

Pope Alexander III:

Be advised that you ought not permit the Jews to build anew synagogues where they have not had them. Indeed if old synagogues fall or threaten to fall, it can be tolerated that the Jews rebuild them. They must not, however, enhance them or make them larger and more pretentious than they were known to be previously. In any case, they should clearly have the right to be tolerated in their old synagogues and observances.

Chapter VIII   Christians should not be in the close service of Jews.

Pope Alexander III:

By the authority of the present letter we order and command that you forbid all Christians who are in your jurisdiction and, if necessary, compel them by ecclesiastical punishment that they not place themselves in the servitude of the Jews for any price. You should also take care to prohibit their midwives and nurses that they not dare to feed the children of the Jews in their houses, because the customs of the Jews and our customs in no way agree. The Jews, moved by their enmity for the human race, through continual conversation and excessive familiarity, bend the souls of the simple to their superstition and perfidy.

Chapter IX   Jews should not be baptized against their will nor forced into baptism nor punished without judicial proceedings nor despoiled of their goods nor disturbed in their festivals nor have their cemeteries violated nor their corpses exhumed.

Pope Clement III:

Just as the Jews, without permission, should not presume to do in their synagogues more than is permitted by the law, so ought they not suffer curtailment in those privileges which have been conceded them. Therefore, although they prefer to remain hardened in their obstinacy rather than acknowledge the prophetic words of the prophets and the secrets of their own scriptures and thus arrive at an understanding of Christianity and salvation, nevertheless, in view of the fact that they begged for our protection and our aid, in accordance with the clemency that Christian piety imposes, we, following in the footsteps of our predecessors of blessed memory, the popes Calixtus, Eugenius, and Alexander, grant their petition and offer them the shield of our protection. We decree that no Christian shall use violence to force them to be baptized as long as they are unwilling and refuse. However, if any one of them seeks refuge among Christians by reason of faith, after his willingness has become quite clear, he shall be made a Christian without subjecting himself to any calumny. For surely one who is known to have come to Christian baptism not willingly, but against his wishes, cannot be believed to possess the faith of Christ.

Moreover, without the judgment of the authority of the land, no Christian shall presume to kill or wound any of them or rob them of their money or change the good customs which they have thus far enjoyed in the place where they live. Furthermore, while they celebrate their festivals, no one shall disturb them in any way by means of sticks or stones. No one shall exact from them forced service, except that which they have been accustomed to perform from ancient times. In opposition to the wickedness and avarice of evil men in these matters, we decree that no one shall dare to desecrate or reduce the cemetery of the Jews or, with the object of extorting money, to exhume bodies there buried. If anyone, however, after being acquainted with the contents of this decree, should presume to act in defiance of it, God forbid, he shall suffer loss of honor and office, or he shall be punished by the penalty of excommunication, unless he shall have made proper amends for his presumption.

Chapter XIII   Jews should not have Christian nurses or servants. Commerce with Christians is to be forbidden to those who do so.

Innocent III to the archbishop of Sens and the bishop of Paris:

Christian piety accepts the Jews who by their own guilt are consigned to perpetual servitude, because they crucified the Lord who their own prophets had predicted would come in the flesh to redeem Israel. Christian piety permits the Jews to dwell in the Christian midst, although, because of their perfidy, even the Saracens who persecute the Catholic faith and do not believe in the Christ whom the Jews crucified cannot tolerate them and have even expelled them from their territory, vehemently rebuking us for tolerating those by whom, as we openly acknowledge, our Redeemer was condemned to the cross. Therefore the Jews ought not be ungrateful to us, requiting Christian favor with contumely and intimacy with contempt. Yet, mercifully admitted into our intimacy, they threaten us with that retribution which, according to the common proverb, the mouse in a pocket, the snake around one's loins, and the fire in one's bosom are accustomed to exhibit to their hosts. For we have heard that the Jews make Christian women nurses for their children, and—something which is an abomination not only to utter but even to think—whenever it happens that on the day of the Lord's Resurrection they take in the body and blood of Jesus Christ, the Jews make these women pour their milk into the latrine for three days before they again give suck to the children. Besides, they commit other detestable and unheard of acts against the Catholic faith, as a result of which the faithful should fear that they are incurring divine wrath when they permit the Jews to perpetrate unpunished such deeds as bring confusion upon our faith.

We therefore asked our dearest son in Christ, Philip the illustrious

king of France, and ordered the noble duke of Burgundy and the countess
of Troyes so to restrain the excesses of the Jews that they shall not dare
raise their neck, bowed under the yoke of perpetual slavery, against the
dignity of the Christian faith. We strictly forbid them to have any nurses
or other kinds of Christian servants in the future, lest the children of a
free woman should be servants to the children of a slave. Rather as
slaves rejected by God, in whose death they wickedly conspired, they
shall, by the effect of this very action, recognize themselves as the slaves
of those whom Christ's death set free at the same time that it enslaved
them. For, as soon as they begin to gnaw in the manner of a mouse and
to bite in the manner of a serpent, one may fear lest the fire that one
keeps in his bosom burn up the gnawed parts. Wherefore we command
you, by this apostolic letter, to take care to warn the aforementioned
king and the others to this effect on our behalf and most zealously to
prevail upon them that henceforth the pèrfidious Jews should not in any
other way dare grow insolent, but should, in servile fear, exhibit always
the shame of their guilt and respect the honor of the Christian faith. If
indeed the Jews do not dismiss the Christian nurses and servants, you,
armed with our authority, should strictly forbid all Christians, under
penalty of excommunication, from daring to undertake any commerce
with them.

*Chapter XIV   A Jew who strikes a cleric must be punished
temporally. If in fact he cannot be punished, commerce with Christians
shall be forbidden to him until he makes amends to the injured.*

Pope Innocent III:
    You asked to be instructed by the Apostolic Throne how you should
proceed against a Jew who had raised a hand of violence against a certain priest. To this request we briefly reply to you that, if the aforementioned Jew lives under your own jurisdiction, you should punish him by
means of a money payment or whatever other secular penalty may be in
order, giving proper satisfaction to the one struck. Otherwise you should
threaten and induce his lord that he should cause fitting amends to be
made to the injured and to the Church. Should his lord neglect to
execute this, you should interdict Christians, by means of ecclesiastical
punishment, not to dare have commercial relations with this Jew until he
makes amends.

Chapter XV   Jews and Saracens of both sexes in Christian lands should wear garb by means of which they can be distinguished from Christians. On Good Friday they should not appear in public, nor should they behave frivolously as an insult to the Creator.

Pope Innocent III in the General Council:

Whereas in certain provinces the difference in their clothes sets Jews and Saracens apart from Christians, in certain other lands there has arisen such confusion that no differences are noticeable. Thus it sometimes happens that by mistake Christians have intercourse with Jewish or Saracen women, and Jews or Saracens with Christian women. Therefore, lest these people, under the pretext of error, find an excuse for the sin of such damnable intercourse, we decree that Jews and Saracens of either sex, and in all Christian lands, and at all times, shall easily be distinguishable from the rest of the population by the quality of their clothes, especially since such legislation is imposed upon them also by Moses.

Moreover, they shall not walk out in public on the Days of Lamentation or the Sunday of Easter. For, as we have heard, certain ones among them do not blush to go out on such days more than usually ornamented and do not fear to poke fun at Christians who display signs of grief at the memory of the most holy Passion.

We most especially forbid anyone to dare to break forth into insults against the Creator. Since we cannot shut our eyes to insults heaped upon Him Who washed away our sins, we decree that such presumptuous persons shall be duly restrained by fitting punishment meted out by the secular rulers, so that none dare blaspheme against Him Who was crucified for our sake.

Chapter XVI   One who appoints a Jew or pagan to public office shall be reproached by the provincial council. Commerce with Christians should be denied to the appointee until he leaves office and returns gains for the use of Christian poor, according to the specifications of the bishop.

Pope Innocent III in the General Council:

Since it is quite absurd that any who blaspheme against Christ should have power over Christians, we, on account of the boldness of the transgressors, renew what the Council of Toledo already has legislated with regard to this. We forbid that Jews be given preferment in public office, since this offers them the pretext to vent their wrath against

Christians. Should anyone entrust them with an office of this kind, he shall be restrained from so doing by the council of the province, which we order to be held every year. Due warning having been given him, he shall be restrained therefrom by such means as the denial of all intercourse, commercial and otherwise, with Christians until they shall have turned for the use of poor Christians, in accordance with the dispositions of the bishop of the diocese, all that they may have earned from the Christians through the office they had undertaken and abandon in disgrace the office which they had so irreverently assumed. This shall apply also to pagans.

Chapter XVIII   Jews and pagans are not to be preferred for public office. If royal rights are sold to them, a proper Christian is to be chosen to collect these dues.

Pope Gregory IX to the bishops of Astorga and Lugo:

Because of the particular affection that we cherish for the illustrious king of Portugal . . . we order you to induce that king not to prefer Jews to Christians in public office, in accordance with the decree of the General Council, and, if by chance he sells his revenues to Jews or pagans, to appoint a Christian under no suspicion of bringing hardships upon clergy and churches through whom the Jews or Saracens might collect the royal dues without injury to Christians.

Chapter XIX   He concludes.

Pope Gregory IX:

No Jew may buy or retain in his service a baptized slave or one who desires to be baptized. If the Jew, for purposes of business, buys an unconverted slave and the slave afterwards becomes or desires to become a Christian, the Jew shall be paid twelve shillings for him, and he shall be withdrawn from service at once. But if he does not put the slave up for sale within three months, or if he buys him for his own service, he shall not presume to sell the slave, nor shall anyone else presume to buy him; rather without any compensation the slave shall be set free.

3 A LEGAL SYNTHESIS: RAYMOND OF PENAFORTE / *SUMMA DE POENITENTIA ET MATRIMONIO*

AS WE HAVE SEEN, *the* Decretales *consists of chronologically ordered papal statements in which key laws are enunciated. One limitation of this basic structure is that conclusions are not arranged topically; the reader is left to synthesize for himself. Other codes of the period, not backed by direct papal authority, but at the same time not bound by the necessity of presenting documents in full, proceeded to a synthetic, topically organized survey of the law.*

An example of this topical approach is the code of the same Raymond of Penaforte who was responsible for the Decretales. *Clearly, many of the views expressed are very close to those found in the* Decretales. *What is strikingly different is the pattern of organization. Raymond begins with an explanation of the term "Jew." He proceeds to emphasize the basic protections promised the Jews in Christendom. This is counterbalanced, however, by heavy emphasis on segregation of the Jews. There is extensive consideration, in particular, of the issue of slaves held by Jews.*

CONCERNING JEWS, SARACENS
AND THEIR SLAVES

WE HAVE DISCUSSED those who blaspheme the Holy Spirit through simony. Now let us deal with those who dishonor God by worshiping vilely, namely Jews, Saracens, and heretics. Let us begin, however, with Jews and Saracens and their servants. Let us therefore examine who are designated Jews and whence; who are designated Saracens and whence; how they are to be attracted to the faith; and how they are to be treated by Christians. Let us then examine the law concerning their slaves, if there still are such who do not wish to become Christian. We shall add a few items concerning the slaves of Christians.

1.　　　Those people are designated Jews who observe the Mosaic law literally, by circumcising themselves and by observing other regulations. They are called Jews by the name of the most exalted tribe, namely by the tribe of the patriarch Judah, which—most bellicose among the tribes—obtained first rank in war and the privilege of kingship. That is to say that the king was to be chosen from that one tribe only, just as were the priests from the tribe of Levi. At first, the Jews were also designated Hebrew, after Eber, whose family observed the cult of one God, while others were defiled by idolatry . . .

2.　　As Gratian indicates, both Jews and Saracens should be induced by authoritative texts, by reason, and by blandishments rather than by harshness, to accept anew the Christian faith. They should not, however, be compelled to do so, for forced servitude does not please God, as in the *Decretum*. The Council of Toledo says the same, as in the *Decretum*. If, however, forced conditionally, for instance by threats or by confiscation of their goods or by flogging or by other similar force, they accept the sacrament of baptism and afterward leave our faith, they must be compelled to return, lest the name of the Lord be blasphemed and the faith which they accepted be held vile and contemptible, as in the *Decretum*. I have said this when they are conditionally forced. For, if they were absolutely forced, for instance if they were violently dragged off and water poured over them, then the essence of baptism is not conferred, as in the decretal collections [early collections of papal decrees].

3.   Christians should behave toward them in this manner. According to certain authorities, they should not eat with Jews nor live with Jews nor accept them at their social functions, as in the *Decretum*. However, we may eat with Saracens, as in the *Decretum*. The reason for this distinction is because the Jews through abuse of Scriptures and their contempt for our food impugn more deeply our faith. Others say indiscriminately and more properly that, just as a Christian should not do the aforesaid with a Jew, so too should he not do so with a Saracen, since Saracens also regularly judaize, whence the same reason for the prohibition and the same danger . . . Likewise Christians should not, in illness, call upon Jews nor receive medicine from them nor bathe with them in the same baths, as in the *Decretum*. Likewise Jews should not be permitted to hold secular dignities or public office among Christians, lest they have occasion to vent their rage against Christians, as in the *Decretum*. Likewise no Christian may leave something to a Jew or a pagan in his will. If he does so, even after death he should be sentenced to excommunication, that is to say he should be excommunicated, as in the decretal collections and in the *Decretum*. Likewise Jews should not be permitted to build new synagogues, but rather to repair old ones, although not to make them larger and more extravagant. They should be permitted to observe their rites and celebrations, as in the decretal collections. Likewise on the Days of Lamentation and of the Passion they should not be permitted to open their windows or to appear in public. They should also be compelled, in all places and at all times, to wear such garb or such signs by means of which they may be easily distinguished from other people, as in the decretal collections. Likewise they are to be compelled to pay to the Church tithes, as in the decretal collections. Likewise Jews seeking baptism should be tested forty days in penitence and abstinence, as in the *Decretum*. Likewise they must be forced to accept Christian witnesses against themselves, as in the decretal collections. Likewise anyone may attract these people to the faith by promises and by gifts and even by graver exaction of payment to be made at the outset of business dealings, as in the *Decretum* . . . Likewise if Jews or Saracens convert to the Christian faith, they shall not be deprived of their possessions, as in the decretal collections.

4.   Transgressors of all the stipulations in the previous section shall be punished in the following manner. If they are clerics and if, once admonished, they do not wish to make amends, they should be deprived of office and benefice. If they are laymen or princes who do not wish to execute these stipulations or others who impose a certain impediment

and if, when admonished, they do not make amends, they should be ex-communicated. If they are Jews or Saracens, then Christians should be removed from commerce and communion with them, under penalty of strict excommunication if necessary, until they release their Christian nurses and servants and return all goods to those who chose the Christian faith over their rite, i.e., Judaism; likewise until whatever was extracted from Christians as the result of an office held over Christians be converted to the use of Christian paupers, according to the stipulation of the bishop of the diocese; and until they abandon in disgrace the office which they had irreverently and improperly assumed. This shall be understood concerning both Jews and pagans. Moreover the Church decrees that those Jews who attempt to subvert those who were infidels and have been baptized be consigned to public flogging. The Church often decrees similar penalties against such malefactors, including sometimes financial penalties, as the nature of the crime demands. Moderation must be employed in administering lashes, concerning which it is decreed that it must not proceed beyond a punishment of blood. Such excessive punishment must be left to the secular arm. All these penalties are indicated in the *Decretum* and in the decretal collections.

5.   It is obvious from the foregoing that the Church may judge those who stand outside it and may inflict numerous penalties upon them. Against this the Apostle says: "What business of mine is it to judge outsiders?" The solution is that the Church cannot judge them, in the sense of inflicting spiritual penalties or imposing the rules of religion. However, it can inflict temporal penalties in such cases and even spiritual penalties indirectly, by removing Christians from communion with them. Likewise the pope judges concerning restitution of inheritance to converts to the faith, against the decretal collections. Note that the pope does this in the name of the faith which they accepted. Now then since Jerome says that, following the advent of Christ, the cult of the law does not differ from idolatry and Origen also says that now one cannot serve God through the law, why is it that the Church gives them the right to sin mortally, since it commands that they not be obstructed from observing their rites? Likewise if they sin mortally in such observance, why should they not be punished as for other crimes? Say to this that the Church does not give them the right to sin, but it grants permission, as Pope Gregory says, lest those whom reason might easily win over be forced back by adversity. Moreover, if Jews were prohibited from this or punished temporally for this, then they would be forced into the faith, which should not be done, as noted above.

6.   It remains to look at their slaves. Note that a Jew's slave is either homeborn, that is, born of a female slave, or purchased. If he be homeborn and wishes to become a Christian, he shall be released immediately into freedom, without paying any price, as in the *Decretum*. If however he is purchased, you must distinguish whether he was already a Christian when purchased or a pagan. If he was a Christian, he should be set free, without any payment made, since commerce in Christians is thoroughly forbidden to the Jews, as in the *Decretum*. Likewise slaves of heretics may with impunity leave their masters and take refuge with the Church. However if he was purchased while he was a pagan, either for the purpose of service or for the purpose of business, in the first case, if he wishes to become Christian, he shall be set free without payment, as in the *Decretum*. In the second case, if within three months the owner does not offer the slave for sale, then subsequently, if the slave wishes to become a Christian, he shall be freed without payment, since it is presumed that the Jew bought him for service. If, however, he exposed the slave for sale within three months and the slave wishes to become a Christian within that period or even afterwards, then since it is not the Lord's fault that he did not sell him within that time, he shall be freed with a payment of twelve shillings by any Christian, as in the *Decretum* and in the decretal collections. This is the case, unless, when the slave said that he wished to become a Christian, the master circumcised him against his will or impressed some sign of the other sect. In that case, because of the injury to his body, he shall be freed without payment, as in the *Decretum* . . . Of what money are the aforesaid twelve shillings? Some say that it is a shilling in place of a gold coin. Others, with whom I agree, say that it is of that money which is in use. Now does the slave become the property of the person who paid? No—rather he returns the purchase price to him and goes free. But if he does not have the purchase price, he may beg from house to house, or he may serve him for a certain time as arbitrated by reliable men or for five years . . .

7.   What of a Christian, may he buy or hold a Jewish or pagan slave? By all means, as in the *Decretum* and the decretal collections, where it is said that Jews are the servants of Christians. However, they should not live together so that they become familiar, as in the *Decretum*. If the Jew wishes to become a Christian, he can. His master should not and cannot prohibit this, for the call of the Holy Spirit removes all chains, as in the *Decretum* . . . But should he remain after baptism a slave of his master? By all means, for servitude has been introduced by divine law, as in Genesis: "Cursed be Canaan, slave of slaves shall he be to his

brothers,'' and has been approved by Roman law, and has been confirmed by canon law, as in the *Decretum*. However, where as a result of good custom Christians are not slaves, as in Catalonia, I would advise that the master release him in remission of his sins or at least, lest the master be excessively damned, that he beg alms from house to house. If he has funds from somewhere else, by means of which he might redeem himself, he shall do so through the arbitration of reliable men, as in the *Decretum*.

8.   When the Jews occupy a certain parish by buying estates and homes which were formerly inhabited by parishioners, can the Church request the Jews to pay what the Christians used to pay? I respond, according to all authorities, that the Church can request all property, tithes and whatever used to be paid on account of the property and even oblations and personal tithes, as in the decretal collections. However, many doctors do not wish to include oblations and personal tithes, in order to preserve the purity of the Church. Also note that, although a Christian should not serve a Jew or live with a Jew in the same house, he is not prohibited from tending the estates of Jews, as in the decretal collections.

4 A THEOLOGICAL SYNTHESIS:
ALEXANDER OF HALES / *SUMMA THEOLOGICA*

THE THIRTEENTH CENTURY *brought dramatic new developments in Christian theology. As western Europe learned more and more of Greek and Arabic philosophic speculation, Christian theology underwent radical revision. As in the area of canon law, the rapid pace of creative activity necessitated continued efforts at reformulation. In thirteenth-century Christian theology, the reformulation took the form of a series of imposing* summae, *broad statements of the foundations of Christian belief. The imposing scope of this effort at defining the essentials of Christian theology meant, among other things, specification of the nature and status of Judaism.*

The summa *which we shall consider is that of Alexander of Hales. A word is in order concerning the form of Alexander's presentation. While it may seem at the outset complex and awkward, Alexander's system is quite simple. What he does is to raise a series of key theological issues. In each case, a question is posed, and then the pros and cons of the question are carefully presented. In some instances the answer appears clearly; in others the merits of both sides require some kind of solution to the apparent conflict. Often Alexander returns to explain away the rejected views. Thus, while ponderous, the mode of exposition does deal with the complexities of accepted ecclesiastical views, does find convincing resolutions to these complexities, and does present succinctly the conclusions.*

In regard to the content of Alexander's views concerning the Jews it is important to note the context within which the discussion takes place. The Jews are treated by Alexander in the section in which he analyzes sins against God, specifically those sins through which divine omnipotence is dishonored. The very placement of the discussion of the Jews is a reflection of highly negative views of Judaism. The first question which Alexander raises is whether, given the nature of Judaism, it should be tolerated in Christendom. From there he proceeds to ask whether the Jewish rite is to be considered idolatrous and whether it may be publicly observed in a Christian society. The last questions deal with pressures for conversion and acceptance of converts. Out of this analysis of the fundamental position of the Jews and Judaism emerges the traditional Church view that Judaism is in fact to be tolerated and that Jews should be free to practice their rites without being coerced into the reigning religion. The place of this exposition within Alexander's system and the extensive quotations of anti-Jewish views, however, vitiate somewhat the doctrine of tolerance. The reader is left with profoundly negative impressions of the Jews and their faith.

❦

CONCERNING OBSERVANCE
OF THE JEWISH RITE

Chapter I.   Whether Jews are to be tolerated.

Concerning this first matter as follows:

It seems that they are not to be tolerated.

1.   They blaspheme against Christ and against the Blessed Virgin; they take revenge on the Catholic faith; they do injury to the sacraments and to ecclesiastics, as is indicated in the *Decretales*. According to the Old Testament, blasphemers are to be subjected to death. Therefore Jews are not to be tolerated, but should be consigned to death, especially those who behave in this fashion.

2.   Moreover, in their book which is called Talmud, many statements are contained which relate to blasphemy of Christ and the Blessed Virgin. Since they must observe the doctrine of that book as law, they along with these books should be dispersed.

3.   Also, Christians persecute those pagans who hold the Holy Land to the death. However, contempt of the Redeemer is a great injury. Therefore Christians ought to persecute to the death those who

perpetrate such contempt. Therefore the Jews are not to be tolerated. That they exhibit such contempt is revealed through that which is said in the *Decretales*.

It seems to the contrary.

a.   Through that which is said in Psalms: "Kill them not, lest my people forget." In regard to this the Glossator says: "This may be applied particularly to the Jews. The Psalmist beseeches, lest the Jews utterly disappear. Rather they are dispersed so that they might be invited to conversion. The Psalmist also prays on their behalf, saying 'Kill them not,' those who killed me; rather let the Jewish people remain with the sign of circumcision." Therefore they are to be tolerated.

b.   Also testimony taken from adversaries is the very best. The Catholic Church takes testimony from the Old Testament, which the Jews observe. To the end that the Catholic Church may have testimony from its enemies, the Jews are to be tolerated. For from the Old Testament, namely from the Law of Moses and the Prophets, testimony is taken concerning Christ which the Jews are unable to negate.

c.   Also in Isaiah 10:22, it is indicated that a remnant of Israel shall turn again. Similarly the Apostle, in Romans 11:5. Now remnants cannot be saved, unless the seed of the Jews remains. Therefore the seed of the Jews must be preserved. Therefore the Jews must be tolerated.

This then must be conceded.

In response to the objections:

1.   To the objection it must be said in rebuttal that, although they perpetrate blasphemy, they believe that they do not sin thereby, since they believe that the messiah has not yet come. In this they err and are consigned to future damnation, unless they recover their senses. As is said in Psalms: "I shall pay them out to the full." In regard to this the Glossator says: "In the present, they shall be dispersed; in the future, they shall be damned." If, however, they persist in open blasphemy, they must be coerced by the secular rulers, as is indicated in the *Decretales*, where it is said: "We most especially forbid anyone to dare to break forth into insults against the Redeemer. Since we cannot shut our eyes to insults heaped upon Him Who washed away our sins, we decree that such presumptuous persons shall be duly restrained by fitting punishment meted out by the secular rulers, so that none dare blaspheme against Him Who was crucified for our sake."

2.   To the second objection, it must be said that their books, in which blasphemies are contained, are to be burned. If they tenaciously persist in blasphemy and are convicted before a tribunal, they are to be punished with a fitting penalty. The same is the case if they blaspheme secretly.

3.   To the third objection, it must be said that the issue concerning those pagans holding the Holy Land differs from that concerning the Jews. Christians persecute those pagans as unjust holders of the Holy Land and as violators of a sacred place, to the injury of Christ. Jews, however, are allowed for many reasons to live and dwell among Christians. This is so, since we have received the Old Testament from the Jews, since Christ came from their seed, since the promise of their salvation when "the Gentiles have been admitted in full strength" has been made. Therefore, if they transgress openly against Christ, they are to be coerced by the proper punishment. It does not seem they should be spared punishment in cases of open sins any more than evil Christians.

Chapter II   Whether the Jewish rite is idolatrous.

Secondly, it is asked whether their rite is idolatrous.

It seems so.

1.   Through that which is said in Galatians 5:1: "Refuse to be tied to the yoke of slavery again." In regard to this the Glossator says: "The servitude of the Law is no lighter than that of idolatry." It thus seems that servitude to the Law is compared to that of idolatry in sinfulness.

2.   Further, it is said in Galatians 4:9: "How can you turn back to the mean spirits?" In regard to this, the Glossator says: "Observance of the Law, to which they had been devoted, became a sin almost equal to service of idols, to which they had been devoted prior to conversion." Whence it seems that observance of the Law is like idolatry. This is explained there by that which follows: "After Christ, the Law is not far removed from ancient idolatry." Therefore it appears clearly that observance of the Law is like idolatry.

To the contrary:

a.   The Law dictates belief in God and service of Him alone. Idolatry demands the opposite, for it serves idols. Thus service of the Law can in no way be equated with the sin of idolatry.

The solution:

1-2.   It must be replied that it is not equally sinful for the Jews to observe the rite of the Law as to engage in idolatry. Rather it is called "a sin almost equal" for those assuming the Christian faith, because in either case it is apostasy, even though it is not equal. Concerning the burden of the sin there is likewise a similarity, for in both cases the sin is grave. Therefore the sacrifices of the Jews are reproved as those of the Gentiles. It is said to be close to idolatry, because in either case it constitutes infidelity. The Galatians, since they had been Gentiles, served idolatrous superstition. When they withdrew from the Catholic faith to the service of the Law, which is prohibited, they fell as it were into infidelity. Moreover, by virtue of the action undertaken, sacrifices, there was a similarity to idolatry, by virtue both of the inclination to sacrifice as well as the superstition in sacrifices. However, it is not a similar sin for the Jews to serve the Law as it was for those who served idols.

Chapter III   Whether Jews are to be permitted to observe their rite in celebrations and in other ways.

Thirdly, it is asked whether they are to be permitted to observe their rite in celebrations and in other ways.

It seems not.

1.   For they sin mortally in observing their rites, since the period of the Law had already elapsed. Jerome says that the Laws are deathly to those who observe them, and Augustine concurs. It therefore remains that they sin mortally by observing the Law. Since the Church does not hinder this action, it seems to consent, particularly since it could hinder. "Anyone who ceases to hinder an open action when he might" seems to consent, according to Augustine. Therefore the Church sins. Therefore it remains that the Church should not permit the Jews to observe their rites through celebrations.

To the contrary:

a.   It seems that the Church should give them permission, since it commands that they not be impeded from observance of their celebrations, as is noted in the *Decretum,* where it is said: "They must have the full right of observing and celebrating all their festivals and holidays, as both they and their ancestors have had for a long time past." The same also appears in that which is said in the *Decretales,* where it is said: "Furthermore, while they celebrate their festivals, no one shall disturb them in any way by means of sticks or stones.'' However, the Church does not give the right to sin. Therefore they do not sin by celebrating their festivities. They are therefore permitted to observe their rites.

b.   This also appears through that which Pope Gregory says: ''Of what use is it to prevent the Jews from the solemnities of their holidays when—although they are prohibited in defiance of long usage—there is no profit toward the conversion of faith. Why should we establish rules for the Jews as to how they should observe their ceremonies, if through such rules we are unable to afford them gain? We should therefore behave in such a way that they wish to follow us by reason and mildness, rather than flee us.'' From them it is accepted that they should be permitted to observe their proper solemnities.

The solution:

It must be said that they should be permitted by tolerance, as indicated in the *Decretales*, where it is said that ''in any case, they should clearly have the right to be tolerated in their old synagogues and observances.'' If they were forbidden to observe their rites, then they would be seemingly forced into the faith, but enforced servitude is not pleasing to God. Moreover, Pope Gregory says: ''Adversity may alienate the mind of those whom a reasonable argument would have been able to attract.''

To the objection:

1.   It must be said to the contrary that the Church, although it permits Jewish observance, cannot be said to consent. For that consent which is considered sin is understood to involve manifest misdeeds, where one is responsible for converting those who are caught up in it, or where the sinners are united in a bond of faith with the one who corrects. This however does not have a place in this issue. Therefore it is not called consent, but rather the permission of tolerance, lest something worse happen and so that, in a different way, good be elicited.

Chapter IV   Whether Jews are to be compelled to the faith.

Fourthly, it is asked whether they are to be compelled to the faith by threats and penalties.

It seems not.

1.   It is said in the Council of Toledo: ''Concerning the Jews the sacred synod ordered that no one henceforth force them to believe. Just

as man, heeding the serpent, perished through the exercise of his own free will, so too, called by the grace of God, one should be saved in faith by the conversion of his own spirit. They are therefore not to be compelled forcibly, but rather they are to be persuaded.'' Pope Gregory says the same thing. It therefore remains that they are not to be forced into the faith.

2.   Likewise Augustine says: ''Although unwilling, we are able to do. However we cannot believe except voluntarily.'' Thus no one should be led to faith by compulsion.

To the contrary:

a.   Augustine says in *Ad Macedonium*: ''Man leads his neighbor to the worship of God by the consolation of kindness and by the correction of discipline.'' Discipline means through lashes. Therefore one should be led to faith by lashes.

b.   Also in the *Decretum*, it is said that ''by the lashes of tribulation evil men are kept from evil and drawn toward the good.'' Therefore one should be forced into faith by lashes.

c.   Moreover, in the *Decretum*, it says that some are to be forced into Christianity, ''as was done at the time of the most pious Prince Sisebut.''

The solution:

It must be said that one thing is understood concerning converts to the faith who never believed and another concerning those who once believed but then left the faith or held it in contempt. In regard to those who never believed, they should never be compelled. If, however, they once believed, they should be compelled to serve the faith or return to it. In this way are the aforesaid authorities to be understood. Moreover, it must be noted that there are two categories of force: absolute and conditional. One who has never believed should never be compelled by absolute force. In this way the authorities who speak of this should be understood, for in this way faith is not gained nor is the nature of baptism imprinted, as noted in the *Decretales*. If the force is conditional, such as through threats or lashes, then in this way faith and the imprint of baptism are received, since there is volition. In this way some have been compelled ''to hold the faith which they accepted under duress, 'lest the name of the Lord be brought to disrepute' and the faith which they accepted be held vile and contemptible,'' as noted in the *Decretum*.

*Chapter V   Whether when they come to the faith
they should be quickly accepted.*

In the light of this question, it is asked whether those who come to the faith from Judaism should be quickly accepted or not. It may be similarly asked concerning the pagans.

It seems not.

1.   Through that which is said in the *Decretum*, where it is said that they shall enter "for eight months among the catechumens of the Church. If they are known to enter in pure faith, only then shall they merit the grace of baptism." The same is also noted there where it is said that "abstinence of forty days is set." In any case a long period is given for probation and for the sake of completing penitence.

However it seems the contrary.

a.   Through that which is said in Acts 2:38, where Peter says to the Jews: "Repent and be baptized, every one of you." Since they were baptized quickly, by that example it does not seem that there should be significant difference between accepting the faith and the sacrament of faith, which is baptism.

b.   It is likewise noted in Acts 10:47-8, where it is said by Peter: " 'Is anyone prepared to withhold the water for baptism from these persons, who have received the Holy Spirit just as we did ourselves?' Then he ordered them to be baptized in the name of Jesus Christ." In the same fashion it is noted concerning the eunuch in Acts 8:36-8. From these instances it seems that a long delay is not appropriate.

The solution:

It must be said that one situation existed in the early Church and another during the development of the Church. For in the early Church, there was the gift of the Holy Spirit, which was demonstrated in a visible sign among the believers. Other signs manifesting faith also occurred among them. Therefore it was not necessary to defer the sacrament of faith. However during the development of the Church, when there were not such signs demonstrating or proving faith clearly and feigning of the heart lurks or might lurk, a delay of time was necessary so that proof of faith and cathechism can be achieved, through which readiness for baptism can be accomplished. Thus at different times differing terms were set, some for the earlier epochs and some for the later, so that one might show aptitude for the faith and so that the readiness to return ''to the Jewish vomit'' be removed. Such terms, according to which it seems more or less wise to proceed, are left to the judgment of wise prelates.

PART TWO

THE CHARTERS OF THE STATE

INTRODUCTION

IN CONTRAST TO THE CHURCH, the states of medieval western Christendom lacked impressive intellectual traditions. There was, in these states, no great sense of a rich heritage from the past and no great drive toward the careful articulation of legal precedents and practices. Such law books as did develop did not normally treat extensively the position of the Jews. To the historian, the most useful materials for ascertaining the position of the State toward the Jews are the charters occasionally extended to individual Jews, to specific Jewish settlements, or to the entire Jewish population of a given area.

The circumstances which occasioned these charters were varied. In many instances, they reflect the founding of a new Jewish enclave; in some cases they signify a shift in political power, with the new ruler promising protection for his Jewish subjects. Often the charters indicate a period of danger and violence, when it seemed appropriate to reassure threatened Jews; on occasion it is impossible to reconstruct the circumstances that gave rise to a particular charter. Since they came into being under specific conditions, these documents cannot be viewed as broad and disinterested formulations of Jewish status. Nonetheless, they remain useful for the insights they provide into the general position taken by the State toward the Jews.

The charters address many diverse issues. Jews are accorded areas of a town in which to settle; the safety of their homes, synagogues, and cemeteries is guaranteed; judicial prerogatives are granted; business rights are specified; religious freedoms are established; the right to self-government within the Jewish community is proclaimed; unwarranted restrictions on the Jews are prohibited. These grants reflect both the needs of the Jews and the commitments of their overlords. How well these promises were fulfilled, how they were tempered by ecclesiastical demands, how they were sometimes broken by avarice and cupidity—these issues will be dealt with in Parts Three through Six of this volume.

BISHOP RUDIGER OF SPEYER, 1084

In 1084, *a fire broke out in the Jewish quarter of Mainz. Fearful of the rage of the burghers, some of the Jews of this illustrious community decided to seek refuge elsewhere. Fortunately for them, the bishop of neighboring Speyer was willing to bring them to his town, accord them security and safety, and grant them the rights necessary to earn their livelihood and to conduct their religious affairs.*

Bishop Rudiger indicates clearly that his intention was to bestow upon these immigrant Jews a generous set of safeguards and rights. His frankly avowed purpose was to attract Jews who would aid in his program of improving the economy of Speyer. First and foremost in his charter was the promise of physical safety. The Jews, fleeing impending violence, were established a distance away from the Christian burghers and were surrounded with a wall. Also crucial to the Jews were business rights—they were allowed freedom of trade throughout the entire area. The remaining issues addressed in the charter include the autonomy of the community in the conduct of its own internal affairs and freedom from certain Church pressures. Although there is no way to assess whether this was in fact "a legal status more generous than any which the Jewish people have in any city of the German kingdom," it certainly does represent a considerable effort on the part of the bishop to afford the conditions for a flourishing Jewish community.

The brief Hebrew account, written by a twelfth-century Speyer Jew, reveals the circumstances under which Rudiger's charter was given. The generosity of his grant accords well with the Jewish report that he "pitied us as a man pities his son."

The Latin Document

IN THE NAME OF THE HOLY AND UNDIVIDED TRINITY. When I wished to make a city out of the village of Speyer, I Rudiger, surnamed Huozmann, bishop of Speyer, thought that the glory of our town would be augmented a thousandfold if I were to bring Jews.

1.　Those Jews whom I have gathered I placed outside the neighborhood and residential area of the other burghers. In order that they not be easily disrupted by the insolence of the mob, I have encircled them with a wall.

2.　The site of their residential area I have acquired properly— first the hill partially by purchase and partially by exchange; then the valley I received by gift of the heirs. I have given them that area on the condition that they pay annually three and one-half pounds in Speyer currency for the shared use of the monks.

3.　I have accorded them the free right of exchanging gold and silver and of buying and selling everything they use—both within their residential area and, outside, beyond the gate down to the wharf and on the wharf itself. I have given them the same right throughout the entire city.

4.　I have, moreover, given them out of the land of the Church burial ground to be held in perpetuity.

5.　I have also added that, if a Jew from elsewhere has quartered with them, he shall pay no toll.

6.　Just as the mayor of the city serves among the burghers, so too shall the Jewish leader adjudicate any quarrel which might arise among them or against them. If he be unable to determine the issue, then the case shall come before the bishop of the city or his chamberlain.

7.　They must discharge the responsibility of watch, guard, and fortification only in their own area. The responsibility of guarding they may discharge along with their servants.

8.　They may legally have nurses and servants from among our people.

9.   They may legally sell to Christians slaughtered meats which they consider unfit for themselves according to the sanctity of their law. Christians may legally buy such meats.

In short, in order to achieve the height of kindness, I have granted them a legal status more generous than any which the Jewish people have in any city of the German kingdom.

Lest one of my successors dare to deny this grant and concession and force them to a greater tax, claiming that the Jews themselves usurped this status and did not receive it from the bishop, I have given them this charter of the aforesaid grant as proper testimony. In order that the meaning of this matter remains throughout the generations, I have strengthened it by signing it and by the imposition of my seal; as may be seen below, I have caused it to be sealed.

This charter has been given on September 13, 1084 A.D.,
in the seventh indiction, in the twelfth year since the
aforementioned bishop began to preside in that city.

The Hebrew Report

AT THE OUTSET, when we came to establish our residence in Speyer—may its foundations never falter!—it was as a result of the fire that broke out in the city of Mainz.

The city of Mainz was the city of our origin and the residence of our ancestors, the ancient and revered community, praised above all communities in the empire. All the Jews' quarter and their street was burned, and we stood in great fear of the burghers. At the same time, Meir Cohen came from Worms, bearing a copy of *Torat Cohanim* [either Leviticus itself or the midrash on Leviticus]. The burghers thought that it was silver or gold and slew him . . .

R. Meshullam said to them: "Fear not, for all this was ordained." We then decided to set forth from there and to settle wherever we might find a fortified city. Perhaps the compassionate Lord might show compassion and the merciful One might exhibit mercy and the All-Helpful might help to sustain us, as in fact He does this very day.

The bishop of Speyer greeted us warmly, sending his ministers and soldiers after us. He gave us a place in the city and expressed his intention to build about us a strong wall to protect us from our enemies, to afford us fortification. He pitied us as a man pities his son. We then set forth our prayers before our Creator, morning and evening, for a number of years.

◈

EMPEROR HENRY IV, 1090

SIX YEARS AFTER *the establishment of the Jewish community of Speyer, its leaders appeared before the emperor, seeking a confirmation of their rights and privileges. The imperial charter granted to these Jews is lengthier and more explicit than that of Bishop Rudiger, although the basic issues remain the same. The emperor outlaws violence against the Jews or their property. Stiff penalties are specified for those guilty of transgression. Concerning the issue of Jewish business rights, the Jews are accorded permission to buy and sell freely, this time throughout the German kingdom. They are freed from a series of tolls and duties, as well as from liability stemming from the purchase of stolen goods. Religious liberty is critical. The Jews are firmly protected from forced baptism and their pagan slaves are similarly safeguarded. Jews are not permitted to hold Christian slaves, although they can have Christian workers. The last major concern is judicial prerogatives. The Jews are to decide internal disputes in their own courts while difficult cases are to be brought before the episcopal court. Most important, the Jews are protected from a number of dangerous judicial procedures, such as trial by ordeal. In sum, Emperor Henry IV confirmed in 1090 the major benefits conferred earlier by the local bishop and at the same time extended and detailed Jewish rights.*

◈

IN THE NAME OF THE HOLY and undivided Trinity, Henry, by divine mercy third august emperor of the Romans, to all the bishops, abbots, dukes, counts, and all subjects of the laws of our kingdom:

Let it be known that certain Jews, Judah b. Kalonymus, David b. Meshullam, Moses. b. Yekutiel, and their associates, came before us at Speyer and requested that we take and hold them under our protection, along with their descendants and all those who seem to hope for security through them. May all our faithful know that this has been done. Therefore through the intervention and petition of Huozmann, bishop of Speyer, we have ordered that this authoritative writ of ours be granted and given to them. Hence by the royal declaration of our majesty, we order and command that:

1.   Henceforth no one who is invested in our kingdom with any dignity or power, neither small nor great, neither free man nor serf, shall presume to attack or assail them on any illicit ground.

2.   Nor shall anyone dare to take from them any of their property, which they possess by hereditary right, whether in land or in
houses or in gardens or in vineyards or in fields or in slaves or in other
property both movable and immovable. If indeed anyone shall perpetrate violence against them in disregard of this edict, he shall be forced to
pay to the treasury of the bishop one pound of gold; also he shall repay
doubly the item which he took from them.

3.   They may have the free right to exchange their goods in just
trading with all men and to travel freely and peacefully within the
bounds of our kingdom in order to carry on their business and trade, to
buy, and to sell. No one may exact from them tolls or demand any
public or private levy.

4.   Guests are not to be lodged in their homes without their consent. No one may requisition from them a horse for a royal or episcopal
journey or for the service of a royal expedition.

5.   If a stolen item be found in their possession and if the Jew
claims that he bought it, he shall substantiate by an oath according to his
law how much he paid and how much he would accept, and in that way
he shall return the item to him to whom it belonged.

6.   No one shall presume to baptize their sons or daughters
against their will. If anyone baptize them against their will or when they
have been carried off by stealth or seized forcibly, he shall pay twelve
pounds to the royal or episcopal treasury. If certain of them wish freely
to be baptized, they shall be held three days, so that it be clearly known if
indeed they repudiate their law because of Christian faith or by virtue of
some injury which they have suffered. Just as they leave behind their
ancestral law, so also are they to leave behind their possessions.

7.   No one shall divert their pagan slaves from their service,
baptizing them under the pretext of Christian faith. If anyone does this,
he shall pay a ban, i.e., three pounds of silver, enforced by the judicial
authority. Moreover he shall return the slave to his master without
delay. The slave must abide by all the commands of his master, except
for the observance of the Christian faith, with whose sacraments he has
been imbued.

8.   It is permissible to have Christians do their work, except on festivals and Sundays.

9.   It is not, however, permissible for them to buy a Christian slave.

10.   If a Christian has a dispute or contention against a Jew concerning any matter or vice versa, each may carry out justice and prove his case according to his law.

11.   No one may force a Jew to judgment by hot irons or boiling water or frigid water or turn them over for stripes or place them in prison. Rather he shall swear by his law after forty days. Nor may he be convicted by any witnesses on any issue. Anyone who wishes so to force them against this edict shall be forced to pay a ban, i.e., three pounds of silver.

12.   If anyone shall wound a Jew, but not mortally, he shall pay one pound of gold. If it be a slave that killed or wounded him, his master shall both pay the impost stipulated and shall hand over the slave for punishment. If, suffering from indigence, he be unable to pay the prescribed amount, the same penalty will be levied by means of which the assassin of the Jew Vivus was punished at the time of Emperor Henry my father, viz., his eyes will be put out and his right hand cut off.

13.   If the Jews have a dispute or a case among themselves to be decided, they shall be judged and convicted by their peers and by none other. If any wicked one among them wishes to hide the truth of an internal affair, he shall be forced, according to their law, by him who stands in charge of the synagogue by appointment of the bishop to confess the truth of the matter in question. If difficult issues or disputes are raised among them or against them, they shall be referred to the presence of the bishop—their peace being preserved in the meantime—so that they might be settled by his judgment.

14.   Moreover, they may have the right to sell their wine and their dyes and their medicines to Christians. As we have stated, no one shall demand from them a money levy or transport services or any exaction public or private.

In order that the authority of this concession remain inviolate for all times, we have ordered that this charter be written and sealed with the impression of our seal.

I Humbert the chancellor, in place of Archchancellor Ruthard, recognize the sign of lord Henry, third august emperor of the Romans.

*Given February 19, 1090 A.D., in the thirteenth indiction, in the
36th year of King Henry and in the sixth year of his imperial rule.
Enacted in Speyer. In the name of Christ, amen.*

EMPEROR FREDERICK I, 1157

IN THE MID-TWELFTH CENTURY, *the Jews of Worms approached
another great emperor, Frederick Barbarossa, and requested confirmation of an
earlier charter. Frederick's grant has survived, and its similarity to Emperor
Henry's privilege of 1090 indicates that a more or less standard set of privileges was
granted by the German rulers of the eleventh and twelfth centuries.*

*Strikingly parallel to the Speyer document of 1090, this Worms charter is
slightly fuller and clearer. However, there is one major shift that may be noted.
Whereas in 1090 power was shared cooperatively between the emperor and the local
bishop, in 1157 Frederick emphatically proclaims imperial rights and prerogatives.
The Jews are bound directly to the emperor, and to him alone. This note is forcefully
sounded in the first clause, where the emperor negates the rights of all other
authorities over the Jews, and it is repeated at a number of subsequent points.*

IN THE NAME OF THE HOLY and undivided Trinity, Frederick,
through the favor of divine mercy august emperor of the Romans. To all
bishops, abbots, dukes, counts, and to all those subject to the laws of our
kingdom, let it be known that we have confirmed, for the Jews of Worms
and their associates, by our authority as an abiding law the statutes of
our great-grandfather Emperor Henry, from the time of Solomon,
bishop of those Jews:

1.   Therefore we wish and command by the authority of our
royal dignity, in order that they look to us in all matters of justice, that

neither bishop nor treasurer nor count nor judge nor anyone—except one whom they themselves choose—presume to deal with them or against them in any affair or exaction related to justice. Only he whom the emperor himself has appointed over them through their election, as we have said, shall do so, since they belong to our treasury, as it pleases us.

2.   No one shall dare to take from them any of their property, which they possess by hereditary right, whether in land or in gardens or in vineyards or in fields or in slaves or in other property both movable and immovable. Concerning the goods which they keep in buildings in the wall of the city, within and without, no one shall impede them. If anyone attempts to disturb them in disregard of this edict, he shall be guilty before our grace, and, if he took anything, he shall repay them doubly.

3.   They may have the free right to exchange silver with anyone, throughout the entire city, except before the minter's house or anywhere else the minters set for exchange.

4.   Within the bounds of our kingdom they may travel freely and peacefully in order to carry on their business and trade, to buy, and to sell. No one may exact from them tolls or demand any public or private levy.

5.   Guests are not to be lodged in their houses without their consent. No one may requisition from them a horse for a royal or episcopal journey or for the service of a royal expedition.

6.   If a stolen item be found in their possession and if the Jew claims that he bought it, he shall substantiate by an oath according to his law how much he paid and how much he would accept, and he shall return the item to him to whom it belonged.

7.   No one shall presume to baptize their sons or daughters against their will. If anyone baptize them while seized forcibly or carried off by stealth or against their will, he shall pay twelve pounds of gold to the royal treasury. If any one of them wish freely to be baptized, he shall be held three days, so that it be clearly known if indeed he repudiates his law because of the Christian faith or by virtue of some injury which he has suffered. Just as they leave behind their ancestral law, so also are they to leave behind their possessions.

8.   No one shall divert their pagan slaves from their service, baptizing them under the pretext of Christian faith. If anyone does this, he shall pay a ban, i.e., three pounds of silver, and shall return the slave to his master. The slave must obey the commands of his master in all matters, except for the observance of the Christian faith.

9.   It is permissible for them to have Christian maidservants and nurses and to have Christian men do their work, except on festivals and Sundays. Neither the bishop nor any other cleric may negate this.

10.   It is not permissible for them to buy a Christian slave.

11.   If a Jew contends against a Christian or a Christian against a Jew, each may carry out justice and prove his case according to his law. Just as it is permitted for any Christian to prove his case and to absolve the sureties set by him for the Jew by his own public oath as well as the public oath of a witness from both faiths, so also shall it be permitted the Jew to prove his case and to absolve the sureties set by him for the Christian by his own public oath as well as that of one Jew and one Christian. He must not be forced to do anything further by either the plaintiff or the judge.

12.   No one may force a Jew to judgment by hot iron or boiling water or frigid water or turn them over for stripes or place them in prison. Rather he shall swear by his law after forty days. No Jew can be convicted in any case except by both Jewish and Christian witnesses. In any case for which they demand royal presence, delay shall be granted to them. Anyone who harasses them in disregard of this edict shall pay the emperor a ban, i.e., three pounds of gold.

13.   If anyone plots against one of them or lies in ambush for one of them, so that the Jew be killed, both the plotter and the assassin shall pay twelve pounds of gold to the royal treasury. If he should wound the Jew, but not mortally, he shall pay one pound of gold. If it be a slave that killed or wounded him, his master shall pay the aforesaid impost and shall hand the slave over for punishment. If because of poverty he be unable to pay the aforesaid, the same penalty will be levied by means of which the assassin of the Jew Vivus was punished at the time of our great-grandfather Emperor Henry, viz., his eyes will be put out and his right hand cut off.

14.   If the Jews have a dispute or a case among themselves to be decided, they shall be judged by their peers and by none other. If a wicked one among them wishes to hide the truth of an internal affair, he shall be forced by the Jews' leader to confess the truth. If they be accused of a serious crime, they may have recourse to the emperor if they wish.

15.   They may have the right to sell their wine and their dyes and their medicines to Christians. As we have stated, no one shall demand from them transport services or any exaction public or private.
In order that the authority of this concession remain inviolate for all times, we have ordered that this charter be written and sealed with the impression of our seal.

The witnesses in this matter are . . .

I, Renaldus the chancellor, in place of the archbishop of Mayence, recognize the sign of lord Frederick, august emperor of the Romans.

Given at Worms, April 6, during the reign of the invincible lord
Frederick, emperor of the Romans, during the fifth indiction,
1157 A.D., the fifth year of his royal authority and the second year
of his imperial authority. Enacted in Christ. Amen.

KING RICHARD OF ENGLAND, 1190

DURING THE TUMULTUOUS FIRST YEAR *of his reign, which witnessed serious attacks on a number of Jewish communities, King Richard found time to grant a charter of rights to a leading English Jew. Although the king refers to the privilege given by his father, this document has never been found and there is some question as to whether such a formal decree was ever enacted. It is likely that the unsettled conditions of Richard's reign stimulated the Jews to seek a written guarantee of their traditional rights.*

The major issue in this rambling and poorly organized grant is judicial procedures. Concerned with stipulating the conditions for litigation between Jew and Christian, the grant emphasizes protection of Jewish interests in a variety of court cases. Touched upon also are security, property rights, and business rights. In all these areas the crown attempts to safeguard the Jews as fully as possible. As always, however, such benevolence comes at a considerable price. In this case, there is protection in exchange for emphasis on the dependent status of the Jews. When the Jews are accorded the right to travel freely, it is noted that they enjoy this right as the king's possession. Likewise when they are freed from customs and tolls, it is because they belong to the crown. For the Jews there was no other option; if the cost of such protections was a measure of degradation, it was a price that had to be paid.

RICHARD, BY THE GRACE OF GOD king of England, duke of Normandy and Aquitaine, and count of Anjou, to the archbishops, bishops, abbots, counts, barons, viscounts, ministers, and to all his faithful in England and Normandy, greetings:

1.   Know that we have granted and, by our present charter, confirmed for Isaac son of R. Joce and his children and their men all customs and all liberties, just as the Lord King Henry our father granted and confirmed in his charter to the Jews of England and Normandy, namely: the right to reside in our land freely and honorably; also the right to hold from us all those properties which the aforesaid Isaac and his children held at the time of our father King Henry in lands and fiefs and pledges and gifts and purchases, viz., Hame, which our father King Henry gave them for their service, and Thurroc, which the aforementioned Isaac brought from the count of Ferrars, and all the houses and properties and pledges which the same Isaac and his sons had in our land at the time of our father King Henry.

2.   If a dispute arise between a Christian and Isaac or any of his children or his heirs, he who summons the other to answer his complaint shall provide the witnesses to prove the matter, namely a proper Christian and a proper Jew.

3.   If the aforementioned Isaac or his heirs or his children shall have a writ concerning the dispute, the writ shall serve them as witness.

4.   If a Christian shall have a dispute against the aforesaid Jews, it must be judged by the peers of the Jews.

5.   If any of the aforementioned Jews shall die, his corpse shall not be detained above ground. Rather his heir shall have his money and his debts. In that way he will not be disturbed, if he has an heir who can answer for him and redress his debts and forfeits.

6.   It is permissible for the aforesaid Jews to accept and purchase, without explanations, all things which may be brought to them, except those which belong to the Church and bloodstained cloth.

7.   If they be summoned by anyone without a witness, they shall be acquitted of that summons by only an oath upon their book. In regard to summons concerning those properties which belong to our crown, they shall likewise be acquitted by an oath on their roll.

8.   If there be a dispute between a Christian and any of the aforesaid Jews or of their children concerning an agreement relating to any money, the Jew shall prove his principal and the Christian the interest.

9.   It is permissible for the aforesaid Jews to sell peacefully their pledges, when it is clear that they have held them for a full year and a day.

10.   They shall not enter into judgment except before us or before those who have charge of those lands in which they reside or where they might be.

11.   It is permissible for them to go wherever they wish with all their possessions, as our property. It is permissible for no one to hold them or to deny them these rights.

12.   If a Christian debtor, who owes money to a Jew, dies and the debtor has an heir, the Jew may not be disturbed, in regard to his debt, because of the minority of the heir, unless the land of the heir be in our hands.

13.   We order that the Jews be acquitted, throughout all England and Normandy, of all customs and tolls and prisage of wine, as our own property.

14.   We order and command you that you guard and defend and protect them.

15.   We forbid anyone, on pain of forfeiture, from bringing the aforesaid Jews to court concerning the aforesaid matters.

Witnesses . . .

Given through the offices of William of Longchamp, bishop of Ely,
our chancellor, at Rouen, on March 22 of the first year of our reign
[1190].

KING ALFONSO I OF ARAGON, 1115

IN 1115, *the Christian forces pressing southward on the Iberian Peninsula captured the city of Tudela. These conquering Christians made two treaties with the residents of the city, one with the Muslims and one with its Jews. While the agreement with the Muslims was harsh in some of its provisions, the charter granted to the Jews was rather generous, designed obviously to reassure the Jews and to draw back those who had fled during the period of conquest.*

The provisions of this charter are brief and general. The Jews are assured physical safety in return for their payment of taxes. The specific details of Jewish legal status and the judicial procedures affecting them were simply borrowed from the neighboring city of Najera.

This charter thus shows us a Jewish community in transition from Muslim to Christian rules, the safeguards extended to these Jews, and the utilization of well-established procedures for a newly conquered area.

IN THE NAME OF THE COMPASSIONATE AND TENDER GOD. This is the charter which King Alphonso—may God protect him —ordered made for you, the Jews of Tudela:

1.   He commanded them by his grace that all those who had left return to Tudela to live, with all their possessions and their goods.

2.   He commanded them by his grace that they shall remain firmly in their homes and that no one may quarter either a Christian or a Moor in their homes.

3.   He commanded them by his grace that the levy which they have to pay they must give in one term annually.

4.   He commanded for them by his order the *fuero* [customs] of the Jews of Najera in all their cases, both for themselves and for all their descendants. They shall not pay customs on all their trade in Tudela, as is the case for the Jews of Najera, neither upon entering the city nor upon leaving it, neither on sales or exchanges. They shall pay all fines and penalties according to the *fuero* of Najera.

5.   The king commanded them by his order that no seigneur nor anyone, living in Tudela or in any other place, who sees this charter, shall contravene it nor do other than stipulated in this charter.

*This charter was enacted in 1115, in the middle of March, during the
reign of our lord Alphonso in Toledo and in Castile and in Aragon . . .
The seal of Emperor Alfonso.*

৪◇৪

COUNT RAYMOND BERENGUER IV
OF BARCELONA, 1149

IN LATE *1148, another major city on the Ebro River fell into Christian hands. This time it was Tortosa, conquered by the count of Barcelona. Once more there was an effort to solidify Jewish settlement. The Jews were accorded a substantial residential area, with the promise of additional land for future Jewish immigrants. Again the detailed status of a neighboring Jewish community was granted. In this instance, the Jews of Tortosa were to live by the customs enjoyed by their coreligionists of Barcelona.*

৪◇৪

1.   LET IT BE PLAIN TO ALL MEN that I Raymond, count of Barcelona, prince of Aragon and marquis of Tortosa, give you, all the

Jews of Tortosa and all your descendants, as a hereditary possession that place in Tortosa which is called *daracina* along with those towers surrounding it, which number seventeen, in order to construct and build there sixty homes. Just as it is bounded and defined by those seventeen towers down to the Ebro River, so I give you that *daracina* along with those aforesaid towers in such a way that you shall build and inhabit sixty houses there and remain there safe and sound with all your goods and possessions for all times. I give you also that entire section which is called *ab Nabicora*, completely with its entrances and exits, along with those plots which are therein contained . . . I give you moreover those two sections which I have in the area of Algaceles, fields and plots and any and all things. I add also for you four areas, which do not have homes . . . All these I give you, that you have them and hold them freely and completely and as your inheritance. In that *daracina* you shall remain and live securely and peacefully with all your goods for all times.

2. If more Jews come to settle, I shall give them homes to occupy and to settle.

3. After you will have lived there for four continuous years, you shall pay no service nor other customs nor usages to me or to any seigneur of Tortosa or to a bailiff, except as much as your own free will chooses. Neither I nor any lord of Tortosa nor bailiff shall require them of you.

4. No Saracen shall exercise over you any authority or command.

5. I grant you those good laws and all customs and usages which the Jews of Barcelona enjoy, as relates to sureties and arbitration and judgments and testimonies and all good customs which the Jews of Barcelona enjoy.

All the above written I grant you and firmly fix for you.
This charter was drawn up on December 23, in the thirteenth year
of the reign of Louis the Younger [1149].

❦

KING SANCHO VI OF NAVARRE, 1170

FIFTY-FIVE YEARS *after the conquest of Tudela and the charter to its Jews, the Jewish community was moved to a fortified area of the city. On this occasion, a new grant was extended, confirming and expanding the earlier pact. The primary focus of this new document was Jewish rights within their new quarter. The Jews were accorded possession of their houses, a cemetery, promise of repair of the walls guarding them, and the right of self-defense within their area. Again the monarch does not spell out in detail Jewish legal status, but repeats the stipulation that the Jews of Tudela live by the procedures operative in neighboring Najera. A few specific points are raised, however, including references to Jewish courts and their authority, as well as to a royal official responsible for Jewish affairs.*

❦

IN THE NAME OF THE LORD. I Sancho, by the grace of God king of Navarre, make this charter of donation and confirmation to the community of Jews of Tudela, both present and future. It has pleased me to do so willingly and spontaneously and because you are moving yourselves to that fortified area which I give and concede to you and which you shall legally hold forever.

1.   First of all, I extend to you your homes which you hold in your quarter, either to sell to whomever you wish or to give or to hold or to do with according to your wishes.

2.   Also I affirm for you the law of Najera and that you shall not pay a market toll in all my land and that you shall not pay a fine, on the condition that you care for the fortified area of Tudela outside of the great tower.

3.   Concerning those oaths which you give to Christians according to that charter in the accustomed manner, the Jew shall respond ten times to the oath and another ten amens and that will suffice.

4.   If certain men attack you violently in that fortress and it shall happen that these men be wounded or killed, on that account the Jews

shall not pay the penalty for homicide nor receive punishment by fine, whether the incident be by day or by night.

5.   If any Christian have a claim against a Jew, it must not be dared to seize him. Rather he must first make his claim before the official who is master of the Jews through royal appointment. If he does not make redress for the Christian claimant, then the Christian should proceed before the court—which is Christian—and the royal court shall arrest that Jew and hold him in prison, until he make redress to his claimant.

6.   The king also gave the Jews a cemetery.

7.   A Moor may not prove his case against a Jew except with a Moor and a Jew as witnesses, as is done between Christians and Moors and Jews.

8.   A Jewish court may not mete out punishment to a Jew except through two Jewish witnesses.

9.   If it should happen that certain walls of the outer perimeter of the fortress fall, the king will see that they be rebuilt, just as he does in regard to the walls of the city.

This charter was drawn up in Tudela, in the month of July, 1170, with King Sancho reigning by the grace of God in Navarre, in Pamplona, in Estella, and in Tudela.

Pedro, bishop of Pamplona.

Seal of the king . . . I Pedro, by the order of my lord the king, made this charter and seal.

KING JAMES I OF ARAGON, 1239

DURING THE THIRTEENTH CENTURY, *the Christian drive in Spain proceeded farther southward, bringing new Jewish communities into the orbit of Christendom. After the conquest of Valencia, a charter was granted to the Jews of the area, extending to them physical protection and the legal status held by the Jews*

of Saragossa. A number of specific judicial issues are singled out for special con-
sideration. Jewish courts are firmly supported; the old principle of mixed testimony
is reaffirmed; Jewish oaths are to be taken on the Torah; cases are to be tried in the
defendant's court. Particularly interesting is the stipulation that Jews must not be
held under arrest or forced to appear in court on their Sabbath.

LET ALL KNOW that we James, by the grace of God king of Aragon, Murcia, and Valencia, count of Barcelona and Urgel, and lord of Montpellier, for ourselves and all our successors, grant and concede to you forever, our faithful Jews living in Valencia and within its environs—those there now and those who will come to live there—that you enjoy in all respects those customs and laws which the Jews of Saragossa enjoy.

1. Particularly, in a case involving Jew against Jew, you shall render judgment in a Jewish tribunal according to your law. No judgment shall be imposed upon you by us or by anyone, except for a judgment of homicide, responsibility for which we retain. Other judgments you shall consider according to your law.

2. Also a Christian may not prove his case against you in any matter, unless by a Christian and a Jewish witness.

3. Also, if a Jew wishes to swear to a Christian, he shall swear on the law of Moses.

4. If a Jew demands something of a Christian, the Jew shall receive justice in a Christian tribunal. If a Christian demands something of a Jew, the Christian shall receive justice in a Jewish tribunal. If he encounters procrastination, then the Jew must dispense justice in a Christian tribunal.

5. If any Jew be seized by a Christian tribunal, he shall be released from seizure and permitted to return home from Friday noon through the following Monday, by giving bond that he will return to captivity. No Jew may be forced to respond to his adversary on the Sabbath or on his festivals.

6.   We take you, all and single, and your property under our protection and custody and our special safeguard for entering, tarrying in, and re-entering all areas of our kingdoms and domain, by land and by sea. No one may dare to harm you or your property anywhere nor to intrude or seize or detain you or your property, except as a result of your debts or crimes.

We order all our subjects present and future that they execute all these stipulations on your behalf and cause them to be observed and that they guard all your goods, protecting and defending them against all men from any damage as though they were our very own. Anyone who transgresses must know that he shall incur our anger and a penalty of one thousand maravedis.

KING JOHN OF ENGLAND, 1201

AT THE OUTSET OF THE REIGN OF KING RICHARD, *English Jewry was suddenly exposed to the first wave of sustained violence in its history. Despite the glamor associated with his name, Richard the Lionheart was in England only infrequently, thus exposing his kingdom and his Jews to substantial insecurity. In 1199, Richard was killed, leaving his domains on both sides of the English Channel to his brother, John. Still badly frightened, English and Norman Jewry elicited a general charter from the new monarch. This set of guarantees is modeled on the charter given by Richard to Isaac son of R. Joce and his entourage. The promise of physical protection, business support, and judicial rights is here extended to all the Jews of England and Normandy.*

JOHN, by the grace of God, etc:

1.   Know that we have granted to all the Jews of England and Normandy the right to reside in our land freely and honorably and the right to hold from us all those properties which they held from King

Henry, our great-grandfather, and all those properties which they now rightfully hold, in lands and fiefs and pledges and purchases. They shall enjoy more fully and quietly and honorably all their liberties and customs, which they enjoyed at the time of the aforesaid King Henry, our great-grandfather.

2.   If a dispute arises between a Christian and a Jew, he who summons the other to answer his complaint shall provide the witnesses, namely a proper Christian and a proper Jew.

3.   If the Jew shall have a writ concerning the dispute, his writ shall serve him as witness.

4.   If a Christian shall have a dispute against a Jew, it must be judged by the peers of the Jews.

5.   When a Jew dies, his corpse shall not be detained above ground. Rather his heirs shall have his money and his debts. In that way he will not be disturbed, if he has an heir who can answer for him and redress his debts and his forfeits.

6.   It is permissible for Jews to accept and purchase without explanation all things which may be brought to them, except those which belong to the Church and bloodstained cloth.

7.   If a Jew be summoned by anyone without a witness, he shall be acquitted of that summons merely by an oath upon his book. In regard to summons concerning those properties which belong to our crown, he shall likewise be acquitted by an oath on his roll.

8.   If there be a dispute between a Christian and a Jew concerning an agreement relating to any money, the Jew shall prove his principal and the Christian the interest.

9.   It is permissible for a Jew to sell peacefully his pledge, when it is clear that he has held it for a full year and a day.

10.   Jews shall not enter into judgment except before us or before those who have custody of our castles, in whose bailliages the Jews live.

11.   Wherever the Jews might be, it shall be permissible for them

to go wherever they wish with all their possessions, as our property. It is permissible for no one to hold them nor to deny them this right.

12.   We order that they be acquitted, throughout all England and Normandy, of all customs and tolls and prisage of wine.

13.   We order and command you that you guard and defend and protect them.

14.   We forbid anyone, on pain of forfeiture, from bringing them to court concerning the aforesaid matters.

Witnesses . . .

Given through the offices of Simon, archdeacon of Wells,
at Marlborough, on the tenth of April, in the
second year of our reign [1201].

KING LOUIS X OF FRANCE, 1315

IN 1306, *King Philip IV expelled the Jews from France. While not the first large-scale expulsion of western-European Jews, this was in many senses the most shattering. Large numbers of Jews, from a wide area of settlement, were sent into banishment. An old Jewish community, the product of centuries of experience and creativity, was destroyed.*

Nine years later, King Louis X decided to reverse the policy of his predecessor and to readmit Jews. While the Jews in France prior to 1306 were deeply rooted in France and never depended on formal charters, the Jewish community created in 1315 was new and weak, in need of whatever formal guarantees might be accorded. As a result, the French king granted the Jews rights of settlement and specified the conditions under which they would live.

This charter opens with an interesting preamble, justifying the reversal in policy that allowed the Jews to resettle. Appeal was made to Scriptures, to the policies of the Catholic Church, to the exalted image of the newly beatified Louis IX, and to the clamor of the populace. Ostensibly for these laudable reasons, but in fact out of largely economic motives, the Jews were permitted to return.

The first set of stipulations (#1-#9) involve issues carried over from earlier Jewish settlement and from the expulsion of 1306. Jews could only reside in those areas previously open to them, they were prohibited from usury, and they were to wear the traditional identifying badge. A number of these clauses then go on to deal with the recovery of Jewish debts and property.

The remaining items (#10-#20) further define the conditions of Jewish existence. The first of these stipulations is striking: The permission to resettle is for only twelve years. When that period elapses, the Jews are to be given a full year to wind up their affairs if permission for continuing settlement is denied. Another interesting set of clauses concern Jewish moneylending. While the king had outlawed Jewish usury, he also made provision for lending at interest if it should resume. There is here, of course, a tacit acceptance of Jewish usury.

This charter then is an important one, setting the conditions for a renewed Jewish presence in France. The fragility of such grants is revealed by the exile of the Jews of France once more seven years later—the guarantees specified by Louis X ultimately meant very little.

LOUIS, BY THE GRACE OF GOD king of France and of Navarre, to all the loyal subjects of our kingdom of France, greetings:

We make known that our dear lord and father—whose soul the Lord now holds—had, while yet alive, with the counsel and the advice of the great men of his council, driven out and expelled the Jews from his kingdom. Subsequently there have been indicated and shown, in the course of complaints both before us and our great council by the aforesaid Jews and by the common clamor of the people, many reasons why they should be tolerated as they were before and as they are in other countries. We have heard these reasons. We have considered particularly that our Mother the Holy Church of Rome tolerates them, both for the perpetual memory of the Passion of our Lord Jesus Christ as well as for saving them from their errors and converting them to the Christian faith. It has often happened that many convert through conversation with Christians. We also note that according to the teaching of Scriptures our Lord rejoices more from a repentant sinner than from many righteous. We note also that our great-grandfather Saint Louis, who through certain advice was moved to expel them, then recalled them and retained them for the aforesaid reasons. We have held full deliberation on this matter with our prelates and our barons and our great council, wishing to follow as far as possible the works and deeds of the aforesaid

Saint Louis on this matter and on all other matters and having heard especially the clamor of the people. For these reasons we have ordained, established, and ordered as follows:

1.   First, that the Jews may return and live in our kingdom for twelve years, in the towns and places where they were permitted to live before they left, but not in those places where they were earlier prohibited.

2.   Likewise, they must live by the labor of their hands or they must trade with good and reliable merchandise.

3.   Likewise, they must wear the badge where they were accustomed to wearing it. It must be as large as a silver *tournois* [a well-known coin] or larger and must be of a color different from the garment, preferably of linen or of silk in order to be seen better and more clearly.

4.   Likewise, they may recover and hold a third—while we hold two-thirds—of the debts which were owed them prior to their expulsion, both those debts which have already been disclosed as well as those which will be demanded and reported. It is to be understood that these debts must be good and reliable. If it should transpire that a Jew makes a demand concerning a debt drawn in the debtor's own name or in another's name, for which one gave surety, and if subsequently the debtor is able to exonerate himself, by proving payment or quittance or the like, the Jew will be held responsible to pay the costs and the damages which the debtor suffered. The debtor will be believed concerning these costs and damages by his oath.

5.   Likewise, they may not be troubled over movable goods or chattel which they took with them, nor over loans or business agreements which they made subsequent to their departure.

6.   Likewise, no one may hold them responsible or pursue them for things which they had previously done.

7.   Likewise, their synagogues and cemeteries shall be returned to them, upon payment of the price for which they were sold to those who bought them, unless there are very large buildings there or other reasons why one may not take them away. If there are any still held by us, which were not sold, they shall be returned to them.

8.   Likewise, if perchance they are unable to recover their synagogues and cemeteries for good reason, we shall see that they receive sufficient buildings and grounds for a suitable price.

9.   Likewise, the books of their law which are still held by us, which were not sold, shall be returned to them, except for the condemned Talmud.

10.   Likewise, when the aforesaid twelve years have passed, we may not drive them out of our kingdom without giving them suitable time, i.e., a year, during which they may transfer their goods safely and under our protection out of the kingdom.

11.   Likewise, no other lord in our kingdom, except us, may hold in his land Jews other than his own by origin and by legal right. If any Jews of another lord by origin and by legal right wish to reside in our territory and we agree, or if any of our Jews wish to reside in the territory of another lord with his assent, nonetheless we shall have the rights and the profits from our Jews, just as though they lived in our territory, and each lord shall likewise enjoy his profits. The conditions of such Jews will in no way be altered.

12.   Likewise, since the Jews must work and labor with their hands or must trade, as has already been said, it is not our wish that they be permitted to lend at interest, and we forbid it expressly. If it should happen that perchance they do lend, they may take no more than two pennies per pound per week.

13.   Likewise, the Jew may reckon with his debtor at the end of the year and not before. Any time the debtor wishes to reckon with the Jew and pay him during the year, the Jew must do this and may not refuse.

14.   Likewise, they may not lend against vessels or ornaments of the Church nor against bloody pledges nor against recently washed pledges, nor may they receive them under any circumstances.

15.   Likewise, they may not lend by document but only against pledges. Payment will not be made except by pledges, save for

documents concerning good and reliable merchandise, which may be executed in the customary way.

16.   Likewise, no one may be forced by us to pay interest of any sort to a Jew. We understand by "interest" whatever is beyond the principal.

17.   Likewise, they may not, under pain of committing a crime, dispute matters of faith with anyone, poor or rich, overtly or covertly.

18.   Likewise, their privileges, if they are found, are to be returned to them. If they cannot be found and transcripts are found, they shall be renewed for them, except insofar as they are contrary to the present ordinance.

19.   Likewise, we appoint two upstanding men of our court as Keepers of the Jews, in order to execute and preserve this present ordinance and in order to deal with the needs of the aforesaid Jews as was customary before they left.

20.   Likewise, the two aforesaid upstanding men should inform themselves, through their own information or through others, of the holdings of the Jews sold at less than half of the proper price and shall set matters right, calling those who must be called, guarding the custom of the land, and seeking out our welfare and the welfare of the aforesaid Jews.

Since we have taken the aforesaid Jews under our special protection and guard, we order you all and individually to preserve and cause to be preserved their goods and their property from force, injury, violence, and all oppression and—as far as pertains to you—to preserve the aforesaid laws and cause them to be executed and preserved, so that the aforesaid Jews need not complain to us of your failures.

In testimony of which we have caused our seal to be placed on this present ordinance.

Given at Paris, July 28, 1315 A.D.

◈

DUKE FREDERICK OF AUSTRIA, 1244

IN 1236, *Emperor Frederick II issued a charter to all of German Jewry, extending to the Jews his protection and at the same time asserting his rights over them. Despite these imperial pretensions, many of the German princes contrived to control Jewish communities of their own. One such ruler, the duke of Austria, issued in 1244 a charter of his own, intended for the Jews of his lands. This privilege was destined to have an enormous impact on the developing Jewries of central and eastern Europe. Copied and occasionally modified by a series of rulers, the charter of 1244 laid the foundation for the legal status of a number of important Jewish settlements.*

The stipulations of Duke Frederick's grant are once more highly protective. The Jews are promised physical safety, business rights, internal autonomy, and religious independence. The issue most fully elaborated is Jewish business rights, specifically a set of safeguards for Jewish pawnbroking. Clearly the recipients of this grant had been exposed to a number of dangerous claims and challenges. In order to buttress their business affairs, the duke promised these Jews the fullest protection. Whenever possible, the onus of proving a claim was placed on the Christian debtor. Every effort was made to assure the Jews that they could collect the sums due to them. This grant thus perpetuates the protective stance already noted, revealing in passing the evolution of Jewish economic life during the thirteenth century.

◈

FREDERICK, **BY THE GRACE OF GOD** duke of Austria and Styria and lord of Carniola, offers greetings at all times to all who will read this letter in the future:

Inasmuch as we desire that men of all classes dwelling in our land should share our favor and good will, we do therefore decree that these laws, devised for all Jews found in the land of Austria, shall be observed by them without violation.

1.   We decree, therefore, first, that in cases involving money, or immovable property, or a criminal complaint touching the person or property of a Jew, no Christian shall be admitted as a witness against a Jew unless there is a Jewish witness together with the Christian.

2.   Likewise, if a Christian should bring suit against a Jew,

asserting that he had pawned his pledges with him and the Jew should deny this, and then if the Christian should not wish to accord any belief in the mere statement of the Jew, the Jew may prove his contention by taking an oath upon an object equivalent in value to that which was brought to him and shall then go forth free.

3.   Likewise, if a Christian has deposited a pledge with a Jew, stating that he had left it with the Jew for a smaller sum than the Jew admits, the Jew shall then take an oath upon the pledge pawned with him, and the Christian must not refuse to pay the amount that the Jew has proved through his oath.

4.   Likewise, if a Jew says that he returned the Christian's pledge as a loan to the Christian, without, however, the presence of witnesses, and if the Christian deny this, then the Christian is able to clear himself in this matter through his own oath.

5.   Likewise, a Jew is allowed to receive as pledges all things which may be pawned with him—no matter what they are called—without making any investigation about them, except bloody and wet clothes which he shall under no circumstances accept.

6.   Likewise, if a Christian charges that the pledge which a Jew has was taken from him by theft or robbery, the Jew must swear on that pledge that when he received it he did not know that it had been removed by theft or robbery. In this oath the amount for which the pledge was pawned to him shall also be included. Then, inasmuch as the Jew has brought his proof, the Christian shall pay him the capital and the interest that has accrued in the meantime.

7.   Likewise, if a Jew, through the accident of fire or through theft or violence, should lose his own goods, together with the pledges pawned with him, and this is established, yet the Christian who has pledged something with him nevertheless brings suit against him, the Jew may free himself merely by his own oath.

8.   Likewise, if the Jews engage in quarreling or actually fight among themselves, the judge of our city shall claim no jurisdiction over them; only the duke alone or the chief official of his land shall exercise jurisdiction. If, however, the accusation touches the person, this case shall be reserved for the duke alone for judgment.

9.   Likewise, if a Christian should inflict any sort of a wound upon a Jew, the accused shall pay to the duke twelve marks of gold which are to be turned in to the treasury. He must also pay to the person who has been injured twelve marks of silver and the expenses incurred for the medicine needed in his cure.

10.   Likewise, if a Christian should kill a Jew, he shall be punished with the proper sentence, death, and all his movable and immovable property shall pass into the power of the duke.

11.   Likewise, if a Christian strikes a Jew, without, however, having spilled his blood, he shall pay to the duke four marks of gold, and to the man he struck four marks of silver. If he has no money, he shall offer satisfaction for the crime committed by the loss of his hand.

12.   Likewise, wherever a Jew shall pass through our territory, no one shall offer any hindrance to him or molest or trouble him. If, however, he should be carrying any goods or other things for which he must pay duty at all custom offices, he shall pay only the prescribed duty which a citizen of that town, in which the Jew is then dwelling, pays.

13.   Likewise, if the Jews, as is their custom, should transport any of their dead either from city to city, or from province to province, or from one Austrian land into another, we do not wish anything to be demanded of them by our customs officers. If, however, a customs officer should extort anything, then he is to be punished for *praedatio mortui*, which means in common language, robbery of the dead.

14.   Likewise, if a Christian, moved by insolence, shall break into or devastate the cemetery of the Jews, he shall die, as the court determines, and all his property, whatever it may be, shall be forfeited to the treasury of the duke.

15.   Likewise, if anyone wickedly throw something at the synagogues of the Jews, we order that he pay two talents to the judge of the Jews.

16.   Likewise, if a Jew be condemned by his judge to a money penalty, which is called *wandel*, he shall pay only twelve pennies to him.

17.   Likewise, if a Jew is summoned to court by order of his

judge, but does not come the first or second time, he must pay the judge four pennies for each time. If he does not come at the third summons, he shall pay thirty-six pennies to the judge mentioned.

18. Likewise, if a Jew has wounded another Jew, he may not refuse to pay a penalty of two talents, which is called *wandel*, to his judge.

19. Likewise, we decree that no Jew shall take an oath on the Torah unless he has been summoned to our presence.

20. Likewise, if a Jew was secretly murdered, and if through testimony it cannot be determined by his friends who murdered him, yet if after an investigation has been made the Jews begin to suspect someone, we are willing to supply the Jews with a champion against this suspect.

21. Likewise, if a Christian raises his hand in violence against a Jewess, we order that the hand of that person be cut off.

22. Likewise, the judge of the Jews shall bring no case that has arisen among the Jews before his court, unless he be invited due to a complaint.

23. Likewise, if a Christian has redeemed his pledge from a Jew but has not paid the interest, the interest due shall become compounded if it is not paid within a month.

24. Likewise, we do not wish anyone to seek quarters in a Jewish house.

25. Likewise, if a Jew has lent money to a magnate of the country on his possessions or on a note and proves this documentarily, we will assign the pledged possessions to the Jew and defend them for him against violence.

26. Likewise, if any man or woman should kidnap a Jewish child, we wish that he be punished as a thief.

27. Likewise, if a Jew has held in his possession, for a year, a pledge received from a Christian, and if the value of the pledge does not

exceed the money lent together with the interest, the Jew may show the pledge to his judge and shall then have the right to sell it. If any pledge shall remain for a year and a day with a Jew, he shall not have to account for it afterwards to anyone.

28.   Likewise, whatever Christian shall take his pledge away from a Jew by force or shall exercise violence in the Jew's home shall be severely punished as a plunderer of our treasury.

29.   Likewise, one shall in no place proceed in judgment against a Jew except in front of his synagogue, saving ourselves who have the power to summon them to our presence.

30.   Likewise, we decree that Jews shall indeed receive only eight pennies a week interest on the talent.

In order that this gracious grant retain perpetual validity, we have ordered the present charter to be written and to be strengthened by the protection of our seal . . .

Given at Starkenberg, A.D. 1244, on the first of July.

DUKE BOLESLAV OF
GREATER POLAND, 1264

THE CHARTER *issued by the duke of Austria for his Jews in 1244 served as the prototype for a series of similar grants for developing Jewish communities of eastern Europe. One of the most famous adaptations of the Austrian model was that bestowed upon the Jews of Greater Poland in 1264. Duke Boleslav repeated, with minor modifications, the first twenty-nine provisions of the Austrian charter, adding seven additional stipulations (#28, #31-6). While many of the modifications represent a softening of the harsh penalties imposed by the Austrian duke for anti-Jewish activities, the basic thrust of the Polish document is toward responsible protection of the Jews. Each of the seven additional clauses represents a significant new safeguard of Jewish rights. This decree of 1264 had a profound impact on subsequent history, serving as the basic constitutional delineation of Polish-Jewish status.*

IN THE NAME OF THE LORD, amen. The actions of the human species quickly dissipate and disappear from memory, unless they are preserved by the voice of witnesses or by the testimony of documents. Therefore we Boleslav, by the grace of God duke of Greater Poland, inform those both present and future whose attention the present charter will reach, that we have caused to be prescribed for our Jews living throughout the area of our domain these statutes and privileges which they have obtained from us, word for word, as contained in the following series:

1.   We decree, therefore, first, that in cases involving money, or movable property, or immovable property, or a criminal complaint touching the person or property of a Jew, no Christian shall be admitted as a witness against a Jew unless there is a Jewish witness together with the Christian.

2.   Likewise, if a Christian should bring suit against a Jew, asserting that he had pawned his pledges with him and the Jew should deny this, and then if the Christian should not wish to accord any belief in the mere statement of the Jew, the Jew may prove his contention by taking an oath upon an object equivalent in value to that which was brought to him and shall then go forth free.

3.   Likewise, if a Christian has deposited a pledge with a Jew, stating that he had left it with the Jew for a smaller sum than the Jew admits, the Jew shall then take an oath upon the pledge pawned with him, and the Christian must not refuse to pay the amount that the Jew has proved through his oath.

4.   Likewise, if a Jew says that he returned the Christian's pledge as a loan to the Christian, without, however, the presence of witnesses, and if the Christian deny this, then the Christian is able to clear himself in this matter through his own oath.

5.   Likewise, a Jew is allowed to receive as pledges all things which may be pawned with him—no matter what they are called—without making any investigation about them, except bloody and wet clothes and sacred vessels which he shall under no circumstances accept.

6.   Likewise, if a Christian charges that the pledge which a Jew has was taken from him by theft or robbery, the Jew must swear on that

pledge that when he received it he did not know that it had been removed by theft or robbery. In this oath the amount for which the pledge was pawned to him shall also be included. Then, inasmuch as the Jew has brought his proof, the Christian shall pay him the capital and the interest that has accrued in the meantime.

7.　　Likewise, if a Jew, through the accident of fire or through theft or violence, should lose his own goods, together with the pledges pawned with him, and this is established, yet the Christian who has pledged something with him nevertheless brings suit against him, the Jew may free himself merely by his own oath.

8.　　Likewise, if the Jews engage in quarreling or actually fight among themselves, the judge of our city shall claim no jurisdiction over them; only we alone or our palatine or his judge shall exercise jurisdiction. If, however, the accusation touches the person, this case shall be reserved for us alone for judgment.

9.　　Likewise, if a Christian should inflict any sort of a wound upon a Jew, the accused shall pay a fine to us and to our palatine, according to that which our grace decides, to be remitted to our treasury. He must also pay the person who has been injured for the care of his wound and for expenses, as the laws of our land require and demand.

10.　　Likewise, if a Christian should kill a Jew, he shall be punished with the proper sentence and all his movable and immovable property shall pass into our power.

11.　　Likewise, if a Christian strikes a Jew, without, however, having spilled his blood, a fine will be required by the palatine according to the custom of our land. He shall also pay the man struck or injured in the manner which is customary in our land. If he has no money, he shall be punished for the crime committed as is just.

12.　　Likewise, wherever a Jew shall pass through our territory, no one shall offer any hindrance to him or molest or trouble him. If, however, he should be carrying any goods or other things for which he must pay duty at all customs offices, he shall pay only the prescribed duty which a citizen of that town, in which the Jew is then dwelling, pays.

13.　　Likewise, if the Jews, as is their custom, should transport any of their dead either from city to city, or from province to province, or from one land into another, we do not wish anything to be demanded of them by our customs officers. If, however, a customs officer should extort anything, then we wish him punished as a robber.

14.   Likewise, if a Christian, moved by insolence, shall break into or devastate the cemetery of the Jews, we wish that he be gravely punished according to the custom and laws of our land and that all his property, whatever it may be, shall be forfeited to our treasury.

15.   Likewise, if anyone wickedly throw something at the synagogues of the Jews, we order that he pay two talents of pepper to our palatine.

16.   Likewise, if a Jew be condemned by his judge to a money penalty, which is called *wandel*, he shall pay him a fine of a talent of pepper, which has been imposed from antiquity.

17.   Likewise, if a Jew is summoned to court by order of his judge, but does not come the first or second time, he must pay the judge for each time the fine which is customary from antiquity. If he does not come at the third summons, he shall pay to the judge mentioned the subsequent fine.

18.   Likewise, if a Jew has wounded another Jew, he may not refuse to pay to his judge a fine according to the custom of our land.

19.   Likewise, we decree that no Jew shall take an oath on the Torah unless it be for important cases which involve fifty silver marks or unless called to our presence. For minor cases, he should swear before the synagogue, before the entrance of the synagogue.

20.   Likewise, if a Jew has secretly been murdered, and if through testimony it cannot be determined by his friends who murdered him, yet if after an investigation has been made the Jews begin to suspect someone, we shall extend to the Jews the protection of justice against the suspected murderer of the Jew, by means of the law of such matters.

21.   Likewise, if Christians raise their hand in violence against a Jew, they shall be punished according to that which the law of our land demands.

22.   Likewise, the judge of the Jews shall bring no case that has arisen among the Jews before his court, unless he be invited due to a complaint. Also the Jews ought to be judged near the synagogues or where they take oaths.

23.   Likewise, if a Christian has redeemed his pledge from a Jew but has not paid the interest, the interest due shall become compounded if it is not paid within a month.

24.   Likewise, we do not wish anyone to seek quarters in a Jewish house.

25.   Likewise, if a Jew has lent money on possessions or on a note for immovable goods, and he to whom the things belong shall offer proof, we order that the money and the pledge of the note be removed from the Jew.

26.   Likewise, if any man or woman should kidnap a Jewish child, we wish that he be punished as a thief.

27.   Likewise, if a Jew has held in his possession, for a year, a pledge received from a Christian, and if the value of the pledge does not exceed the money lent, the Jew may show the pledge to his judge. If the pledge is not good, he shall show it to our palatine or his judge. He shall then have the right to sell it. If he shows the pledge to his judge before a year passed, then he shall subsequently have the right to sell it. If any pledge shall remain for a year and a day with a Jew, he shall not have to account for it afterwards to anyone.

28.   We wish that no one dare to force a Jew to payment of pledges on his holiday.

29.   Likewise, whatever Christian shall take his pledge away from a Jew by force or shall exercise violence in the Jew's home shall be severely punished as a plunderer of our treasury.

30.   Likewise, one shall in no place proceed in judgment against a Jew except in front of his synagogues or where all the Jews are judged, saving ourselves and our palatine who have the power to summon them to our presence.

31.   According to the ordinances of the pope, in the name of our Holy Father, we firmly order that henceforth no Jews in our domain be accused of using human blood, since according to the precept of their law all Jews refrain from any blood. If any Jew be accused of killing any Christian child, he should be convicted by three Christian witnesses and as many Jewish witnesses. After he has been convicted, he should be punished by the proper penalty for the crime committed. If, however, the aforesaid witnesses and his innocence exonerate him, then the Christian accuser should undergo the punishment which the Jew would have had to suffer, for slander.

32.   Likewise, we order that whatever the Jew lends, whether it be gold or coins or silver, that the same thing should be repaid or returned to him along with required interest which has accrued.

33.   We wish that the Jews accept horses as pledges openly and by daylight. If any stolen horse be found in a Jew's possession by any Christian, the Jew shall exonerate himself by his own oath, saying that he took that horse openly and by day as a pledge for a certain amount of money which he gave and that he believed that it was not stolen.

34.   We order that the minters living in our domain dare not to detain or seize Jews with false coins or other things by themselves, without our representative or that of our palatine or without honest citizens.

35.   We order that, if any Jew, compelled by dire necessity, cries out at night and if the neighboring Christians do not bother to provide the proper aid or heed the cry, every neighboring Christian shall be responsible to pay thirty shillings.

36.   We also order that Jews may sell and buy all things freely and may touch bread as do Christians. Anyone who impedes them shall be obliged to pay a fine to our palatine.

In order that all the foregoing attain the powers of perpetual validity, we have given them the present document with the addition of witnesses as security, fortified by the protection of our seal. The witnesses of this matter are . . .

PART THREE

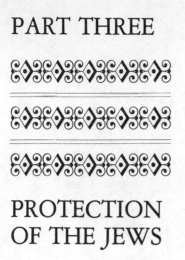

PROTECTION
OF THE JEWS

INTRODUCTION

FROM THE POINT OF VIEW OF THE JEWS, the most important safeguard the authorities could offer was protection of life and property. The Jews were always conscious of the hostilities surrounding them and knew that protection by the duly constituted authorities was utterly indispensable. The Church played an important, although secondary, role in affording such protection. As the shaper of the goals of western Christendom, the Church often spoke out forcefully for law and order and against the anarchy of popular violence. In regard to the Jews specifically, the Church had, as we have seen, developed a stance that emphasized the fundamental legitimacy of Jewish existence. The first chapter presents statements of major churchmen condemning violence against the Jews. What lends added poignancy to these denunciations of persecution is that, in most instances, the violence was set in motion by Church-sponsored programs, most prominently the Crusades. Thus the Church, on many occasions, initiated undertakings out of which attacks on the Jews developed and then took the lead in attempting to repress the unwarranted persecution which had been spawned.

All things considered, however, the Church's role in repressing violence was a limited one; ultimately it was the State that was decisive. The methods adopted by the State varied. Obviously for the Jews the best possible alternative was to forestall any outbreak of violence. Where potential catastrophe could be detected, committed and powerful governmental authorities could make an effort to thwart violence before it erupted. Evidence of the State's efforts to protect the Jews from possible violence is presented in the second chapter. In some cases, such efforts were successful; in other cases, they were not. Where violence did overtake an area and its Jewish settlements, governments could intervene to suppress the outbreak, as indicated in the third chapter. The decision to take such action was normally a difficult one. Often the masses participating in the uprising were imposing, and the risks involved in attempting to suppress the insurgence were substantial. Particularly during massive upheavals many key political leaders chose discretion over valor and watched passively while mobs decimated Jewish quarters. On the other hand, there were powerful factors which stimulated armed intervention. Unchecked violence against the Jews was apt to spill over against other elements in society as well, leading in the direction of general lawlessness. Moreover, the Jews represented substantial income and wealth and were not to be sacrificed lightly. Finally, there certainly were rulers moved by general humanitarian concerns and by specific obligations undertaken toward their Jews.

Of course, the decision to intervene did not mean automatic repression of the outbreak. The texts reflect a mixed record of success and failure. When an outbreak went unchecked, there remained yet one more avenue for effective governmental action. If, in the wake of violence, governments exhibited their concern by serious efforts to identify and punish malefactors, then future outbursts might be minimized. As the texts in the fourth chapter indicate, this too was no easy task.

7 ECCLESIASTICAL ADMONITIONS
AGAINST VIOLENCE

POPE ALEXANDER II, 1060S

IN THE 1060s, *a revitalized northern-European society began to show the first signs of an aggressive expansionism which would eventually push the Muslims from their European enclaves and bring about the impressive early successes of the Crusades in the Near East. The first area of Christian attack was the Iberian Peninsula where Muslims had long dominated the weak Christian states of northern Spain. Possessed of new military power and fired by new zeal, Christian knights from the north aided the Spanish Christians in beginning the long process of reconquest.*

It is not surprising that the hostility unleashed against the Muslims should have spilled over against the Jews: In periods of intense violence it is difficult to hold hatreds in narrowly defined channels. Pope Alexander II was unwilling, however, to acquiesce in such violence against the Jews. He wrote a series of letters decrying attacks upon the Jews and lauding those who had labored to protect the endangered Jews of Spain.

POPE ALEXANDER to all the bishops of Spain:
    We are pleased by the report which we have heard concerning you, that you have protected the Jews living among you, lest they be slain by

those who set out to war against the Saracens in Spain. These warriors, moved surely by foolish ignorance and strongly by blind cupidity, wished to bring about the slaughter of those whom divine charity has perhaps predestined for salvation. In the same manner Saint Gregory also admonished those agitated for annihilating them, indicating that it is impious to wish to annihilate those who are protected by the mercy of God, so that, with homeland and liberty lost, in everlasting penitence, damned by the guilt of their ancestors for spilling the blood of the Savior, they live dispersed throughout the various areas of the world. The situation of the Jews is surely different from that of the Saracens. Against the latter, who persecute Christians and drive them out of their cities and homes, one may properly fight; the former, however, are prepared to live in servitude.

BERNARD OF CLAIRVAUX, 1146

DESPITE THE SIGN *of an early tendency toward crusading violence against the Jews, the Church seems to have been caught unawares by the massive destruction which accompanied the First Crusade of 1096. While the bishops of the Rhineland, largely in their role as secular authorities, labored with greater or lesser success to protect their Jews, the higher echelons of Church leadership appeared to remain silent. No document parallel to the letter of Alexander II has been preserved from the pen of Urban II. When the terrible spring months had passed, however, the Church could no longer harbor any doubts as to the potential dangers stemming from the exhilaration of crusading mobs.*

After the victories of the late 1090s, the fortunes of the crusader principalities in the East began quickly to decline. The shocking fall of Edessa in 1144 aroused western Christendom and inspired a new Crusade. The great abbot of Clairvaux, Saint Bernard, led the way, convincing an inspiring array of political figures to band together and commit themselves to the Crusade. The result was an impressive military force that, unfortunately for Christendom, accomplished virtually nothing.

In calling forth the Second Crusade, Bernard and Pope Eugenius III were fully aware of the dangerous developments associated with the First Crusade. They were determined to preclude similar distortions of the crusading call and to avert the resultant tragedies. In his broadly distributed missive, composed to arouse the warriors of western Christendom to set off on the Crusade, Bernard describes the crisis and exhorts the knights of Europe to respond. He emphasizes the accepted channels in which violence is to flow—the war is to be waged against the Muslims of the East. He specifically warns against a repetition of the assaults on the Jews.

Bernard's warnings are clearly sincere and were generally heeded, a circumstance for which the Jews were deeply grateful. At the same time, it must be noted that there were significant negative implications in Bernard's message concerning the Jews. While demanding physical safety for the Jews, Bernard bases his demands on the notion that the Jews serve as witnesses to the truth of Christianity. We have already noted a variety of such doctrines, of which Bernard chooses some of the most debasing. He notes that "the Jews are for us the living words of Scripture, for they remind us of what our Lord suffered." It was precisely this association of the Jews with the crucifixion that branded them as enemies and prepared the ground for the murderous hostility of the Crusaders. Bernard further suggests that the fact of Jewish dispersion serves as a proof of God's punishment of the Jews' crime—once more a rationale not designed to endear the Jews to their neighbors. In sum, Bernard did insist upon Jewish safety, for which the Jews were grateful. The call, however, was marred by a harsh depiction of the Jews, which may well have reinforced some of the animus which it sought to suppress.

⚬

I ADDRESS MYSELF TO YOU, the people of England, in the cause of Christ, in whom lies your salvation. I say this so that the warrant of the Lord and my zeal in His interests may excuse my hardihood in addressing you. I am a person of small account, but my desire for you in Christ is not small. This is my reason and motive for writing; this is why I make bold to address you all by letter. I would have preferred to do so by word of mouth had I but the strength to come to you as I desire.

Now is the acceptable time; now is the day of abundant salvation. The earth is shaken because the Lord of Heaven is losing His land, the land in which He appeared to men, in which He lived among men for more than thirty years; the land made glorious by His miracles, holy by His blood; the land in which the flowers of His resurrection first blossomed. And now, for our sins, the enemy of the Cross has begun to lift his sacrilegious head there, and to devastate with the sword that blessed land, that land of promise. Alas, if there should be none to withstand him, he will soon invade the very city of the living God, overturn the arsenal of our redemption, and defile the holy places which have been adorned by the blood of the immaculate lamb. They have cast their greedy eyes especially on the holy sanctuaries of our Christian religion, and they long particularly to violate that couch on which, for our sakes, the Lord of our life fell asleep in death.

What are you doing, you mighty men of valor? What are you doing, you servants of the Cross? Will you thus cast holy things to the dogs, pearls before swine? How great a number of sinners have here confessed with tears and obtained pardon for their sins since the time when these holy precincts were cleansed of pagan filth by the swords of our fathers! The evil one sees this and is enraged; he gnashes his teeth and withers away in fury. He stirs up his vessels of wrath so that if they do but once lay hands upon these holy places there shall be no sign or trace of piety left. Such a catastrophe would be a source of confusion and endless shame for our generation. What think you, my brethren? Is the hand of the Lord shortened and is He now powerless to work salvation, so that He must call upon us, petty worms of the earth, to save and restore to Him His heritage? Could He not send more than twelve legions of angels, or even just say the word and save His land? Most certainly He has the power to do this whenever He wishes, but I tell you that God is trying you. "He looks down from heaven at the race of men, to find one soul that reflects, and makes God its aim," one soul that sorrows for Him. For God has pity on His people and on those who have grievously fallen away and has prepared for them a means of salvation. Consider with what care He plans our salvation, and be amazed. Look, sinners, at the depths of His pity, and take courage. He does not want your death but rather that you should turn to Him and live. So He seeks not to overthrow you but to help you. When Almighty God so treats murderers, thieves, adulterers, perjurers, and such like, as persons able to find righteousness in His service, what is it but an act of exquisite courtesy all God's own? Do not hesitate. God is good, and, were He intent on your punishment, He would not have asked of you this present service or indeed have accepted it, even had you offered it. Again I say, consider the Almighty goodness and pay heed to His plans of mercy. He puts Himself under obligation to you, or rather feigns to do so, so that He can help you to satisfy your obligations toward Himself. He puts Himself in your debt so that, in return for your taking up arms in His cause, He can reward you with pardon for your sins and everlasting glory. I call blessed the generation that can seize an opportunity of such rich indulgence as this, blessed to be alive in this year of jubilee, this year of God's choice. The blessing is spread throughout the whole world, and all the world is flocking to receive this badge of immortality.

Your land is well known to be rich in young and vigorous men. The world is full of their praises, and the renown of their courage is on the lips of all. Gird yourselves therefore like men and take up arms with joy and with zeal for your Christian name, in order to "take vengeance on the heathen, and curb the nations." For how long will your men continue to shed Christian blood; for how long will they continue to fight among themselves? You attack each other, you slay each other, and by each other you are slain. What is this savage craving of yours? Put a stop to it now, for it is not fighting but foolery. Thus to risk both soul and body is not brave but shocking, is not strength but folly. But now, O mighty soldiers, O men of war, you have a cause for which you can fight without danger to your souls—a cause in which to conquer is glorious and for which to die is gain.

But to those of you who are merchants, men quick to see a bargain, let me point out the advantages of this great opportunity. Do not miss them. Take up the sign of the Cross and you will find indulgence for all the sins which you humbly confess. The cost is small; the reward is great. Venture with devotion and the gain will be God's kingdom. They do well therefore who have taken up this heavenly sign, and they also will do well, and profit themselves, who hasten to take up what will prove to be for them a sign of salvation.

For the rest, not I but the Apostle warns you, brethren, not to believe every spirit. I have heard with great joy of the zeal for God's glory which burns in your midst, but your zeal needs the timely restraint of knowledge. The Jews are not to be persecuted, killed, or even put to flight. Ask anyone who knows the Sacred Scriptures what he finds foretold of the Jews in the Psalm. "Not for their destruction do I pray," it says. The Jews are for us the living words of Scripture, for they remind us always of what our Lord suffered. They are dispersed all over the world so that by expiating their crime they may be everywhere the living witnesses of our redemption. Hence the same Psalm adds, "only let Thy power disperse them." And so it is: dispersed they are. Under Christian princes they endure a hard captivity, but "they only wait for the time of their deliverance." Finally we are told by the Apostle that when the time is ripe all Israel shall be saved. But those who die before will remain in death. I will not mention those Christian moneylenders, if they can be called Christian, who, where there are no Jews, act, I grieve to say, in a manner worse than any Jew. If the Jews are utterly wiped out, what will become of our hope for their promised salvation, their eventual conversion? If the pagans were similarly subjugated to us then, in my opinion, we should wait for them rather than seek them out with swords. But as they have now begun to attack us, it is necessary for those of us who do not carry a sword in vain to repel them with force. It is an act of Christian piety both "to vanquish the proud" and also "to spare the subjected," especially those for whom we have a law and a promise, and whose flesh was shared by Christ Whose name be forever blessed.

BERNARD OF CLAIRVAUX, 1146

WHILE THE CALL OF SAINT BERNARD *to the Second Crusade had widespread impact, his warnings concerning the Jews were not always heeded. In particular, a popular preacher by the name of Radulph began to incite Crusaders against the Jews in the Rhineland area, which was precisely the scene of the worst atrocities of the First Crusade. Concerned over the potential for violence, the archbishop of Mainz wrote to Bernard, describing the actions of Radulph and seeking guidance. Bernard replied with a stinging condemnation of the preacher and his message.*

TO THE VENERABLE LORD and most dear father Henry, archbishop of Mainz, that he may find favor before God, from Bernard, abbot of Clairvaux:

I received your kind letter with due respect, but my answer must be brief because of the press of business. By revealing to me your troubles, you have given me a sure sign and pledge of your affection and, what is more, a mark of your humility. Who am I, or what is my father's house, that I should have referred to me a case of contempt for an archbishop and of damage to his metropolitan see? "I am no better than a child that has no skill to find its way back and forth." Yet ignorant though I be, I am not unmindful of those words of the Most High: "It must needs be that scandals come, but nevertheless woe to that man through whom the scandal comes." The fellow you mention in your letter has received no authority from men or through men, nor has he been sent by God. If he makes himself out to be a monk or a hermit and on that score claims liberty to preach and the duty of doing so, he can and should know that the duty of a monk is not to preach but to pray. He ought to be a man for whom towns are a prison and the wilderness a paradise, but instead of that he finds towns a paradise and the wilderness a prison. A fellow without sense and void of all modesty! A fellow whose foolishness has been set up on a candlestick for all the world to see!

I find three things most reprehensible in him: unauthorized preaching, contempt for episcopal authority, and incitation to murder. A new power forsooth! Does he consider himself greater than our father Abraham who laid down his sword at the bidding of Him by Whose command he took it up? Does he consider himself greater than the Prince of the Apostles who asked the Lord: "Shall we strike with our swords?" He is a fellow full of the wisdom of Egypt which is, as we know, foolishness in the sight of God. He is a fellow who answers Peter's question differently to the Lord who said: "Put back thy sword into its place; all those who take up the sword will perish by the sword." Is it not a far better triumph for the Church to convince and convert the Jews than to put them all to the sword? Has that prayer which the Church offers for the Jews, from the rising up of the sun to the going down thereof, that the veil may be taken from their hearts so that they may be led from the darkness of error into the light of truth, been instituted in vain? If she did not hope that they would believe and be converted, it would seem useless and vain for her to pray for them. But with the eye of mercy she considers how the Lord regards with favor him who renders good for evil and love for hatred. Otherwise where does that saying come in, "Not for their destruction I pray," and "When the fullness of the Gentiles shall have come in, then all Israel will be saved," and "The Lord is rebuilding Jerusalem, calling the banished sons of Israel home"? Who is this man that he should make out the prophet to be a liar and render void the treasures of Christ's love and pity? This doctrine is not his own but his father's. But I believe it is good enough for him, since he is like his father, who was, we know, "from the first a murderer, a liar, and the father of lies." What horrid learning, what hellish wisdom is his! A learning and wisdom contrary to the prophets, hostile to the apostles, and subversive of piety and grace. It is a foul heresy, a sacrilegious prostitution "pregnant with malice, that has conceived only spite, and given birth only to shame!" I should like to say more, but I must forbear. To sum up briefly what I feel about this fellow: He is a man with a great opinion of himself and full of arrogance. He shows by his works and teaching that he would like to make a great name for himself among the great of the earth, but that he has not the wherewithal to achieve this.

༄༅

BERNARD OF CLAIRVAUX, 1146

EVEN A SPECIFIC LETTER OF REBUKE *failed to halt the preaching of Radulph. Committed to preventing violence, Bernard went in person to the affected area, confronted the recalcitrant preacher, and forced him to halt his agitation. The successful efforts of Saint Bernard reflect the firm intention of the ecclesiastical leadership of the Second Crusade to prevent a recurrence of the bloodshed associated with its predecessor.*

In this instance we have a parallel set of depictions, one Christian and one Jewish, of the activity of Saint Bernard. The Christian perspective is presented by the historian Otto of Freising. The Jewish point of view is presented by Ephraim of Bonn, who some years after the Second Crusade wrote a recollection of the major events of 1146, featuring prominently the intervention of Bernard of Clairvaux.

༄༅

The Report of Otto of Freising

MEANWHILE THE MONK RADULPH, a man who did indeed wear the habit of religion and shrewdly imitated the strictness of religion, but was only moderately imbued with a knowledge of letters, entered those parts of Gaul which touch the Rhine and inflamed many thousands of the inhabitants of Cologne, Mainz, Worms, Speyer, Strasbourg, and other neighboring cities, towns, and villages to accept the cross. However, he heedlessly included in his preaching that the Jews whose homes were scattered throughout the cities and towns should be slain as foes of the Christian religion. The seed of this doctrine took such firm root and so grew in numerous cities of Gaul and Germany that a large number of Jews were killed in this stormy uprising, while many took refuge under the wings of the prince of the Romans. So it came about that not a few of them, fleeing from such cruelty, to save their lives betook themselves to a town of the prince which is called Noricum or Nuremburg and to other of his municipalities.

But the aforesaid abbot of Clairvaux, giving instruction to beware of such teaching, dispatched messengers and letters to the peoples of Gaul and Germany to point out clearly by the authority of the sacred page that the Jews were not to be killed for the enormity of their crimes, but were to be scattered. In this connection he called attention also to the testimony of the writer of Psalms who says in the fifty-seventh Psalm: "God shall let me see my desire upon mine enemies. Slay them not." And also, "Scatter them by thy power."

Now, when countless throngs in western Gaul had been aroused for the expedition across the sea, Bernard decided to turn his attention to the eastern kingdom of the Franks, to stir it with the plowshare of preaching, both that he might by the word of sacred exhortation move the heart of the prince of the Romans to accept the cross, and that he might silence Radulph, who in connection with the Jews was moving the people in the cities to repeated outbreaks against their lords. Hearing of this, the prince called a general assembly to be held at the city of Speyer at the time of the Lord's Nativity. The aforesaid abbot, coming there, persuaded the king with Frederick, his brother's son, and other princes and illustrious men to accept the cross, performing many miracles both publicly and in private.

Coming to Mayence also, he found Radulph living there in greatest favor with the people. He summoned him and warned him not to arrogate to himself on his own authority the word of preaching, roving about over the land in defiance of the rule of the monks. Finally he prevailed upon him to the point where he promised to obey and to return to his monastery. The people were very angry and even wanted to start an insurrection, but they were restrained by regard for Bernard's saintliness.

The Report of Ephraim of Bonn

LET THIS BE WRITTEN for all generations,
In order to accord praise to the Lord on High.
For Satan came forth to despoil Israel and Judah,
Who had to leave their communities and encamp in fear,
In the year 4906,
When oppression came forth to persecute the Jews.
For the evil Radulph
Wickedly pursued the Jews.

A priest of the idolatrous faith, he rose up against the Jews, to destroy, to kill, and to decimate, like the evil Haman. He went forth from France and traveled throughout Germany—may the Lord preserve it!—to call the Christians to the cross. He went about preaching—he was a preacher in the name of Jesus—that they must go to Jerusalem to battle the Muslims. Wherever he went, he spoke evilly of the Jews in the area, arousing against us snakes and dogs. He said: "Avenge the Crucified upon his enemies who live among you. Afterwards you shall journey to battle against the Muslims." We heard this and our hearts melted. Our spirits fell because of the fury of the oppressor who was preparing to destroy us. We called out to the Lord, saying: "Behold, O Lord our God. Not yet fifty years have passed since our blood was spilled for the unity of Your revered name, at the time of the great slaughter. Will You forsake us forever, O Lord? Will Your anger last throughout the genera-tions? Such tribulation should not recur twice!" Then the Lord heard our sigh, turned to us, and pitied us with His great mercy and kindness. Thus He sent after the evil priest a decent priest, a great man and the mentor of all the priests, one who knows and understands their faith. His name was Abbot Bernard, from the city of Clairvaux in France. He then preached as is their wont. Then he said to them: "It is fitting that you go forth against the Muslims. However, anyone who attacks a Jew and tries to kill him is as though he attacks Jesus himself. My pupil Radulph who advised destroying them did not advise properly. For in the Book of Psalms it is written concerning the Jews: 'Kill them not, lest my people forget.' " Everyone esteemed this priest as one of their saints. Moreover we have found no indication that he took a bribe for speaking up on behalf of the Jews. When the Christians heard this, many ceased their plotting to kill us. In addition we gave our money as redemption for our souls, since the Lord had pity upon us, to allow us a remnant in their land and to preserve us. Whatever they requested from us, silver and gold, we did not withhold. Were it not for the mercies of our Creator, Who sent the aforesaid abbot and his letters, there would not have been a remnant or survivor among the Jews. Blessed be He who redeems and saves us, blessed be His name.

എ൹

POPE GREGORY IX, 1236

APART FROM THE MAJOR CRUSADES *of the eleventh, twelfth, and thirteenth centuries, less significant crusading ventures often had important implica-tions for the Jews as well. One of these crusading waves developed in western France* *in the mid-1230s, and while it achieved none of its ostensible goals, it did perpetrate devastating assaults on the Jews of western France.*

Revealing references to these attacks are found in a pair of papal letters, the first addressed to the archbishops and bishops of the affected area and the second to the pious king of France, Louis IX. In these letters, Pope Gregory IX presents the Crusaders' rationales for such attacks and resolutely rejects them. Instead, he emphasizes strongly the Church's traditional policy of physical safety for the Jews. On this basis, he then calls upon the prelates and the king, each in his own way, to stem the tide of violence.

In random complaints gathered by royal inquisitors in the late 1240s there are references to allegedly unjust penalties imposed by royal officials upon Crusaders. It seems likely that some of these complaints may be related to the events of 1236 and that Saint Louis may in fact have taken resolute action against unwarranted violence, as requested by the pope.

Letter to the Bishops of Western France

To THE ARCHBISHOP OF BORDEAUX and to the bishops of Saintes, Angouleme, and Poitiers:

We have received a tearful and pitiful complaint from the Jews who live in the kingdom of France. The Crusaders of your districts and dioceses should have prepared heart and body to fight the battles of the Lord and to liberate the heritage of Christ from the hands of pagans, who, because of the enormous sins of the Christian people, hold and defile the Temple of God. To the extent that such a battle is especially Christ's, so much the more humbly should they embrace the fear and love of His name, lest, God forbid, they steep themselves in their evil desires and arouse against themselves divine displeasure. Yet these Crusaders, along with others, plot impious designs against those Jews and pay no heed to the fact that proofs for the Christian faith come, as it were, from their archives and that, as the prophets testify, although they should be as the sands of the sea, yet in the end of days a remnant of them shall be saved, because the Lord will not forever spurn His people. These Crusaders try to wipe the Jews almost completely off the face of the earth. In an unheard of and unprecedented outburst of cruelty, they have slaughtered in this mad hostility two thousand and five hundred of them—old and young, as well as pregnant women. Some were mortally wounded and others trampled like mud under the feet of horses. They burned their books and, for greater shame and disgrace, they exposed the bodies of those thus killed as food for the birds of heaven and their flesh to the beasts of the earth. After foully and shamefully treating those who remained alive after this massacre, they carried off their goods and consumed them. And in order that they may be able to hide such an inhuman crime under the cover of virtue and in some way justify their unholy cause, they claim to have done the above and threaten to do worse, on the ground that the Jews refuse to be baptized. They do not sufficiently consider that, when a storm arose in this great and spacious sea and humankind was endangered by this tempest, then the true Jonah, Jesus Christ, the Son of God, came into these depths and permitted Himself to be submerged in this storm, so that by His blood he might win us back to God and renew us through the font of regeneration which is consecrated by it. He did not make distinctions of condition of life or of sex, as a result of which anyone of any people can be raised into adoption among the children of God. But those to whom God wants to be merciful are not to be compelled to the grace of baptism, rather they must want it voluntarily. Just as man fell of his own free will when he succumbed to the serpent's guile, even so, when called by the grace of God, he ought to bring about his own rise in complete freedom of will.

Wherefore, placed as under a new Egyptian enslavement, and fearing their extermination, the Jews humbly had recourse to the mercy of the Apostolic Throne. Therefore, lest such great temerity, if unpunished, continue to injure still others, we command that each one of you force the inhabitants of your dioceses who commit such excesses, to bring proper satisfaction for the crimes perpetrated against the Jews and for the property stolen from them. After giving due warning you may use ecclesiastical punishment without appeal.

Given at Reate, on the fifth of September, in the tenth year [1236].

Letter to the King of France

TO THE KING OF FRANCE:

We have received a tearful and pitiful complaint from the Jews who live in the kingdom of France. The Crusaders of the districts and dioceses of Angers, Poitiers, Le Mans, Tours, and Bourges should have prepared heart and body to fight the battles of the Lord and to liberate the heritage of Christ from the hands of pagans, who, because of the enormous sins of the Christian people, hold and defile the Temple of

God. To the extent that such a battle is especially Christ's, so much the more humbly should they be filled with fear and love of His name, lest, God forbid, they steep themselves in their evil desires and arouse against themselves divine displeasure. Yet these Crusaders, along with others, plot impious designs against those Jews and pay no heed to the fact that proofs for the Christian faith come, as it were, from their archives and that, as the prophets testify, although they should be as the sands of the sea, yet in the end of days a remnant of them shall be saved, because the Lord will not forever spurn His people. These Crusaders try to wipe the Jews almost completely off the face of the earth. In an unheard of and unprecedented outburst of cruelty, they have slaughtered in this mad hostility two thousand and five hundred of them, old and young, as well as pregnant women. Some were mortally wounded and others trampled like mud under the feet of the horses. They burned their books and, for greater shame and disgrace, they exposed the bodies of those thus killed as food for the birds of heaven and their flesh to the beasts of the earth. After foully and shamefully treating those who remained alive after this massacre, they carried off their goods and consumed them. And in order that they may be able to hide such an inhuman crime under the cover of virtue and in some way justify their unholy cause, they represent themselves as having done the above and threaten to do worse, on the ground that the Jews refuse to be baptized. They do not sufficiently consider that, when a storm arose in this great and spacious sea and humankind was endangered by this tempest, then the true Jonah, Jesus Christ, the Son of God, came into these depths and permitted Himself to be submerged in this storm, so that by His blood He might win us back to God and renew us through the font of regeneration which is consecrated by it. He did not make distinctions of condition of life or of sex, as a result of which anyone of any people can be raised into adoption among the children of God. But those to whom God wants to be merciful are not to be compelled to the grace of baptism, rather they must want it voluntarily. Just as man fell of his own free will when he succumbed to the serpent's guile, even so, when called by the grace of God, he ought to bring about his own rise in complete freedom of will.

Wherefore, placed as under a new Egyptian enslavement and fearing their extermination, the Jews humbly had recourse to the mercy of the Apostolic Throne. However, it is for the kings to render judgment and justice, for in the words of the prophet, "The glory of a king is love of justice," and "His throne is built upon righteousness and justice," and "Rescue the victim from his oppressor." Therefore, we ask and warn and urge Your Royal Excellency in the name of the Lord to use the

power with which God entrusted you, to correct and to punish those who
in their rashness dare commit these crimes so unspeakably and terribly
offensive to God in Whose image the victims were created and so injurious to the Apostolic Throne whose privileges they have been granted.
Force the Crusaders to restore to the Jews all that has been stolen—that
you may prove yourself by an exhibition of good works to be one who
hates iniquity and loves justice. Thus may we be able to commend to
God the zeal of your sincerity.

Given at Reate, on the fifth of September, in the tenth year [1236].

8 GOVERNMENTAL PROTECTION PRIOR TO THE OUTBREAK OF VIOLENCE

EMPEROR HENRY IV, 1096

THE MOST SERIOUS EARLY DISASTER *to strike medieval Jewry in western Christendom was the First Crusade. While Pope Urban II sought and elicited a scrupulously organized military expedition which would journey eastward and conquer the holy sites of Christendom, the fervor unleashed by the call to the Crusade went far beyond the carefully defined papal objectives and engulfed a series of northern-European Jewish communities as well. The elements participating in the First Crusade were three in number: the well-armed barony, the vast hordes aroused and led by the charismatic Peter the Hermit, and the smaller and more violent groups stirred up in the wake of Peter's preaching. Only the first force reached the Holy Land and achieved Urban's goals of conquest. Interestingly, the Jews in the West suffered little from this successful crusading army. One story, preserved in the longest of the extant Hebrew chronicles, tells of a threat to Jewish security from a major baronial figure in the Crusade and of imperial intervention to quell the incipient danger.*

AT THAT TIME A DUKE named Godfrey—may his bones be ground up—arose, in a mood of savagery. For a capricious spirit had misled him into joining the Crusaders. He then swore wickedly that he

113

would not depart without avenging the blood of the Crucified by spilling the blood of the Jews. He swore that he would leave neither a relic nor a remnant of those bearing the name Jew; he was filled with wrath against us.

Indeed a protector arose—the exemplar of the generation, the God-fearing, sacrificed eventually on the inner altar—R. Kalonymus the *parnas* [communal leader], of the community of Mainz. He anticipated these troubles and sent a messenger to Emperor Henry in the kingdom of Apulia—for he had tarried there nine years—and told him of all these events. Then the emperor was extremely angry and sent letters throughout all the districts of his empire, to his officials, to the bishops, to the barons, and to Duke Godfrey, ordering that they guard the Jews in such a way that no one harm them and ordering that they serve the Jews as an aid and refuge. Then the wicked duke swore that he had never intended to do the Jews any harm. Nonetheless the Jews bribed him with five hundred silver talents in Cologne; they likewise bribed him in Mainz. He then promised on his staff to behave peaceably toward them.

❧

KING LOUIS VII OF FRANCE AND
COUNT HENRY II OF CHAMPAGNE, 1171

A WAVE OF ANTI-JEWISH *accusations, first heard in England, quickly spread through European society during the twelfth century. The claim that Jews slew innocent Christian youngsters was often believed within the Christian populace, but governmental authorities normally rejected the charges and protected their Jews.*

A major turning point occurred in the Blois affair of 1171. In this instance, no body was ever found; the entire tragedy sprang from the testimony of a Christian servant who claimed he had seen a Jew throwing a corpse into the Loire River. Despite the flimsy basis for the murder accusation, it was accepted not only by the populace, but by the authorities as well. Stirred up by the political and religious advisors, the Count of Blois ordered the execution of over thirty Jews, whose death profoundly shocked their coreligionists.

Because of the frightening precedent involved and the danger that their leaders might also follow the example of Theobald of Blois, the Jews of northern France, under the guidance of R. Jacob Tam, undertook a concerted campaign of political negotiation. Fortunately, some of the correspondence of this campaign has survived. The first of the following three letters details the meeting between the leaders of

Parisian Jewry and the most important political figure in the area, King Louis VII of France. Fortunately for the Jews, the king roundly condemned the actions of his brother-in-law Theobald. Noting his familiarity with the new accusation, Louis firmly rejected it and promised his Jews enhanced protection. The entire tone of this letter is one of joyous reassurance. The second letter stems from another major Jewish community, that of Troyes. Addressed to the Jews of the Rhineland, this epistle preserves a condensed account of the successful negotiations with the king as well as a report of an equally productive discussion with Theobald of Blois' brother, the powerful count of Champagne.

In the Troyes letter, there is a brief reference to other negotiations, aimed at securing burial for the Jewish martyrs and redemption for those still held captive. A report on the achievements of this discussion with yet another of Theobald's brothers, William of the White Hands, archbishop of Sens and bishop of Chartres, is included in the third and final letter. Here too there is a pleased reference to the royal stance. More important is the full account of the Jews' approach to the archbishop and the meeting's success.

The Paris Letter

THIS IS THE LETTER from the leaders of Paris Jewry:

Today is a day of glad tidings from the Great King to His people Israel, for He has inclined the heart of the earthly king in our favor. We journeyed to the king at Poissy to fall before his feet concerning this matter. When we saw that he extended greetings, we indicated that we would like to speak to him privately. He responded: "Speak openly!" Then he himself called forth all his ministers stationed in the fortress and said to them: "Listen all of you to what Count Theobald has done—may he and his descendants be barren throughout the entire year! If he has acted properly, then well and good; but if he has behaved improperly, may he be punished. For I too am frightened over what he has done. Now then, you Jews of my land, you have no cause for alarm over what that persecutor has done in his domain. For people have leveled the same accusation against the Jews of Pontoise and Janville, but, when the charges were brought before me, they were found false." Then the king told the Jews of the Pontoise incident and Robert who was beatified in Paris and indicated that it was completely unfounded—likewise in the present instance. "Therefore be assured, all you Jews in my land, that I harbor no such suspicions. Even if a body be discovered in the city or in the countryside, I shall say nothing to the Jews in that regard. Therefore be not frightened over this issue.''

Nonetheless we can still not go there. In any case, thank the Lord, the king has drawn up a sealed charter to be circulated throughout his domain, that the Jews remain tranquil and undisturbed and that all his officials treat the Jews respectfully and protect their persons and property more carefully than heretofore. In fact much more transpired than we have written to you. Praise and thanks to the Great King.

The Troyes Letter

THIS IS WHAT OUR BRETHREN in Paris have written to us. Their letter is no longer in our hands, for it has been sent elsewhere. However, I have composed a summary.

When the king returned from Flanders, the leaders of Paris Jewry and other Jewish communities went forth to meet him. They asked the king's servants to speak with the king. The king's servants replied: "Enter." When the king saw them, he offered greetings and they responded, rejoicing silently. They said: "Our lord king, we wish to speak privately." He replied: "I shall not speak with you privately. Rather I shall speak openly. For Theobald has sinned grievously. It is a serious matter and I am fearful. I do not believe that the Jews ever killed a Christian—neither Robert of Pontoise, who was beatified, nor that of Theobald. Fear not, for I shall enhance the respect accorded you." He then announced throughout his kingdom that the Jews must be respected doubly and that their persons and property must be protected more carefully than heretofore.

The *haver* [advanced student] R. Nathan b. Rabbi Meshullam is attempting by a bribe of 220 pounds to gain burial for those slain and to redeem those held captive. Perhaps he will be successful.

Count Henry, the brother of the wicked Theobald, is remorseful over the incident and says: "We find nowhere in Jewish law that it is permissible to kill a Christian. Recently, just before Passover, an accusation was made in Épernay and I did not believe it." In any case we gave money to quash the accusation.

The Letter of Nathan ben Rabbi Meshullam

THAT WHICH MAY BE REVEALED I shall communicate to Rabbi Yom Tov, so that he may reveal it by letter to our sacred teacher, that we might give thanks to our Savior Who has inclined the king's heart in our favor. For when he learned of this terrible matter, he remained stunned momentarily and said to the queen: "Today your brother has disgraced my crown, for we are warned by the sacred authorities to protect zealously the persons and the property of the Jews." What Theobald did troubled the king, as he indicated to all. His officers then asked if they were to do likewise. He answered: "It is not proper to do this. Indeed it is my intention to honor the Jews doubly." He then sent a decree throughout his domain to his officials, ordering them to guard zealously the Jews' persons and property.

Yesterday I came before the bishop of Sens, to attempt to release those imprisoned by his brother, the wicked count, and those forcibly converted. I paid the bishop a bribe of 120 pounds, with a promise of 100 pounds for the count, for which I have already given guarantees. The count then signed an agreement to release the prisoners from confinement. Concerning the young people forcibly converted, he asked that they be permitted to return to the Lord. Thus they emerged safely. All those imprisoned, however, escaped the clutches of the wicked one with their clothes only, for he retained possession of all their goods—both capital and loans. He also signed an agreement that there would be no further groundless accusations. All of this the Lord has performed on our behalf.

❦

EMPEROR FREDERICK I, 1188

IN 1187, *the achievements of a century of crusading were suddenly wiped out by the startling successes of Saladin. News of the stunning turn of events in Outremer quickly reached western Christendom, arousing Church and secular leaders. A great new Crusade was quickly organized, although the accomplishments of the Third Crusade eventually proved quite limited. Reports of Crusader reverses penetrated the Jewish quarters of Europe as well, eliciting a mixed reaction of elation and trepidation. The Jews well knew that the new agitation meant grave dangers once more.*

The accompanying report, composed by a Jewish leader, R. Elazar b. Judah, reveals three stages in the tribulations of Mainz Jewry. In the fall of 1187, while dramatic events were unfolding in the Near East, the Jewish community of Mainz was beset by another in the series of murder accusations already noted. In this instance, the Jews were spared from violence, although they were, as usual, forced to pay a high price for the protection accorded them. As soon as the news of Saladin's victories reached Germany, the Jews of Mainz faced a far graver threat. According to R. Elazar, the Christian response was: "Behold! The day which we have demanded has come—the day on which to kill all the Jews." With this cry, Christians invaded the Jewish quarter of Mainz. Fortunately for the Jews, the authorities proved resolute and drove off the attackers. In the face of deepening tensions, the Jews decided finally to adopt again the techniques which had proven successful during the Second Crusade. They left their homes and possessions and retreated to outlying fortifications, where they might fully protect themselves.

The third and final stage of the trials of Mainz Jewry involved a small but important group of Jews who decided to remain in the city. It was precisely in Mainz that Emperor Frederick too the cross on March 27, 1188. A courageous band of Jews jeopardized their own safety by staying in Mainz in order to negotiate with Frederick directly. The information on this group and its achievements comes directly from a letter written from Mainz by R. Elazar's brother-in-law and appended by R. Elazar to his narrative. This letter depicts the deepening tension in Mainz, with occasional outbursts against individual Jews. In all instances, the authorities remained strong and protected their Jews. Eventually a full-scale invasion of the Jewish neighborhood was mounted and repulsed. The emperor responded with a major declaration: "Anyone who harms a Jew and causes an injury, his hand shall be cut off. Anyone who kills a Jew shall be killed." This edict was buttressed by the support of the assembled ecclesiastical dignitaries. All of this was fully paid for by the Jewish representatives who had endangered themselves in order to carry on these delicate and crucial negotiations.

※

I SHALL RECOUNT WHAT HAPPENED to us at Mainz in the year 4947 [1187], during the month of Elul. A Christian went through the cemetery on Friday and claimed that a Jew attempted to kill him. The bishop spread this tale, until the community came to an agreement and gave the bishop more than one hundred talents. On the second day of Rosh Hashanah, when they were brought to the bishop's palace, they swore that they had done nothing to the Christian; they also swore that they do not kill Christians on the eve of Passover. The Jews also gave much money.

While we were still involved in this incident, the entire world saw a sign in the sun. In 4947, on the eve of Rosh Hashanah, in the morning, we saw that the sun was as small as a half moon and was very dark. Afterwards, the sun reddened, and the earth looked entirely green. At the end of a third part of the day, the sun was restored. After Sukkot and prior to Hanukah, we heard that the Muslims had gone out and conquered Acre, had killed all the inhabitants of Acre, and had captured all the environs of Jerusalem—from Acre and Ekron to Jerusalem. On the eve of Rosh Hashanah, on the day when the sun was eclipsed, the Muslims had killed more than four thousand Frankish knights. They had also captured a relic upon which Jesus—may his bones be ground up—was crucified and brought it with them to their land. After Hanukah they captured the sepulcher and killed all the inhabitants of Jerusalem. They took out the tomb of the Crucified and destroyed the inside of the sepulcher. Afterwards the news reached all areas of Germany, and the Christians said to all the Jews: "Behold! The day which we have demanded has come—the day on which to kill all the Jews." This happened during the days of Lent.

When we heard, a very great trembling seized us, and we took up the arts of our forefathers, decreeing fasting, weeping, and mourning. On Friday, the twenty-eighth of the month of Shevat, 4948 [January 24, 1188], the Christians gathered to kill us and came into the Jews' street. The Jews then shut themselves up in their houses. The Christians broke through one of the Jews' roofs. Finally heavenly forces had pity upon us, and the chamberlain's men came and drove the Christians off. Thus our Creator—may He be blessed—saved us from all our enemies. Meanwhile the Christians were taking the sign of the cross by the hundreds, by the thousands, and by the ten thousands, double and treble the number of those leaving Egypt, continually threatening to kill us. Our sages and elders told us: "Let us fast and beseech our God. Perhaps our God will come to our aid." Then at the afternoon service of the Sabbath, on the thirteenth day of Adar I [February 13], after the Torah scroll had been rolled up, my father R. Judah b. Kalonymus ascended the wooden platform and said: "Let every man repent of his wicked ways. Perhaps the Lord, in His mercy and grace, will deal kindly with us. Let us accept upon ourselves a fast and let us seek mercy." Likewise R. Moses b. Mordechai and all our elders and my brother-in-law R. Moses the cantor exhorted tearfully, enjoining the Jews to fast every Monday and Thursday until the month of Nisan, to give charity on the night of these fasts, to utter the penitential prayers, and to seek forgiveness—every man from his friend and every woman from her neighbor. Thus we begged tearfully for our lives, for our wives, and for our children, lest the wicked kill them or baptize them with their impure waters. All the Jews were in deep distress. Finally we decided to flee to fortifications—all the Jews of Mainz, Speyer, Strasbourg, Worms, Wurzburg, and all the neighboring areas where Jews lived. We, the Jews of Mainz, left Torah scrolls, our beloved treasures, along with books and all our wealth, with the ravenous wolves, the burghers, in order to make it easier to flee for our lives. In the year 4948 [1188], during the month of Adar II, we fled to Munzenberg. Everywhere the Jews divided themselves up, fleeing to four villages or to five fortifications. Meanwhile the royal court was at Mainz, and the Crusaders continued to take the cross by the thousands and the ten thousands—an innumerable host. A few Jews remained in Mainz in their homes.

Today, on Friday, the second day of Nisan [April 1, 1188], Elazar the Small, the secretary of my brother-in-law R. Moses b. Elazar ha-Cohen the cantor, arrived. This is the letter he brought:

Let me give thanks and acknowledge divine glory with stringed instruments to the Lord Who has given us life and sustained us. For this year, on the week prior to the beginning of Nisan, we were suspended between life and death. For the Crusaders ground their teeth, prepared to swallow us as one swallows up fish. Had it not been for the mercies of the Almighty, we would have been lost. Blessed is the Lord Who has saved us from their swords. The Crusaders gathered on our street to assault us and to attack us. But the Lord saved us, as we shall indicate.

First, however, let me tell all that has happened to us here. From the eighth day of Adar II [March 9], they began to come to the royal court. We remained in great danger until the twenty-fourth of Adar II [March 25]. On Friday, a Jewish lad came with me to the market to buy bread for the Sabbath. They threw him to the ground, trampled him in the dirt, and placed a knife at his heart, asking him whether he was willing to deny the living God. He responded: "No!" They then continued to beat him until he fled to a church. They ran after him, but the priests would not allow them to harm him. He finally escaped through another door. They ran after him and almost killed him, when a knight happened by and saved him with great difficulty. Fortunate is the eye which was spared all these sights! For they cast lots against us—this was to die in one manner and this in another, this by plucking out his eyes and this by the sword. They did not cease day or night, grinding their teeth in preparation for swallowing us alive. We had to listen to abuse, behaving like the deaf who do not hear. We remained shut up in our homes. On the Sabbath, the marshal assured us that we might open our homes, which we did fearfully. On Sunday, two marshals came to the *nadiv* [wealthy community leader] R. Moses b. Joseph ha-Cohen and told him to close up the doors of his house. We were very frightened; we were seized with trembling and breathless until the aforementioned Moses ha-Cohen—may he be remembered for good and for life—returned. For had he not stepped into the breach and comforted us and consoled us, we would have died of fear. We prayed regularly in the synagogue early in the morning, but not on Saturday evening or Sunday morning. The old king and his son the duke and all their officials took the cross, along with an innumerable multitude. On Monday, a knight wished to enter the synagogue, but a marshal came and struck him with a stave so that he almost died. God—may He be blessed—did many such things on our behalf; who could relate or write them? We are not properly appreciative of His great miracles. If it were not forbidden to add new festivals, we should establish a second Purim. For all the nations beat their hands, in preparation for destroying us and obliterating our memory. Only the old king and his son, the young king—may he live—were beneficent toward the Jews. More than ten thousand took the cross, really only to kill themselves and to gather booty. But the kings continually spoke well of the Jews. Then the enemy turned about and returned to their lands shamedfacedly.

On the Sabbath prior to the month of Nisan [March 26], the Crusaders gathered in our street to assault us and to attack us. One arose, with a sword in his hand, and attempted to smite a Jew. Then the marshal came . . . and seized him by the hair, pulling it, and smote him with a staff until his blood spilled to the ground. The rest fled to the marketplace and told their fellow Crusaders what had been done to them on account of the Jews. They all gathered, by the thousands and the ten thousands, and wished to take a standard and advance upon our street. The matter was revealed to the marshal; with a staff in his hand, he took his servants with him and smote the Crusaders and beat them, until they had all dispersed. We were in very grave trouble—almost fatal—from Friday until Tuesday. Blessed is the Lord and may His memory be exalted forever, for He provided relief prior to the blow. The officers understood clearly, saying: "How beloved are the Jews in the eyes of the king!" May the name of the Lord be blessed from now and forever and may His memory be honored to eternity, for He has done all this not because of our righteousness but because of His great Name which is to be blessed forever. On Tuesday, the emperor extended peace to the Jews, announcing: "Anyone who harms a Jew and causes an injury, his hand shall be cut off. Anyone who kills a Jew shall be killed." The bishops then excommunicated all who lift their hands to kill a Jew. Even crusading would not exempt one from this penalty. The king further ordered an edict circulated both written and oral, that the Jews be protected carefully, even more than had been done heretofore. All of this was paid for fully. The *nadiv* R. Moses ha-Cohen rode with the king and wrote out the edict extending peace to the Jews.

We left Munzenberg on the twenty-seventh of Nisan [April 26]. When we had advanced a mile and a half, the Crusaders came out to meet us by the hundreds, with their crosses and their standards, and beat upon our wagons . . . But the Lord saved us.

⬥

KING JOHN OF ENGLAND, 1203

IN THE MID-ELEVENTH CENTURY, *the Norman conquerors of England brought with them a small Jewish community. These Jews proved highly useful to the English economy and particularly to the English monarchy. By and large they lived quietly and peacefully down through the end of the twelfth century. It was the crowning of King Richard and the exhilaration associated with his departure for the Third Crusade that sparked a wave of violence against English Jewry.*

By the early thirteenth century, the agitation against the Jews had quieted and relative tranquillity had returned. A letter from King John reveals, however, that London Jewry was still somewhat insecure. John's epistle, which speaks of the general security of England's Jews and of the specific problems in London, was intended to forestall any new outbreak of violence. It is a warning to the authorities in London to protect their Jews. This protection is seen as part of the normal royal concern for peace and justice. Included is an exceedingly uncharitable reference to the Jews—"for if we gave our peace to a dog it should be inviolably observed." The appeal, then, is based on no special fondness for the Jews; it is a demand that the well-being of English society be preserved and that all violence be suppressed.

⬥

THE KING, etc., to the mayor and barons of London, etc.:
We have always loved you greatly and have caused your laws and liberties to be carefully observed. Therefore, we believe that you love us

in a special way and that you freely wish to do those things that enhance our honor and the peace and tranquillity of our land. Indeed, as you know that the Jews are under our special protection, we are amazed that you permit harm to be done to the Jews residing in the city of London, since this is obviously against the peace of the kingdom and the tranquillity of our land. In fact, we are further amazed and concerned because other Jews, wherever they dwell throughout England, live in peace, except those who reside in your city. We say this not only for our Jews, but also for our peace, for if we gave our peace to a dog it should be inviolably observed. Therefore, we commit henceforth the Jews residing in the city of London to your care, so that, if anyone attempts to do them harm, you shall defend them, affording them assistance by force. We shall require their blood of your hands, if perchance, through your failure, any harm befalls them, Heaven forbid. Indeed we well know that such things happen through the fools of the city and not through its wise men. However, the wise must restrain the folly of the fools.

With myself as witness, at Montford, July 29.

EMPEROR FREDERICK II, 1236

BY THE TWELFTH CENTURY, *the widespread animosity toward the Jews found new avenues of expression. Charges alleging Jewish malevolence and hatred of Christianity and Christians were broadly disseminated. Most of these allegations related to the Easter season and the traditional imputation to the Jews of the guilt of deicide. During the 1230s, a new twist was added: It was claimed that as part of their own spring ritual, the Jews utilized Christian blood. This baseless slander, which was destined for a long career in medieval and modern Christendom, profoundly frightened German Jewry, who found little solace in the inherent irrationality of the charge. These Jews turned to their major protector, the emperor, in order to elicit the safeguards which would forestall violence.*

Emperor Frederick responded in two ways to the entreaties of his Jews. He first confirmed an older charter of protection, accorded to the Jews of Worms by his distinguished grandfather Frederick I, and extended this charter to all Jews throughout the empire. He then buttressed this broad protection by attacking the new slander directly. He personally gathered lay and ecclesiastical leaders and initiated an exhaustive inquiry into the issue. His goal was to discover the truth, which seems to have been rather obvious to him, and to convince the masses of it, which was a good deal more difficult. To these ends he utilized expert information, particularly from recent converts who possessed both information and, often, a strong desire to show Jews and Judaism in the most damaging possible light. When this investigation led to the conclusion that Jewish utilization of human blood was impossible on many grounds, the emperor emphatically warned against any violence which might be rationalized on the basis of the discredited slander. Frederick's decree is unusually careful and vigorous; it was one of the most significant charters accorded the Jews during the Middle Ages. Lamentably it did not deal a death blow to the new slander, which remained influential long after this imperial edict was forgotten.

As always the Jews paid a price for protection. In this case their needs were exploited by the emperor to reemphasize his full control over them and their total dependence upon him. The Jews are recurrently designated imperial serfs throughout the charter. While the emperor enjoins safety and well-being, it is the safety accorded to serfs as a sign of esteem for their master. Once more the Jews' needs thrust them more tightly into the grasp of their overlords.

✲❖✲

IN THE NAME OF THE HOLY AND UNDIVIDED TRINITY, Frederick II, through the favor of divine mercy august emperor of the Romans and king of Jerusalem and Sicily:

Although the preeminence of this august dignity is obligated to extend the arm of its protection to all subjects of the Roman Empire and although it is fitting, for the protection of the faith which stems from celestial dispensation, to treat the faithful of Christ with special favor, nonetheless, for the proper management of justice, it is required that we rule the non-believers properly and protect them justly, as a special group committed to our care. Thus, living with the faithful under the protection of our majesty, they shall not be violently oppressed by those stronger than themselves. Therefore, it is by the contents of the present letter that present and future generations shall know that all the serfs of our court in Germany have beseeched our majesty that we deign by our grace to confirm for all the Jews of Germany the privilege of our divine grandfather Frederick, granted to the Jews of Worms and their associates. These are the contents of that privilege . . . :

Providing then for the security and peaceful status of the Jews of Germany, we cause this special grace to be extended to all Jews who belong directly to our court. That is to say, copying and adhering to the edicts of our aforesaid grandfather, we confirm for the Jews by our natural mercy the above privilege and those stipulations contained in it, in the same manner as our divine and august grandfather granted to the Jews of Worms and their associates.

Moreover, we wish that all present and future know the following. When a serious crime was imputed to the Jews of Fulda concerning the death of certain boys of the town, because of that terrible incident the harsh opinion of the neighboring populace, spawned by recent misfortune, was projected against the rest of the Jews of Germany, although covert attacks were not yet in evidence. In order to clarify the truth concerning the aforesaid crime, we had many of the princes and magnates and nobles of the empire, along with abbots and clerics, convened to provide counsel. When diverse views on the matter had been expressed, not adequate to produce clear counsel, as is fitting, we concluded that one could not proceed more properly against the Jews accused of the aforesaid crime than through those who had been Jews and had converted to the cult of the Christian faith. They, since opposed to Judaism, would not withhold whatever they might know against the Jews, whether through the Mosaic books or through the contents of the Old Testament. Although through the authority of many books, which our majesty distributed, our conscience had the innocence of the aforesaid Jews reasonably proven, in order to provide satisfaction for both the populace and the law, by our counsel and that of our princes, magnates, nobles, abbots, and clerics, with unanimous agreement, we sent special messengers to all the kings of the West, through whom we had many experienced experts in Jewish law sent from their kingdoms to our presence. When they had tarried in our court for some time, we commanded, in order to ascertain the truth of this matter, that they diligently conduct a study and instruct our conscience whether there survives any belief leading to the perpetrating of any act regarding human blood, which might impel the Jews to commit the aforesaid crime. When their findings were published on this matter, then it was clear that it was not indicated in the Old Testament or in the New that Jews lust for the drinking of human blood. Rather, precisely the opposite, they guard against the intake of all blood, as we find expressly in the biblical book which is called in Hebrew, "Bereshit," in the laws given by Moses, and in the Jewish decrees which are called in Hebrew, "Talmud." We can surely assume that for those to whom even the blood of permitted animals is forbidden, the desire for human blood cannot exist, as a result of the horror of the matter, the prohibition of nature, and the common bond of the human species in which they also join Christians. Moreover, they would not expose to danger their substance and persons for that which they might have freely when taken from animals. By this sentence of the princes, we pronounce the Jews of the aforesaid place and the rest of the Jews of Germany completely absolved of this imputed crime. Therefore, we decree by the authority of the present privilege that no one, whether cleric or layman, proud or humble, whether under the pretext of preaching or otherwise, judges, lawyers, citizens, or others, shall attack the aforesaid Jews individually or as a group as a result of the aforesaid charge. Nor shall anyone cause them notoriety or harm in this regard. Let all know that, since a lord is honored through his servants, whoever shows himself favorable and helpful to our serfs the Jews will surely please us. However, whoever presumes to contravene the edict of this present confirmation and of our absolution bears the offense of our majesty.

In order that the present confirmation and absolution remain in unimpaired and perpetual validity, we have ordered that the present privilege be drawn up and be sealed with the golden seal bearing the symbol of our majesty.

KING JAMES II OF ARAGON, 1294

THE SLANDERS *already noted became increasingly widespread during the thirteenth century, exposing the Jews to constant danger and necessitating resolute governmental protection. A letter written by the king of Aragon at the end of the century reveals both the credulity of the masses, the recognition of danger by the Jews, and the firm stand of some political authorities.*

The incident at Saragossa began with the disappearance of a young boy. When all efforts to locate him failed, the municipal authorities permitted the use of magic. Through a magician, a young girl was alleged to have reconstructed a supposed Jewish crime. She claimed that the Jews had killed the youth, had extracted his heart and his liver, and had burned the corpse. Armed with this information, the authorities searched the house where the crime was supposed to have been committed and the body interred. Although they found nothing, tensions remained high. The Jews sought to protect themselves by instituting a search of their own, culminating in the discovery of the boy in Calatayud. The king ended his lengthy description of the incident with a clear and unequivocal warning. The entire affair was scandalous, both for the dangers that it entailed for the Jews and for the use of magic which had long been prohibited. Those guilty of fomenting this incident were to be sought out and punished. Most important, King James prohibited any repetition of such slander, threatening offenders with drastic punishment. Such positive action by a powerful monarch represented a major safeguard for Jewish security.

JAMES, etc., to the judge and the officials of Saragossa, etc.:

The following has been presented before us by the *aljama* [community] of the Jews of the aforesaid city. Recently a certain Christian woman was unable to find a certain lad, her son. In order to discover him, she had him searched throughout the said city, but she did not find him. It was then suggested that the said *aljama* had seized or abducted the aforesaid boy. As a result, it is reported, the officials of the said city commanded a certain man who, it is said, knows magic to discover where the said boy was. A certain Christian girl, who, it is reported, was familiar with the Jews' houses, was chosen. The man then caused her to look into a certain magic instrument which he had prepared. This girl, we understand, said that she saw a certain Christian woman who had carried the said boy to the house of a certain Jew and that the Jews took him up to a certain chamber and that they beheaded him and took from his body the liver and the heart and that they buried the corpse in a certain room of the house. When all this had been said by the said girl, then the aforesaid officials came to the house of the said Jew with the aforesaid girl and searched, along with her, that house. They dug up that place where the said girl indicated that the said boy was interred. However they found nothing. As a result of all the aforesaid, a strong rumor developed among the Christians of the said city, to the extent that the Jews did not dare to appear among those Christians. As a result of the Jews' fears, they had the aforesaid boy sought throughout the various areas of Aragon and Navarre. He was discovered, the Jews claim, at Calatayud, in the keep of a certain alms-collector who had gone there on business. The said alms-collector, when arrested and questioned, claimed that the boy was his son and that he had sired him through a certain woman of Saragossa. When the discovery of the aforesaid boy reached the ears of the aforesaid officials, they ordered that woman, by whom the alms-collector claimed that he had fathered the boy, to tell the truth. The woman said that the said boy was not her son and that she knew nothing of those things which the said alms-collector had reported.

Such efforts against the said Jews are highly irregular, since scandal from these matters might develop in the said city, as a result of which our *aljama* might be destroyed, and since this was done illegally, because magic and all incantations are prohibited according to our law. Such behavior should not be tolerated by us, since it is totally improper. Therefore, we order and command you that you inform yourselves carefully concerning the aforesaid incident and that you punish those whom you find guilty. In this way their punishment will serve as an example to others wishing to attempt similar efforts. We order that henceforth such incantations not be carried out in the said city and that henceforth such efforts not be attempted against the said Jews. The matter is a grave one to us and we shall seriously punish such excesses.

Given at Barcelona, November 16, 1294 A.D.

§◆§

KING PETER IV OF ARAGON, 1348-49

ONE OF THE MAJOR DISASTERS *to strike European Jewry occurred in the wake of the devastating bubonic plague of 1348-49. Few regions were spared the impact of a calamity which took the lives of perhaps as many as a third of the population of western Christendom. Unable to fathom or control the spread of the dread disease, Europe's inhabitants sought understanding and perhaps a measure of control by turning to the folklore and mythology of past centuries. In the desperate quest to halt the plague, a series of agents responsible for the disease were identified, the Jews most prominently. Thus, 1348-49 became a double disaster for European Jewry. As inhabitants of the affected areas, the Jews were afflicted with all others and perished in substantial numbers. As scapegoats identified as the agents of the devil in spreading disease, Jewish communities were subjected to human attack and decimation.*

In the accompanying royal letters, the king of Aragon notes one such assault on the Jewish community of Barcelona. In his first epistle, Peter indicates with satisfaction the efforts of the municipal authorities to halt the violence and protect the Jews. Concerned, however, with the possible recurrence of such outbreaks, the monarch both praises the municipal leaders for their resolute stand and orders continued vigilance, so that his Jewish subjects be exposed to no further suffering.

Shortly after sending this letter to the municipal authorities of Barcelona, King Peter posted a second missive to Barcelona addressed to the ecclesiastical leadership. Again, the recent incident is mentioned, this time in greater detail. The king repeats his praise for the extensive efforts to dampen the passions in Barcelona and to suppress the violence. Once more the focus of the letter is an exhortation to stand firm against any further outbreaks. In the second epistle, an additional issue is raised. The king bids the ecclesiastical leaders insure that the preaching in their churches in no way contribute to the deterioration of an already tense situation.

As time passed, the crimes perpetrated in Barcelona went unpunished, the result of the unsettled conditions of the period. With the approach of the ensuing Holy Week, fears of renewed violence spread. Concerned with these rumors, the king once more turned to the municipal authorities, noting plaintively that justice had not been done and that this tardiness might well encourage repetition of the crimes. The main focus of the message is a call for renewed vigilance and protection.

The First Letter

PETER, etc., to the beloved and faithful councilors and citizens of the city of Barcelona, greetings, etc:

Through information supplied to us by the Jews of the *aljama* of the aforementioned city, we have learned that recently, when the populace of the aforesaid city had been aroused, certain men of that city, indifferent to the sting of our punishment, invaded the Jewish quarter and there killed several of the Jews of the aforesaid *aljama*. We have learned that you, zealous for justice and our honor, lest further damage be done to the aforesaid Jews, caused the aforesaid quarter to be carefully protected through personal intervention and through proper guards. This seems exceedingly praiseworthy, and therefore we commend your adroit and watchful diligence.

In this regard, we wish that the aforesaid Jews, who live under our special protection, be preserved unharmed as our royal subjects from improper oppression and disturbance. Entreating earnestly for the continuation of your fine resolution in these matters, as is fitting, we order and command that you defend the oft-mentioned Jewish quarter and its Jews and protect them completely from injury. You may be certain that such action, through which you perform pleasing homage to us, will surely arouse gratitude and appreciation in our sight.

Given at Valencia, May 24, 1348.

The Second Letter

PETER, etc., to the venerable and beloved vicars spiritual and temporal of the venerable bishop of Barcelona and to the chapter of Barcelona greetings, etc:

From the contents of certain letters sent to us by our beloved and faithful councilors and citizens of the city of Barcelona, we have learned that recently a corpse was carried through Saint Jacob Square and that, from the direction of the Jewish quarter of the aforesaid city, an arrow struck. When the aforesaid corpse had been removed, those who had borne the deceased along with many others, rashly stirring up the populace and indifferent to the sting of our punishment, invaded the aforesaid Jewish quarter and killed by sword several Jews of that quarter. Since we perceive that you are concerned for our honor and profit, recognizing that the aforesaid Jews are our royal subjects and live under our special protection and care, to the extent of your power you must make provisions through which the Jews of the aforesaid quarter might be protected from undeserved persecution. In this regard, commending the zeal of your good will, which you have exhibited and do exhibit in this matter, we require and entreat, since you care to provide in such a manner for the dignity of our honor, that the sermons offered by preachers and others in the churches of the aforesaid city, through which incitement against or danger to the aforesaid Jews might develop, be completely suppressed. We require and entreat you that, to the extent of your power, as already noted, the aforesaid Jews remain safe and protected from unwarranted attacks. This assuredly will arouse gratitude in us and we shall be indebted to you.

Given at Valencia, June 3, 1348.

The Third Letter

PETER, etc., to his beloved and faithful councilors and citizens of the city of Barcelona, greetings, etc:

The recent affair and the shortness of time force us to recall firmly to ourselves and to you the rash intrusion carried out this year against the *aljama* of the Jews of the aforesaid city by several men of that city. We are impressed deeply with the gravity of the matter, which we are unable to remove from the depths of our heart, since the justice by virtue of which we live and reign has not yet been done. Indeed—what is worse—those intruders despise the sting of our aforesaid discipline as a result of this lack of punishment for their crime and continue their evil design. They do not hesitate to spread covertly threats against those Jews, that during the coming Holy Week they will attack them and destroy them totally.

We know certainly that during that intrusion you defended strongly those Jews. If your forces had not been opposed to the intruders in that way, they would have caused the *aljama* and all its members a grave disaster. We do not believe that they would have been able to recover from it.

Therefore, since serious consideration has been given to these matters, we wish and we indicate to you and we order you that you continue your good counsel. You must take care to make such provisions and ordinances concerning these matters as may seem necessary to you, so that the aforesaid *aljama* and all its members will be protected from all unwarranted damage. Having special confidence in you concerning the aforesaid matters, we commit to you the custody and protection of that *aljama* and all its members through the present letter. We command you that you take particular care that, during this Holy Week, they might not be attacked by anyone nor disturbed in any way. Moreover, through the present letter we expressly enjoin all our officials and each of them singly and all those who take their place, both present and future, that they afford you counsel and aid in these matters, when they are asked.
Given at Valencia, February 26, 1349 A.D.

9 GOVERNMENTAL INTERVENTION DURING PERIODS OF VIOLENCE

THE BISHOP OF SPEYER, 1096

DURING THE FIRST CRUSADE *the Jews of western Christendom suffered less at the hands of the barony or the enthusiastic masses aroused by Peter the Hermit than at the hands of the violent crusading bands that sprang up in Germany in the wake of Peter's preaching. These groups, poorly organized and poorly provisioned, quickly turned unruly. Although the proper object of crusading zeal was defined as the Muslims who controlled the holy sites of Christendom, the mobs soon vented their hostility upon the Jews, who were, in their words, both closer and more reprehensible than the Muslims: "Indeed we set forth on a long journey to seek the Holy Sepulcher and to avenge ourselves upon the Muslims. But behold the Jews who dwell among us, those Jews whose ancestors groundlessly slew and crucified Jesus. Let us take our revenge upon them first. Let us obliterate them entirely, so that the name Israel no longer be recalled. Or else let them become like us and acknowledge Jesus."*

The threat of mob violence severely tested the political authorities of Germany. Unfortunately for the Jews, the authorities by and large failed during this period of crisis. One of the major exceptions was the bishop of Speyer. Bishop John's predecessor, Rudiger, had invited the Jews to settle in Speyer a decade earlier and had promised them extensive protection. In 1096, Bishop John fulfilled the promises made by his predecessor, meeting the crusading threat directly and saving the bulk of his threatened Jewish community.

133

AND IT CAME TO PASS on the eighth day of the month of Iyar [May 3, 1096], on the Sabbath, that divine justice began to descend upon us.

For the Crusaders and the burghers rose up first against the saintly and pious of Speyer, plotting to capture them as a group in the synagogue. But the Jews were forewarned, rose early on the Sabbath, prayed quickly, and left the synagogue. When the Crusaders and the burghers saw that their plan to capture the Jews as a group had failed, then they rose up against the Jews and killed eleven of them. From there the persecution began, in order to fulfill the verse: "Begin at my sanctuary."

When Bishop John heard of this, he came with a large force and helped the community sincerely; he gathered them indoors and saved them from their enemies' hands. He took a few of the burghers and chopped off their hands. Indeed he was a saintly one among the Gentiles, and the Lord brought about merit and salvation through him. R. Moses b. Yekutiel the *parnas* also stood in the breach and exerted himself on the Jews' behalf. Through him all those forcibly converted who had remained here and there in Henry's empire returned to Judaism.

Through the emperor, Bishop John removed the remainder of the community of Speyer to his fortified towns—the Lord was concerned with these Jews because of His great name. Then the bishop hid them until the enemies of the Lord passed by. The Jews remained there, fasting and crying, mourning and fearing deeply for their lives. For every day, the Crusaders and the Gentiles and Emicho—may his bones be ground up—and the populace gathered in order to seize the Jews and to destroy them. Through R. Moses the *parnas*, Bishop John saved them. Indeed the Lord moved his heart to succor them without a bribe. For all this was the Lord's doing, in order to afford us a relic and a remnant through Bishop John.

THE BISHOP OF WORMS, 1096

WHEN THE NEWS *of the attack at Speyer reached Worms, the Jews were profoundly shaken. Many members of the Jewish community turned to the authority that had proven relatively effective in Speyer, the local bishop. Others, yet more trusting, accepted the reassurances of their Christian neighbors and remained in their homes.*

The latter group was quickly disabused of its confidence. A slanderous accusa-

tion against the Jews circulated rapidly, cries for revenge broke out, and an assault was launched on those Jews who had chosen to remain in their houses. Many lives were lost, with a group of Jews deciding finally to accept baptism in order to bury the dead and regain control of captured youngsters.

Meanwhile the majority of the community remained safely protected in the bishop's fortress. After two weeks had passed, a combined force of Crusaders and burghers initiated an attack against the Jews gathered in the bishop's castle. This time, a fateful turn of fortune took place—the bishop of Worms was unable to afford the promised protection. A large number of Jews fell victim to the Crusader attack, some at the hands of the attackers and some at their own hands to avoid capture and forced conversion. A catastrophic precedent was set: A major ecclesiastical and temporal leader had proven incapable of stemming Crusader violence. A series of communities would soon be left exposed to the fate of the Jews of Worms.

WHEN THE EVIL TIDINGS—that some of the community of Speyer had been slaughtered—reached Worms, the Jews called out to the Lord, crying bitterly, for they saw that a harsh edict had been decreed in heaven and that there was no possibility of flight. Then the community divided itself into two segments; some fled to the bishop and his towers, while the rest remained in their homes. For the burghers had falsely reassured the latter Jews—they are broken reeds, intent upon evil and not good! Indeed the burghers joined the Crusaders in destroying us totally. They extended vain and meaningless comforts: "Fear not the Crusaders. Any who kills one of you will be held fully responsible." They gave us no options for flight. The Jews entrusted all their funds to the burghers; therefore the burghers betrayed them.

On the tenth day of Iyar [May 5, 1096], a Monday, the burghers conspired against the Jews. They took a corpse, which had been buried a month earlier, and carried it through the city, saying: "See what the Jews have done to our comrade! They have taken a Gentile, have immersed his corpse in boiling water, and have then poured those waters into our cisterns in order to kill us." When the Crusaders and the burghers heard this, they shouted in rage. Then all those bearing arms—both great and small—gathered and said: "Behold, the time has now come to avenge the Crucified, whom the Jews' ancestors slew. Now let neither a relic nor a remnant escape—neither a youngster nor a suckling in the crib." They then came and smote those who had remained in their homes. Fine young men and lovely young women, old men and old women—all of them stretched forth their necks; even manumitted slaves and serving-women were killed along with them for the sanctification of the Divine Name . . . When these remaining Jews saw their brethren lying naked and the modest Jewish women lying naked, then under great duress they heeded the Crusaders. For the Crusaders had threatened not to leave the Jews a relic nor a remnant. Some of the Jews then said: "Let us do their will for the moment, so that we may go and bury our brethren and save our children from them." For the Crusaders had captured the few remaining children, saying: "Perhaps these will become part of our faith." But these converts never really abandoned their Creator. Their hearts were not inclined in the direction of the Crucified; rather they remained loyal to the Lord on High. Meanwhile the rest of the community, which remained in the bishop's chambers, sent clothes to cover the corpses through those who had been saved—for they were most charitable. The heads of the community remained there, and the majority of the community was saved on this first occasion. These Jews sent consolations to those who had been forcibly converted: "Do not fear and do not be perturbed by what you have done, for if the Holy One saves us from our enemies we shall be fully rejoined. Only veer not from following the Lord."

On the twenty-third day of Iyar [May 18, 1096], the Crusaders and the burghers said: "Behold those who remained in the courtyard and the chambers of the bishop—let us take vengeance on them as well." Then men gathered from all the surrounding villages, along with the Crusaders and the burghers; they besieged the Jews and battled against them. There ensued a very great battle—one side against the other, until the Christians seized the chambers where the Jews were. When the Jews saw the fighting raging on every side—the decree of the King of Kings, then they accepted the decree, trusted in their Creator, and offered up pious sacrifices. They took their children and willingly slaughtered them for the unity of the revered and awesome Divine Name . . .

❦❧

THE BISHOP OF MAINZ, 1096

THE LEADING RHINELAND JEWISH COMMUNITY *during the eleventh century was undoubtedly the Jewry of Mainz. In fact the Jews of France, who were the first to hear of the preaching of the First Crusade, responded to the frightening news by sending requests to the important communities of the period, particularly to the community of Mainz, for prayers and fasting. It was commonly felt that no entreaties would be so efficacious as those of the pious and scholarly Jews of Mainz. In responding to this request, Mainz Jewry, blithely unaware of the new threat, wrote back: "All of the communities have decreed a fast. We have done that which is within our power. May the Lord spare us and you from all trial and tribulation. We are deeply fearful for you. For ourselves, however, there is less to fear. We have not even heard rumors of danger." Half a year later, while French Jewry had in fact been spared serious suffering, the Jewish community of Mainz lay decimated.*

The Hebrew description reveals growing tension in Mainz, with the burghers of the town divided in their reaction to the threat against their Jewish neighbors. The Jews, for their part, lived in increasing fear. When news of the assaults at Speyer and Worms reached Mainz, the Jewish response, depicted in both the Hebrew and Latin sources, was to turn to the bishop for his protection. The serious crisis was precipitated by the arrival at Mainz of a band of Crusaders led by Count Emicho. Again both Jewish and Christian sources agree in their evaluation of the cruelty and fury of this force. Although the Jews related to Emicho as they would toward any responsible political figure and attempted to initiate negotiations, their overtures were useless. On the third of Sivan, the day on which the Israelites of old had begun their preparations for receiving the Torah at Sinai, the pious Jews of Mainz were brutally assaulted. The initial attack was against those Jews gathered in the bishop's castle. The bishop's own men deserted quickly, leaving the badly outnumbered Jews to battle alone against the crusading forces. When the tide swung against the Jews, a massacre took place, in which many Jews chose to die by their own hands. The last stages of the tragedy involved an assault on the burgrave's palace, followed by pursuit of the isolated remainder of the once-proud community.

Both Hebrew and Latin records of this catastrophe remain. There is substantial agreement between the Jewish and Christian narratives, but the most striking contrast is in the evaluation of those Jews who chose the alternative of ritualized suicide. While to the Jewish observer this was an act of martyrdom, reflecting both the courage and the faith of the pious Jews of Mainz, to the Christian chronicler it was an act of incomprehensible cruelty.

※

The Hebrew Report

WHEN THE SAINTLY and pious ones—the holy community of Mainz—heard that some of the community of Speyer had been killed and the community of Worms had suffered a second time, their spirits dropped and their hearts melted. Then they cried out to the Lord, saying: "Alas O Lord God! Do You intend to destroy completely the remnant of Israel? Where are all Your wonders which our forefathers related to us, saying: 'Did You not bring us up out of Egypt, O Lord?' But now You have abandoned us, turning us over to the Gentiles to be destroyed." All the Jewish leaders gathered out of the community and came before the bishop and his officers and his servants. The Jews said to them: "What shall we do about the rumor which we have heard concerning our slain brethren in Speyer and Worms?" They responded to the Jews: "Listen to our advice. Bring all of your wealth to our treasuries and to the treasury of the bishop. Then bring yourselves, your wives, your children, and all your possessions to the courtyard of the bishop. Thus will you be spared from the Crusaders." They gave this advice in order to gather us up and to surrender us, holding us fast like fish trapped in a net. Indeed the bishop collected his officers and servants —his great officers, the nobles of the land and its leaders—in order to aid us and to save us from the Crusaders. For at the outset it was his intention to save us, but ultimately he failed.

On a certain day, a Gentile woman came, bringing with her a goose which she had raised from the time it hatched. This goose went wherever the woman went. She said to all those passing by: "Behold! The goose understands my intention to go on the Crusade and wishes to go with me." Then the Crusaders and the burghers gathered against us, saying: "Where is your protection? How will you be saved? Behold! These wonders the Crucified performs for us." Then all of them came forth with swords and spears to destroy us. But some of the burghers came and would not permit this. At that time they stood together and attacked one another on the banks of the Rhine, until the burghers killed one of the Crusaders. Then they said: "All this the Jews have caused," and they almost united against us. When the saintly ones saw all these things, their hearts melted. The Christians spoke harshly against them, threatening to attack them. When the Jews heard the Christian threats, then they all—both great and small—said: "Would that we might die at the hand of the Lord, rather than dying at the hands of the enemies of the Lord. For the Lord is a merciful God, the sole king in the universe." They then left their homes empty, not even coming to the synagogue except on the Sabbath . . .

At the beginning of the month of Sivan, Emicho the Wicked—may his bones be ground up on iron millstones—came to the outskirts of the city with a large force, consisting of Crusaders and riffraff. He too had said: "It is my intention to go on the Crusade," but he became our chief persecutor. He had no pity—neither on the old nor on the young, neither on youngsters nor on infants, not even on the ill. He turned the Lord's people into dust to be ground up. He slaughtered young men by sword and split open pregnant women. Their troops camped outside the city for two days. The heads of the Jewish community said: "Let us send him money, and let us give him a letter ordering the Jewish communities in his path to do him honor. Perhaps the Lord in his great mercy will help." For previously they had spread about their money, giving it to the bishop and to the burgrave, to their officers and servants, and to the burghers—approximately four hundred marks. All this was done in order to save them, but it was fruitless. We were not even as fortunate as Sodom and Gomorrah. For in their case ten righteous men were sought in order to save them. For us, however, nothing was sought—neither twenty nor ten.

On the third day of the month of Sivan [May 27, 1096], the day on which Moses said: "Prepare yourselves for the third day," on that very day the crown of Israel toppled . . . At midday, Emicho the Wicked—may his bones be ground up—came forth, along with all his troops. The burghers opened the gate for him. Then the enemies of the Lord said to each other: "Behold! The gate has opened by itself. All this has been done for us by the Crucified in order to avenge himself on the Jews." Then they came with their banners to the gate of the bishop's courtyard, where the Jews were; they came in force, as numerous as the sands on the banks of the sea. When the saintly and God-fearing Jews saw this enormous mob, they trusted and clung to their Creator. They then donned their armor and took up their weapons—all of them, both great and small, with R. Kalonymus b. Meshullam at their head. There was a pious man, one of the greatest of that generation, R. Menahem b. R. David ha-Levi, who said to the community: "Sanctify the revered and awesome Name wholeheartedly . . ." They responded as our forefathers had responded when they received the Torah at this same season on Mount Sinai: "We shall do and we shall understand." They called out loudly: "Hear O Israel! The Lord is our God; the Lord is One." Then they all approached the gate, to do battle against the Crusaders and the burghers. One side fought against the other at the gate. But, as a result of our sins, the enemy triumphed and captured the gate. Indeed, the bishop's men, who had promised to help, fled at the outset, in order to turn the Jews over to their enemies; for they are broken reeds. Then the enemy advanced into the courtyard and found R. Isaac b. Moses, whom they smote mortally. They failed, however, to find fifty-three men who fled with R. Kalonymus through the bishop's chambers. These men emerged into a long room and remained there. The enemy entered the courtyard on the third day of the month of Sivan, a Tuesday, a day of darkness and dusk, a day of clouds and mist . . .

Then the Crusaders began to commit desecrations in the name of the Crucified. They raised their banners and turned to the remnant of the community, in the courtyard of the burgrave. They besieged these Jews also and fought against them. They captured the entrance to the gate and smote the Jews. There was a man named Moses b. Helbo, who called to his sons and said: "My sons, Helbo and Simon. At this moment, hell is open before you and paradise is open before you. Into which do you wish to enter?" They answered: "Lead us into paradise." They then stretched out their necks, and the enemy smote them—the father along with his sons. In the same room, there was a Torah scroll. The Crusaders came into the room and found it, tearing it to bits. When the saintly and pure Jewish women saw that the Torah had been ripped, they called out loudly to their husbands: "Behold! Behold the holy Torah! The enemy is ripping it!" Then all together—both men and women—cried: "Woe for the holy Torah, the most perfect beauty and the light of our eyes—to which we bowed in the synagogue, which we kissed and revered. How has it now fallen into the hands of the filthy Gentiles." When the men heard the cries of their saintly women, they became exceedingly zealous for the Lord our God and for His holy and precious Torah. A young man named David b. R. Menahem happened to be there; he said to them: "My brethren. Tear your clothes over the sullied glory of the Torah." They then tore their clothes, as is the command of our teachers. They then found a Crusader in one of the rooms. They all—both men and women—rose up and stoned him and he fell dead. When the burghers and the Crusaders saw that the Crusader had died, they did battle against the Jews. They ascended the roof, under which the Jews were gathered; they broke through the roof; and they shot the Jews with arrows and pierced them with spears . . .

The Latin Report

NOT LONG AFTER THIS, they started upon their journey, as they had vowed, and arrived in a great multitude at the city of Mainz. There Count Emicho, a nobleman, a very mighty man in this region, was awaiting, with a large band of Teutons, the arrival of the pilgrims who were coming there from diverse lands by the king's highway.

The Jews of this city, knowing of the slaughter of their brethren and aware that they themselves could not escape the hands of so many, fled in hope of safety to Bishop Rothard. They put an infinite treasure in his guard and trust, having much faith in his protection, because he was bishop of the city. Then that excellent bishop of the city cautiously set aside the incredible amount of money received from them. He placed the Jews in the very spacious hall of his own house, away from the sight of Count Emicho and his followers, that they might remain safe and sound in a very secure and strong place.

But Emicho and the rest of his band held a council and, after sunrise, attacked the Jews in the hall with arrows and lances. Breaking the bolts and doors, they killed the Jews, about seven hundred in number, who in vain resisted the force and attack of so many thousands. They killed the women also, and with their swords pierced tender children of whatever age and sex. The Jews, seeing that their Christian enemies were attacking them and their children and that they were sparing no age, likewise fell upon one another, brothers, children, wives, and sisters, and thus they perished at each other's hands. Horrible to say mothers cut the throats of nursing children with knives and stabbed others, preferring them to perish thus by their own hands rather than to be killed by the weapons of the uncircumcised.

From this cruel slaughter of the Jews a few escaped; and a few, because of fear, rather than because of love of the Christian faith, were baptized. With very great spoils taken from these people, Count Emicho, Clarebold, Thomas, and all that intolerable company of men and women then continued on their way to Jerusalem, directing their course toward the kingdom of Hungary, where passing along the royal highway was usually not denied the pilgrims.

THE SHERIFF OF NORFOLK, 1144

THE DEVASTATION *associated with the First Crusade did not dampen the animosity of the masses toward the Jews of western Christendom. As already noted, the ongoing hatred of the Jews expressed itself in a dangerous set of slanders, all based on the fundamental notion of the Jew as the enemy of Christians and Christianity.*

The first major expression of these views occurred in Norwich in 1144. An extensive report on the life, death, and miracles of William of Norwich, penned by a

monk at the local monastery, affords substantial information on both the events and
perceptions of 1144. The sweet childhood of William is extensively described,
serving as a backdrop for the horror of the crime perpetrated against him. The monk
Thomas then depicts in lurid detail the alleged torture and murder of William. The
section of the monk's report presented here describes the apprehension of the Jews,
supposedly discovered while hiding the body.

As soon as the body of the boy was discovered, suspicions fell upon the Jews.
With passions at a fever pitch, the Jews of Norwich were in mortal danger; they
hastened to seek out the key royal official in the area, Sheriff John. Fortunately for
them, the sheriff was equal to his responsibility and resolutely protected the Jews
entrusted to his care.

THE MORROW DAWNED, when everywhere the Christian religion
specially celebrates a day of solemnity by reason of the sacramental rite
of the Adoration of the Cross [Good Friday]. On that day it is the
custom among all Christians with sparing diet to abstain from all
amusements and pleasures and, while going around the churches of the
saints, to be diligently engaged in devout attendance at the prayers. At
daylight therefore on this day the Jews who had been chosen the day
before, namely Eleazar and another, tied up the body of the blessed
martyr William in a sack and carried it out. And when they had left the
city with the body and were just entering Thorpe Wood, it chanced that
a certain citizen of Norwich, one of the most eminent and richest of the
citizens, met them. His Christian name was Aelward and his surname
was Ded. He, after visiting all the churches in the city during the
previous night, was returning from the Church of Saint Mary Magdalene,
which is the church of the sick folk whose abode is near the aforesaid
wood, and was making his way with a single servant to Saint Leonard's
Church, along the edge of the wood. This happened by the ordaining of
God's grace and in order that a lawful witness might be forthcoming, so
that when the body was afterwards discovered the matter might not be
concealed from the Christians. So Aelward, coming upon the Jews as
they were going along, recognized them, but could not tell what it was
that one of them was carrying before him on his horse's neck. However,
being in doubt and considering what the passers-by were about and what
it could possibly be which they were carrying with them and why they

should have gone so far from home on a day when it was not the custom for the Jews to leave their houses, he halted for a moment and asked them where they were going. Then, going nearer and laying hands thereupon, he touched what they were carrying with his right hand and he found it was a human body. But they, frightened at having been discovered and in their terror not having anything to say, made off at full gallop and rushed into the thick of the wood. Whereupon a suspicion of some mischief suggested itself to the mind of Aelward; yet he recalled his thoughts to the road which he had been pursuing when he was engaged in his devotional employment.

Meanwhile the Jews, picking their way through the tangled thickets of the wood, hung the body by a thin flaxen cord to a tree and left it there and then returned home by another path. And because they were extremely terrified and conceived new fears at every meeting with anyone that they saw, I conjecture that there occurred with them that which usually happens with very timid people who are conscious of guilt. For they who are in such a case look with suspicion at everybody that comes in their way, and they see pitfalls everywhere, and they suppose that the stones and trees in the distance are men. At any rate the Jews, when they got back, told the others the mishap that had occurred to them on the road.

The enemies of the Christians, being very much alarmed, were quite at a loss as to what course to take. And in despair, while one was suggesting this and another that measure for their common safety, they determined at last to make advances to John the Sheriff, who had been wont to be their refuge and their one and only protector. So by common consent it was arranged that certain of them who were their chief men in influence and power should go to him and deal with him so that, supported by his authority, they should hereafter have no cause for alarm. So they went and, passing within the castle walls, were admitted to the presence of the sheriff. They said that they had a great secret to divulge and wished to communicate secretly with him alone. Straightway, when all who were present had withdrawn, John bade them forthwith to say what they wanted, and they replied, "Look you, we are placed in a position of great anxiety, and, if you can help us out of it, we promise you a hundred marks." He delighted at the number of marks and promised that he would both keep close their secret and that, according to his power, he would not fail to give them his support on any occasion . . .

On that same Saturday, after sunrise, Henry de Sprowston, the forester, whom I mentioned before, mounting his horse went into the wood to see if he could find anyone who might be doing mischief by cutting down anything in the wood without license. And it came to pass that either chance or, as I rather believe, the divine will inclined his mind as he went along toward the place where he had seen the beams of the bright light gleaming on the day before. While he was passing hither and thither in that part of the wood, suddenly he observed a man cutting wood who said that he had discovered there a boy who had been slain. Whereupon, going with the peasant as his guide, Henry found the boy, but who he was or how he had got there he could not understand. But when he had looked at him carefully to find out if by any chance he knew him, he perceived that he had been wounded, and he noticed the wooden torture in his mouth. Becoming aware that he had been treated with unusual cruelty, he now began to suspect, from the manner of his treatment, that it was no Christian but in very truth a Jew, who had ventured to slaughter an innocent child of this kind with such horrible barbarity. So, observing the place very carefully and taking note of the outlook, he became certain that this was the same place where on the day before he had seen the rays of light gleaming and flashing upwards. Accordingly, when he had pondered over these things with much wondering, Henry went back and told his wife and all his household all he had seen. Then, summoning a priest, he announced to him that the body of a little innocent who had been treated in the most cruel manner had been discovered exposed in the wood. He said that he very much wished to take it away from there and, if the priest approved, to bury it in the churchyard of Sprowston. After very earnestly deliberating about the carrying out of this intention, they came to the conclusion that, inasmuch as the festival of Easter was coming next day [March 26, 1244], they should defer their arrangement till the third day and so carry into effect their devout intention more fittingly.

So the business of burying him was put off. But in the meantime, as one man after another told others their several versions of the story, the rumor was spread in all directions. When it reached the city, it struck the heart of all who heard it with exceeding horror. The city was stirred with a strange excitement; the streets were crowded with people making disturbance. Already it was asserted by the greater part of them that it could only have been the Jews who would have wrought such a deed, especially at such a time. And so some were standing about as if amazed by the new and extraordinary affair; many were running hither and thither, but especially the boys and the young men; and, a divine impulse drawing them on, they rushed in crowds to the wood to see the sight. What they sought they found. On detecting the marks of the torture on the body and carefully looking into the method of the act, some suspected that the Jews were guilty of the deed; also some, led on by what was really a divine discernment, asserted that it was so. When these returned, they who had stayed at home got together in groups, and, when they heard how the case stood, they too hurried to the sight. On their return they bore their testimony to the same effect. And thus all through Saturday and all through Easter day, all the city everywhere was occupied in going backward and forward time after time, and everybody was in excitement and astonishment at the extraordinary event.

And so the earnestness of their devout fervor was urging all to destroy the Jews. They would there and then have laid hands upon them, but, restrained by fear of the Sheriff John, they kept quiet for a while.

A FRENCH BARON, 1147

THE SECOND CRUSADE *was quite a different experience from the First Crusade, both for Christians and for Jews. Fully aware of the dangers involved, the Church, the political authorities, and the Jews themselves took steps to avoid a repetition of the disasters that had accompanied the Crusade of 1096. As we have seen, the prime protector of the Jews was the great spiritual force behind the Crusade, Bernard of Clairvaux. In his missives to all areas of Christendom, Bernard prohibited improper and unwarranted violence against the Jews. When necessary, Bernard personally suppressed threats to internal security and to the Jews. The Jews, for their part, had learned much also. They immediately arranged well-fortified refuges for themselves, preferring fortresses which would be totally turned over to them. This combination of vigilance on both sides was by and large successful in squelching the occasional symptoms of incipient violence.*

Nonetheless, sporadic incidents did take place. One of the most frightening occurred in the small French town of Ramerupt. Although the attack involved only one person, his significance to mid-twelfth-century Jewry was so great that the assault and its fortunate outcome were carefully recorded in R. Ephraim of Bonn's chronicle of Jewish fate during the Second Crusade. The victim of the assault was R. Jacob Tam, a grandson of the famed R. Solomon b. Isaac of Troyes (Rashi). R. Jacob was a major intellectual leader in French Jewry and a key Jewish political spokesman. Fortunately, a passing knight extended the necessary protection and the life of R. Jacob Tam was spared.

ON THE SECOND DAY OF SHAVUOT [May 8, 1147], the French Crusaders gathered at Ramerupt, entered the home of Rabbenu Jacob —may he live!—and took everything in his house. They ripped up a Torah scroll in his presence and then took him out to the field. They spoke strongly against his faith and prepared to slay him. They struck him five times on the head, saying: "You are the Jews' leader. Therefore we shall take the revenge of the Crucified upon you, and we shall smite you as you smote our deity, five times." Indeed that pure soul was almost laid to rest, had it not been for the mercies of our Creator Who had pity on His Torah. For the Lord sent a great baron to the aid of R. Tam, through that very field. Our rabbi called out to the baron and bribed him with a horse worth five talents. The baron went and spoke to the Crusaders, convincing them with his argument. He said to them. "Today permit me to speak to him. Perhaps he will be moved and we might win him over. If he remains obstinate, you may be certain that tomorrow I shall turn him over to you." They did so, and the evil hour was averted. Through the pity of the Lord for His people, He had mercy on their great teacher of His holy Torah.

In the remaining communities of France, we have not heard of anyone killed or forcibly converted. But the Jews lost much of their wealth. For the king of France commanded: "All who volunteer to go to Jerusalem shall have their debts forgiven, if they are indebted to the Jews." Since most of the Jews' loans in France are by charter, they lost their monies.

❧❀❧

THE COURT OF WINCHESTER, 1190

DURING THE EXCITEMENT *fostered by the Third Crusade and the internal upheaval occasioned by the accession of Richard the Lionheart, England's Jews suffered severe persecution. The accompanying text describes a potential disaster in the city of Winchester, where the Jews were accused of murdering a young French lad who worked among them. In this instance, the accusation was brought before the proper judicial authorities and quashed.*

In this account, the notion of Jewish crimes against Christian youngsters plays a prominent role. From the earliest stages of this slander in the 1140s, down through the 1190s, the allegations became increasingly common. In Winchester, by 1190, it was obviously widely believed, although in this particular case violence was avoided.

BECAUSE WINCHESTER should not be deprived of its just praise for having kept peace with the Jews, as is told at the beginning of this book, the Jews of Winchester, zealous, after the Jewish fashion, for the honor of their city (although what was done greatly lessened it), brought upon themselves, according to the testimony of many people, the widely known reputation of having made a martyr of a boy in Winchester. The case was thus. A certain Jew took into the bosom of his family as a helper a certain lad who was an apprentice to the cobbler's art. He did not work there continuously, nor was he allowed to finish anything big at one time, lest his dwelling there should later point to his murder, which was already planned. Since he was better paid there for a little work than for a great deal of work elsewhere, he freely frequented the devil's house, seduced by his gifts and his wiles. He was French by race, a minor and an orphan, of low condition and of extreme poverty. When he had bitterly bewailed these miseries in France, a certain French Jew persuaded him by frequent exhortations to go to England, a land flowing with milk and honey. He declared that the English were generous and had an abundance of all good things; there no one who strove to make an honest living would die poor. The lad, prompt, as is natural to Frenchmen, to try anything you please, took with him a companion of his own age and country. He girded himself to set forth on his journey with nothing in his hands but a staff and nothing in his scrip but an awl . . .

The lads, who took everything in a good sense, arrived at Winchester. Their awls were sufficient to secure the necessities of life for him and his companion, and, thanks to the Jew's letter, horrible sweetness and lisping kindness were their comfort. Wherever these poor lads worked or ate away from each other by day, every night they slept together in the same bed in the same old hut of a poor old woman. Day followed day and month followed month; and for our lad, whom we have so carefully brought thus far, time hastened on, whether he was present or absent. The day of the Adored Cross [March 23, 1190] came, and the lad, working that day at his Jew's shop, did not appear that night, however he had been kept out of the way. It was, to be sure, near Passover, a holy day of the Jews. His companion, wondering at his absence when he did not return to his bedroom that evening, was terrified that same night by many dreams. When he did not find him after having looked for several days in every corner of the town, in his simplicity he went to the Jew to ask him if he had sent his friend anywhere. He was greeted with extraordinary harshness in place of yesterday's kindness. Noticing the change in the Jew's words and looks, he become inflamed against him. Since he was of a sharp voice and wonderful eloquence, he burst into a quarrel, accusing him with loud cries of having done away with his companion. "You son of a dirty whore," he said, "you thief, you traitor, you devil, you have crucified my friend! Alas, why haven't I the strength of a man? I would tear you to pieces with my hands!" The cries of the lad shouting in the room were heard in the streets, and Jews and Christians ran up from all directions. The lad insisted, and, already surer of himself because of the crowd, he addressed those present and began to plead for his companion. "O you men who gather together," he said, "see if there is a grief like unto my grief. This Jew is a devil; this man has torn the heart out of my breast; this man has cut the throat of my only friend, and I presume he has eaten him, too. A certain son of the devil, a French Jew—I do not understand or know what it is all about—that Jew gave my companion a fatal letter to this man. He came to this city, led or, rather, misled by him. He often worked for this Jew here, and he was last seen in his house." He had a witness to some of this, for a Christian woman who, contrary to the canons, took care of some Jewish children in that same house, steadfastly swore that she had seen the lad go down into the Jew's storeroom without returning. The Jew denied the story, and the matter was referred to the judges. The accusers failed: the boy because he was under age; the woman because her being employed by Jews made her infamous. The Jew offered to clear his conscience by oath concerning the infamy. Gold won the judges' favor.

THE BAILIFF OF GRENADE, 1320

THE ECCLESIASTICAL *and lay leadership of Christian Europe had, by the late thirteenth century, largely abandoned its commitment to the Crusades. Yet popular hopes for the conquest of the Holy Land dissipated more slowly. From time to time, charismatic preachers stirred the masses to set forth and do battle. Such movements, nourished by the frustrations of the lower classes, usually vented their hostilities on immediate targets, such as the wealthy, the clergy, and the Jews.*

One of the most savage of these popular uprisings was the Shepherds' Crusade of 1320. Stirred by exhilarating preaching, masses gathered in northern France and began to move south. Jews again were the first victims of the unrestrained passions of the mobs, although the clergy and the affluent were soon threatened. It required a determined and coordinated effort on the part of the Church and the State to put down this bloody insurrection.

A curious source stemming from this period of upheaval is the Latin record of the trial of a Jew named Baruch at the court of the bishop of Pamiers. Baruch was accused of having converted during the uprising and then of reverting to Judaism. His first line of defense was to argue that his conversion under duress was undertaken with the clear conviction on his part that such an act was not binding. Baruch's conviction derived from a similar case involving a Jewish acquaintance; in this earlier instance Baruch and the Jew who had converted were formally told that forced conversion was invalid. While Baruch recounted the story of Solomon of Ondes for his own purposes, for us it reveals yet another example of governmental intervention at a time of crisis. Unfortunately for Solomon, the bailiff of Grenade was unable to make good on his promise of protection, although the bailiff supposedly showed his good faith by offering to die along with Solomon. Such gestures of good faith were rare; the guarantee to provide protection, the effort to do so, and humiliating failure were not.

⚜

IN THE YEAR OF OUR LORD 1320, the 13th of July, the reverend father in Christ, lord Jacques, by the grace of God bishop of Pamiers, having learned that Baruch the German—at one time a Jew, who had abandoned Jewish blindness and pervasion of faith, became a convert, and received the sacrament of baptism in the city of Toulouse during the persecution of the shepherds—had now, like a dog returning to his vomit, gone back to the rites of Judaism and, taking advantage of his opportunity, was living as a Jew with the Jews of the city of Pamiers, had him arrested and held in his prison. On this day he had him brought before him into the chamber of the episcopal court of Pamiers. Present also were: Friar Gaillard de Pomies, lieutenant of the lord inquisitor of Carcassonne, Bernard Saxerius, a civil official of Pamiers and a man of distinction, as well as David of Troyes, a Jew who had been called for the purpose of acting, if necessary, as interpreter from the Hebrew for the lord bishop. The bishop interrogated Baruch concerning the above matters, Baruch having first taken an oath on the law of Moses that he would tell the whole and unvarnished truth both about himself as principal and about others as witnesses.

Having taken an oath, Baruch spoke up and confessed as follows: That same year, on Thursday, a month earlier, shepherds wearing the cross had come from Bragayrac to the town of Grenade and threatened to kill the Jews. Solomon of Ondes, a Jew, then went to the bailiff of Grenade, and with him went the Jew Eliezer, Solomon's scribe. As Solomon later recounted to Baruch, he asked the bailiff whether he could guarantee his safety from the shepherds. The bailiff said he could. Later, however, when a great multitude of the shepherds arrived, the bailiff told Solomon that he could not keep him in safety, but that he should embark in a boat on the Garonne and go to Verdun, where there was a royal fortress.

Embarking in the boat, Solomon went down toward Verdun. The shepherds, seeing and hearing about this, pursued him in a small vessel and, taking him out of the water, led him back to Grenade. There the shepherds told Solomon that he must either baptize himself or they would kill him. The bailiff, who was present, said that, if they killed Solomon, they should kill him, too. Hearing this, the Jew said that he did not want the bailiff to suffer anything on his account. He then asked the shepherds what they wanted of him. The shepherds replied that he must baptize himself or have himself baptized or they would kill him. Thereupon the Jew said that he would rather be baptized than killed. Solomon was there baptized along with Eliezer, his scribe.

On the next day, Solomon and Eliezer, now baptized, came to Toulouse, to him, the narrator, and recounted all that had befallen them. They said that they had been baptized, but not from the heart, and that, if they could, they would willingly return to Judaism. He, the narrator, answered them that, while he knew Jewish law, he did not know Christian law and could not therefore advise them whether they could without punishment return to Judaism; he would, however, inquire of Friar Raymond of Junac, lieutenant of the lord inquisitor of Toulouse, whether this could be done. Then he, the narrator, along with Bonet of Agen, a Jew, went to the said Friar Raymond and to Master Jacques, notary of the lord inquisitor of Toulouse, and told them of Solomon's case. He asked them whether baptism, not from desire or willingness to accept it, but purely out of terror, was valid. They—so the narrator said—answered that such baptism was not valid. The narrator understood them to say that such baptism, so received, was not baptism. They hastily returned to Solomon and Eliezer and told them what Friar Raymond and Jacques had said, namely, that such baptism was not baptism and that they could openly return to Judaism.

10 GOVERNMENTAL REPRISALS
IN THE WAKE OF VIOLENCE

⧓⧓⧓⧓⧓⧓⧓⧓
⧓⧓⧓⧓⧓⧓⧓⧓
⧓⧓⧓⧓⧓⧓⧓⧓

KING STEPHEN OF ENGLAND, 1144

AS WE HAVE ALREADY SEEN, *in Norwich in 1144 a dangerous new accusation was levelled against the Jews. Accused of torturing and murdering a Christian youth, the Jews were saved from calamity by the determined intervention of the local sheriff.*

The full account of the incident and its aftermath as penned by Thomas of Monmouth reveals a related incident in which a Norwich Jew was killed and subsequent efforts were made to secure justice. The description of the trial held by the king is unusually rich in detail. The Jews emphasize their utility both to the king and to the realm. They plead for justice, arguing that in its absence they are likely to be exposed to further violence—"if an act certainly illegal be left unpunished, we doubt not that there will be many who will be imitators of this man's audacity and that hereafter things will become worse than they are."

While there were certainly good reasons for the king to respond to this appeal, other factors could often interfere. In this case, the local bishop, who had agreed to speak on behalf of the defendant, introduced the issue of the allegedly martyred William of Norwich, accused the Jews of perpetrating that crime, and thus forced a postponement of the immediate proceedings. Thus the same disabilities that exposed the Jews to violence in the first place made it difficult to secure redress after the fact as well.

151

FOREMOST AMONG THESE INSTANCES must I describe the death of the Jew Eleazar, in whose house, as I have mentioned in the previous book, the blessed martyr William was mocked and slain. When the martyr was dead, this Eleazar carried him away to be concealed in the wood. If the manner in which this was brought about be diligently attended to, it will be considered an argument of very great weight for the truth of the story.

In truth, that Jew was the richest Jew of them all. He had got into his clutches a certain Simon de Nodariis who owed him a large sum of money, and, as the time for payment was drawing near, he kept very frequently pestering the knight to pay the money. So the knight being in straits, inasmuch as he had not the means to pay the debt, kept on from day to day making new excuses for deferring payment. His squires, however, seeing their lord to be in such great difficulties, took secret counsel among themselves as to how they might extricate him. So they laid their heads together, and one of them, as a result of their conspiracy, was sent to fetch the Jew, who was ignorant of the plot, as if for the repayment of the debt. The others meanwhile—whether their lord was privy to it or not, I know not, God knows—hid themselves in a wood through which he had to pass. When the Jew arrived there, the squire leading him on, he was immediately seized by the others, dragged off, and killed. When the other Jews heard of the murder, as the news was commonly reported, they took the corpse and carried it to London for burial.

Let the careful reader here observe how just was the judgment of God which permitted this to happen and how worthily He dealt out retribution. The Jew had with wicked hands enticed a Christian into his house and killed him. When he had killed him, he had flung him into a wood and there had exposed him to the dogs and the birds. This same man was enticed out of his own house, was killed by the hands of Christians in a wood, and exactly in the same way was left in the open air and exposed to be torn to pieces by dogs and birds.

However, when some time had passed and the king had come to Norwich, the Jews assembled together before the king and lodged their complaint regarding the aforesaid Jew. Ascribing the guilt of the whole act to the forementioned knight, they accused him in manner following.

"Hear us, most gracious king. Thy well-known clemency, which is proclaimed throughout the world, is withheld from none that deserves it and is the means of procuring peace and quiet for us. Behold, we who trust in thy patronage have betaken ourselves to thee as to our one and only refuge and, with every confidence in thy justice, have come before thee as the just judge and faithful follower of right and equity. Wherefore we, looking for the justice that is our due for a wrong and injury done us and demanding too the shield of thy protection against the fear of a like misfortune, will set forth in few words what the wrong is that has been done us and what our wishes are.

"We are thy Jews. We are thy tributaries year by year; we are continually necessary to thee in thy necessities, since we are always faithful to thee and by no means useless to thy realm. Truly thou rulest us leniently and quietly. The audacity of this Simon whom we see standing there opposed to us—an audacity which deserves to be punished—has presumed to disturb our tranquillity, in an atrocious way. For this man, having as his creditor one of our brethren, thy servant, a Jew, and having sent to him a squire on pretence of paying his debt, called him out of the city into the country and caused him to be murdered on the road. What more? It is certain, O lord the king, that thy Jew was slain, and we complain that the fact is so. We lay our charge against this Simon de Nodariis as answerable for the homicide of this man. We assert that by his counsel and device a deed so wicked was planned, aye, and carried out. But what so base a deed deserves, that the wisdom of so righteous a judge well knows. But that thou mayest believe that so it was, let the following arguments for the truth be considered: (1) the treacherous leading him astray, (2) the road that was marked out through a lonely spot, (3) the convenience of time and place, (4) and the facility for carrying out the business according to what was desired.

"(1) The squire was sent by the knight as his deputy and was well known to the creditor, the Jew. This Jew he invited as if to receive his debt and led him away. (2) The path took a long and tortuous route and so obviated the fear of any chance encounter. (3) A wood on the road and the silence of the dark night afforded the opportunity. (4) The squire's sword and a crowd of his comrades, as report indicates, lying in wait to do the deed, afforded facility for the commission of the crime. What other purpose could the knight have had—since he was in such great financial difficulties and unable to pay—except that, by ridding himself of the bondage of his long-standing embarrassment, he might get freedom for himself, and by this act he might make an end of the worrying exactions?

"To make the matter plainer, this knightly debtor either would pay and could; or he would and could not; or he would not and could; or lastly, he neither would nor could.

"If he would and could, why did he not pay, and why did he continue in this long embarrassment? If he would and could not, no wonder if his lack of power gradually suggested to his mind the desire to get free. If he would not and yet could, observe how the thoughts of his evil mind conceived the evil deed. But if, as is more credible, he neither would nor could pay, it is plainly manifest that the working of his crafty thoughts brought forth the plot of a wickedness of this character. Again, if he did not wish for the murder of the Jew which is laid to his charge, if he was not aware of it, if he did not plan it, why did he not, in order to turn away from himself all suspicion of the crime, pay the debt to the dead man's wife or his relations when they asked for it? Why did he wantonly neglect the engagement by which he was bound to his creditor? On the contrary he has become now so insolent and contumacious that, when we call upon him to fulfil his engagement, he hurls at us calumnies and abuse and aims at us continual threats, though we deserve them not. We think therefore that the guilt of this murderous knight has been sufficiently made out, since the motive of the murder, the manner of it, the insolence of the assassin, and the audacity of his menaces have been set forth.

"We by no means believe that it is lawful for any Christian whoever he be to slay with impunity according to his pleasure any Jew who behaves as he ought. If an act certainly illegal be left unpunished, we doubt not that there will be many who will be imitators of this man's audacity and that hereafter things will become worse than they are. Furthermore we, fearing this kind of treatment for ourselves and sorrowing over the undeserved death of our brother, beseech thee for thy clemency, O righteous king, that thou provide for our living in peace and security and that thou do not suffer the undeserved death of thy Jew to go unpunished."

The knight, having been accused in this manner, first denied that he was guilty of anything of the sort. Then, having obtained leave of the king, he retired to consult with his friends before making a detailed answer to the charge. And inasmuch as the knight was under the bishop's jurisdiction, as the term is, Bishop William by license of the king went to the conference to consult for the knight's safety. Since all perceived that in so difficult a cause the pleading would require a special kind of defense, it was determined that in this cause the bishop should represent the knight as his defender, in order that the high position of the advocate might make the king (who seemed already convinced of the truth of the charge) give a favorable hearing and so that, the charges of his adversaries being weakened, the bishop's accomplished eloquence, in which he surpassed all others, might get the knight acquitted.

So the prelate, prevailed upon by many petitions, at length complied. As he observed that both the king and the audience were already indignant, he decided that in the kind of cause which he had to plead it would be best to make use of a brief statement to begin with, so as to win over insensibly the hostile minds of his hearers by skilled oratory. Once their goodwill was thus gained, he might employ the remainder of his speech in making a countercharge. Thus armed, as I may say, he rose to engage in the pleading of his cause, returned from the conference with his friends, and began his speech before the king in the following terms:

"We agree perfectly with our accusers on one point: that men who deceive creditors who deserve well of them or who, after deceiving, kill them merit detestation, nay, condign punishment. And we account that they should be most strictly pursued who habitually break faith, make light of the crime of fraud, think nothing of lying, and have neither will nor skill to find a remedy for their debts save the one way of contriving the death of another.

"Now, the Jew of whose death the knight Simon is accused had, while he lived, many debtors besides Simon: some owed him less, some as much, some again far more than Simon did. If, then, anyone was desirous of his death in order to be rid of the annoyance of debt, it seems more likely to have been planned by one who was saddled with a heavy debt than one who owed less. But can anyone believe that Simon should have desired the death of his creditor? The man's death was productive of great loss to him; his life had been the means of repeated advantages to him. With what show of reason can it be made out that I should be desirous of the death of one whose premature removal I regard with fear and whose life I earnestly desire to see prolonged as being in every way advantageous to me? So with this knight, who is charged with murdering his creditor. If while he lived he cherished him as being of great use and advantage to him; if now that he is dead he has not yet ceased to bemoan him—as how should he not mourn the loss of that which he had possessed with such affection?—who can contend that he rejoices over the loss of this man or that he desired his death, when he is so much affected by that loss?

"Now, as to the charge that is brought against the squire, the squire denies his guilt completely. In regard to the real facts of the matter, I will briefly explain what they were, as I have learned them from him. The knight, whom I am much surprised to find as the object of such an accusation, since I have always known him to be of good report, a peaceable, kind and law-abiding man, was detained at home by urgent private affairs, could not come to Norwich, and certainly did send by a squire for his creditor, that the latter might receive his debt. The squire, according to the arrangement of the Jew, left the city in his company in the quiet of night and took the safest route he knew in order to avoid the notice of evil-disposed persons under cover of the darkness and to escape all suspicious encounters. They accomplished a good part of the way and were suspecting no sort of ambush, when they fell among thieves. These men came, seized them, threw them from their horses, and dragged them violently away to despoil them. Upon this, the Jew, while attempting to defend himself with the sword which he carried, fell slain by a hostile weapon. The squire, naturally, in the interests of his own safety, while the rest were busied about the Jew, escaped from the hands of his captors and saved his life by flying swiftly through the thick wood which was at hand. In this way it appears that the Jew lost his life, my lord king, and you need not doubt that the knight who is charged with the guilt of his death is clear from it. Upon hearing of the deed he was at once powerfully affected by its atrocity and by the undeserved fate of so valued a friend; but never, to this hour, though he has shown himself a most zealous investigator of the matter, has he been able to ascertain the perpetrators of this great crime. I am not surprised that rumor has deviated from the path of truth in this case, but, as we see that false reports become current every day, we must not lend a ready belief to all the reports we hear. In fact, whereas the knight is accused of employing threats and abuse, he is not a little surprised at the charge, for he has always respected the Jews and been much attached to them.

"However, to wind up the whole case shortly, the knight is present here, prepared to prove with all constancy, in whatever way this court shall prescribe, that he neither desired the death of the Jew in question nor planned it nor knew of it in any other wise than has been stated and that he never abused the Jews in any way.

"But, meanwhile, O most just king, we are desirous of signifying to your most serene discretion that it is our opinion that we Christians should not have been called upon to reply to an accusation of this kind from the Jews, before they themselves were purged of the murder of one of us, a Christian, of which they are known to have been accused and not purged. To lay before your most Christian clemency in a plain and concise fashion the whole case—it is a matter which concerns all Christians —that Jew, of whose death the knight, though innocent, is accused, did, in conjunction with the other Jews then in the city, in his house, as report says, miserably torment, kill, and hide in a wood a Christian boy. And when, in the days of my predecessor, Bishop Eborard, the Jews had been accused of this in full synod by a priest, yet because the Sheriff John opposed us and maintained them, the Christians were unable to have justice executed upon them. We have, furthermore, at this day the same priest ready to prove them guilty of the crime aforesaid at such time and under such conditions of trial as you please. On this account, if it be not displeasing to your Royal Majesty, it seems to us fitting and right that, just as the death of the Christian, done in reproach and derision of the Passion of Christ, preceded the death of the Jew, and the injury inflicted on us preceded that inflicted on them, so the priest's accusation ought to come first and the purgation of the knight afterwards. Let the rigor of justice be no longer deferred; for we complain bitterly that so foul a crime has remained unpunished to this day, and we earnestly pray that it may no longer be put off. Yet, let everything be so handled that Christ be first considered in all things and due reverence be paid, as is right, to the law of Christianity.''

As the bishop ended his speech, the effect, and indeed conviction, produced in the minds of the king and his assessors was so great that they decreed that the ghastly outrage of the Jews must be at once punished and gradually were worked up more and more to take vengeance. But, since the matter seemed to be one affecting all classes of Christians, the king commanded that it should be postponed until the general council of the clergy and barons (which was near at hand) should be assembled at London, and this was done.

KING RICHARD OF ENGLAND, 1189

THE CORONATION *of Richard the Lionheart, a gala event in English history, was for the Jews of the British Isles catastrophic. During the course of the festivities, the London populace, exhilarated with the coronation itself and by the preparations for a new Crusade which the young monarch was to lead, vented its hatred upon the Jews. The impunity with which this attack was carried out emboldened Englishmen elsewhere to repeat the London atrocity. After Richard departed, a wave of assaults swept across the islands, destroying a number of Jewish communities.*

The accompanying texts depict the London disaster from both a Christian and Jewish perspective. In the more detailed account of William of Newburgh, the inability of the royal authorities to quell the attack is clearly portrayed. According to William, the royal forces dispatched by Richard recognized the power of the mob and swiftly withdrew. Equally important was Richard's inability to impose justice in the wake of the crisis. The new king realized that punishment must be meted out; to

*fail to do justice "seemed an action unworthy of a king and injurious to the realm."
Again, however, the forces arrayed against the Jews were so potent as to make proper
punishment impossible. For William of Newburgh, this was only fitting; for the
Jews and for many Christians, it was an exceedingly inauspicious beginning to the
new reign.*

*The Hebrew report offers an interesting contrast. While the essential details are
the same, the Jewish author views the victims in quite a different light, as martyrs to
the truth of their faith. The Jewish chronicler is also concerned with the aftermath of
the incident, choosing to see the king in a more positive light, as capable of punishing
at least some of those responsible for the massacre.*

The Report of William of Newburgh

ON THE DAY appointed for his coronation, almost all the nobility of
the kingdom and the parts beyond the sea came to London, together with
a great number of men of distinction. Richard—the only monarch of the
age who bore that name—was consecrated king at London and solemnly
crowned by Baldwin, archbishop of Canterbury, on the third day of
September, a day which, from the ancient superstition of the Gentiles, is
called Evil or Egyptian, as if it had been a kind of presage of the event
which occurred to the Jews. For that day is considered to have been fatal
to Jews and to be Egyptian rather than English, since England, in which
their fathers had been happy and respected under the preceding king,
was suddenly changed against them, by the judgment of God, into a
kind of Egypt where their fathers had suffered harshness. Though this is
an event that is fresh in our memory and known to all who are now living, yet it is worth the trouble to transmit to posterity a full narration of
it, as proof of an evident judgment from on High upon that perfidious
and blasphemous race.

Not only Christian nobles, but also the leading men among the
Jews, had come together from all parts of England to witness the solemn
anointing of the Christian sovereign. For those enemies of the truth were
on the watch, lest, perchance, the prosperity which they had enjoyed
under the preceding monarch should smile upon them less favorably
under the new king. They wished that his first acts should be honored by
them in the most becoming manner, thinking that undiminished favor
would be secured by ample gifts. But whether it was that they were less

acceptable to him than to his father, or whether he was on his guard against them, from some cause (of which I am ignorant), through a superstitious precaution, advised by certain persons, he forbade them (by a proclamation, it is said) to enter the church while he was being crowned or to enter the palace while the banquet was being held after the solemnity of the coronation. After the celebration of the mass was finished, the king, glorious in his diadem, and with a magnificent procession, went to the banquet; but it happened that, when he was sitting down with all the assembly of the nobility, the people, who were watching about the palace, began to crowd in. The Jews, who had mingled with the crowd, were thus driven within the doors of the palace. At this, a certain Christian was indignant; and, remembering the royal proclamation against them, he endeavored, as it is said, to drive away a Jew from the door and struck him with his hand. Aroused at this example, many more began to beat the Jews back with contempt, and a tumult arose. The lawless and furious mob, thinking that the king had commanded it and supported them, as they thought, by his royal authority, rushed like the rest upon the multitude of Jews who stood watching at the door of the palace. At first they beat them unmercifully with their fists; but soon becoming more enraged, they took sticks and stones. The Jews then fled away; and, in their flight, many were beaten, so that they died, and others were trampled under foot and perished. Along with the rest, two noble Jews of York had come thither, one named Joce and the other Benedict. Of these, the first escaped; but the other, following him, could not run so fast, while blows were laid upon him. He was caught and, to avoid death, was compelled to confess himself a Christian. Conducted to a church, he was there baptized.

In the meantime, an agreeable rumor, that the king had ordered all the Jews to be exterminated, pervaded the whole of London with incredible celerity. An innumerable mob of lawless people, belonging to that city, and also from other places in the provinces, whom the solemnity of the coronation had attracted there, soon assembled in arms, eager for plunder and for the blood of a people hateful to all men, by the judgment of God. Then the Jewish citizens, of whom a multitude reside in London, together with those who had come there from all parts, retired to their own houses. From three o'clock in the afternoon till sunset, their dwellings were surrounded by the raging people and vigorously attacked. By reason of their strong construction, however, they could not be broken into, and the furious assailants had no engines. The roofs, therefore, were set on fire; and a horrible conflagration, destructive to the besieged Jews, afforded light to the Christians who were raging in their nocturnal work. Nor was the fire destructive to the Jews alone, though kindled especially against them; for knowing no distinction, it caught some of the nearest houses of the Christians also. Then you might have seen the most beautiful parts of the city miserably blazing in flames, caused by her own citizens, as if they had been enemies. The Jews, however, were either burnt in their own houses or, if they came out, were received on the point of the sword. Much blood was shed in a short time, but the rising desire for plunder induced the people to rest satisfied with the slaughter they had committed. Their avarice overcame their cruelty for they ceased to slay. But their greedy fury led them to plunder houses and carry off the Jews' wealth. This, however, changed the aspect of affairs and made Christians hostile to Christians; for some, envying others for what they had seized in their search for plunder, were led to spare neither friends nor companions.

These events were reported to the king as he was banqueting in festivity with all the assembly of nobles. Ranulph de Glanville, who was justiciary of the realm—a man both powerful and prudent—was thereupon sent from his presence, with other men of equal rank, that they might turn aside or restrain the audacity of the mob. But it was in vain, for in so great a tumult no one listened to his voice or showed respect to his presence. Some of the most riotous began to shout against him and his companions and threatened them in a terrible manner if they did not quickly depart. They, therefore, wisely retired before such unbridled fury, and the plunderers, with equal freedom and audacity, continued to riot until eight o'clock on the following day. At that same time satiety or weariness of rioting, rather than reason or reverence for the king, allayed the fury of the plunderers . . .

Certainly the new king, who was of a lofty and fierce disposition, was filled with indignation and grief that such events had occurred, almost in his presence, amidst the solemnities of his coronation and at the commencement of his reign. He was irritated and anxious as to what he ought to do upon this occasion. To overlook so great and unexampled an affront to his royal dignity and to let it pass unpunished seemed an action unworthy of a king and also injurious to the realm, since his connivance at an atrocity so great would encourage the audacity of evil-doers to attempt similar acts of violence in the hope of impunity. However, it would be utterly impossible to enforce the rigor of royal censure upon such an indefinite multitude of guilty persons. For hatred toward the Jews and the hope of plunder had united in the performance of the work, which I have mentioned, almost all the retainers of the nobles who had come with their lords to the solemnity of the coronation, besides the nobles themselves, who were feasting with the king, of whom the number was so great that the ample space of the royal palace seemed all too small for them. It was, therefore, necessary to connive at that which could not be punished. Without doubt, it was ordained by God that those who were the ministers of divine vengeance upon the perfidious and the blasphemous should not be subjected to human judgment on account of this. The design of that watchfulness which is on High demanded that those blasphemers who, in the time of the late sovereign, had been beyond measure stiffnecked and perverse toward Christians, should be humbled at the commencement of the reign of his successor.

The Report of Ephraim of Bonn

IN THE YEAR 4950 [1190], disaster for the Jews was decreed from on High, when a new king was enthroned on the island called England. On the day he was installed as king and the royal crown placed upon his head in London, in the palace outside the city, a large crowd from France and from England gathered. Jews also came—the leaders and the wealthiest of them—to present the king with a gift. The wicked began to say: "It is not proper that the Jews come to see the royal crown with which the priests shall adorn the king on his coronation day." They therefore pushed the Jews aside and struck them. The king, however, did not know. Then a rumor spread through the city, indicating: "The king has commanded to destroy the Jews." They then began to smite the Jews and to destroy their houses and towers. They killed about thirty Jews; some slaughtered themselves and their children. There the famous rabbi, R. Jacob of Orléans, was killed for the sanctification of the Divine Name. The king knew nothing of all this, for, when he heard the noise of the mob in the city, he had asked: "What is that tumult?" His gatekeeper had responded: "It is nothing—only the lads playing and enjoying themselves." Subsequently, when the truth was revealed to the king, he ordered that the gatekeeper be tied to the tails of horses and dragged through the streets and marketplaces until he expire. Thus he died a painful death. Blessed is the Lord Who provides revenge.

THE DUKE OF AUSTRIA, 1196

THE INCIDENT DESCRIBED *in the accompanying text stemmed from the aftermath of the Third Crusade. The Jewish victim, R. Solomon, is portrayed as unusually affluent and influential, with very strong ties to the duke of Austria. One of R. Solomon's servants took both the cross and some of his master's funds. R. Solomon had the offender imprisoned, an act which raised legal questions and grave practical dangers. As a result, R. Solomon and fifteen of his fellow Jews were slain. In this instance, the aggrieved overlord, the duke of Austria, was sufficiently determined and sufficiently strong to secure death for the ringleaders, although he remained cautious about extending the punishment to others for fear of provoking the Crusaders.*

THERE WAS A MAN in Austria, named R. Solomon. That man was pure and upright and God-fearing, performing righteous acts at all times and caring for the poor. The duke appointed him over all his tolls and over his provisions. This Jew had servingmen and servingwomen, both Christian and Jewish. The following came to pass in the year 4956 [1196], in the month of Tammuz—during the 256th cycle, during which we hoped for joy and gladness, but which was transformed into mourning. For in that year as well, innumerable Christians took the cross, in order to journey to Jerusalem and to make war against the Muslims. One of R. Solomon's servants, who had taken the cross, stole twenty-four talents from him. R. Solomon then went and put the offender in prison. On a certain holy day, the wife of the imprisoned Crusader complained in church about the plight of her husband, who had been imprisoned by the Jew. Then the Crusaders in that city arose and went forth in great anger. They came to the house of the righteous R. Solomon and slew him, along with fifteen other Jews. Subsequently the matter was revealed to the duke, who commanded that the two leaders of the murderers be captured and decapitated. The duke did not wish to kill more of them, for they were Crusaders. See our tribulations, O Lord, and avenge Israel.

﹡

EMPEROR HENRY VI, 1196

THE ATTACKS *described in the following report may have been related in part to the Crusades of the 1190s, although the Jewish author makes no reference to crusading fever. In the Jewish chronicles, this is yet another in the lamentable series of persecutions sparked by the widely circulated slanders concerning Jewish enmity and maliciousness. The discovery of a corpse in the vicinity of Speyer immediately raised suspicion of Jewish complicity in a murder. The body of a recently interred Jewess was unearthed and publicly exhibited, to the shame and indignation of the Jews of Speyer. When the girl's father, R. Isaac b. Asher, was successful in bribing the authorities to call a halt to this barbarity, the house of Rabbi Isaac was attacked and a group of nine Jews slain. Extensive damage was done in the Jewish quarter, although most of the Jews managed to escape. A week after the assault, there was a similar outbreak in Boppard, in which eight Jews fell victim.*

What is particularly striking in these two related incidents is the alacrity and severity with which the authorities responded. The emperor's brother, Count Otto of Burgundy, had ordered prior to the violence that Jews not be harmed. When this order was so openly flaunted, the enraged count besieged Speyer, doing serious damage in the environs of the city. With the approach of the emperor himself, the siege was lifted. The emperor also showed signs of grave displeasure, fining those responsible heavily. Interestingly, much of the money thus realized was turned over to the Jews, in order to assist in reconstructing the public and private facilities of the Jewish community of Speyer. The same was done in the wake of the attack on the Jews of Boppard. While details are not provided, it is clear that a key intermediary in the imperial court was Hezekiah b. Reuben of Boppard, and it seems quite likely that the emperor's generosity may have related in no small measure to the efforts of R. Hezekiah.

﹡

IT HAPPENED IN THE DAYS OF EMPEROR HENRY, the son of Emperor Frederick, the Lord was angered with His people, smote them mightily, and punished them painfully. For in the year 4956 [1196], during the month of Adar, a Gentile woman was found murdered about three miles from the city of Speyer. The Gentiles became excited needlessly, circulating a rumor that the Jews had murdered her. The Gentiles rose up as if to swallow the Jews alive. They removed the corpse of the daughter of R. Isaac b. Asher ha-Levi from its grave during the period of mourning and hung it naked in the market-place, with a rat hanging in the strands of her hair as a mockery and humiliation to the Jews. Her father ransomed the corpse through bribery and returned it to the grave. The following day, the burghers— those men of Sodom—surrounded the rabbi's house, breached it, and killed him, along with eight other Jews. They also burned all the Jews' homes. The Jews ascended the chamber above the synagogue and after-wards pulled up the ladder by means of which they had ascended. There they found refuge until aid might arrive. During the night, they lowered the ladder, descended, and left the city. The enemy despoiled everything in the Jews' homes. They threw books and Torah scrolls into the water and burned the synagogue.

Prior to this slaughter, Duke Otto, the emperor's brother, had ordered, through bribery, that the Jews not be harmed. When he heard the news of the slaughter, he was enraged. He gathered troops and besieged Speyer. He burned all the villages belonging to the wicked bishop and the burghers; he cut down their trees, tore up their vine-yards, and trampled their grain totally. Had he not heard that his brother the emperor was on his way back from Apulia, he would not have lifted his siege until the walls of the city had been destroyed. Subse-quently, the emperor came and captured the murderers, until they paid him great sums of money. They gave the Jews approximately five hun-dred talents and rebuilt their homes and synagogue as before.

In that year many in the Jewish community of Speyer died at their own hands. The Jewish community of Worms was exceedingly kind to both the living and the dead—may their Creator bless them. Finally the remaining Jews returned to their city. All of this salvation, as well as the saving of other communities, was through the *nagid* R. Hezekiah b. Reuben of Boppard and R. Moses b. Joseph ha-Cohen. May they be remembered for thousands upon thousands of blessings for the kindness and the effort and the expense which they extended on behalf of all the Jewish communities.

Whom has woe befallen? Who has suffered needlessly? Those who tarry in their exile—those who anticipate salvation, but find instead a sharp sword at their throat—those who proceed from catastrophe to catastrophe. For seven days after the Lord smote us in Speyer, the enemy came to Boppard on Saturday evening and killed R. Solomon the cantor, along with seven others. Then the Lord roused Otto, the emperor's brother, and he blinded two of the murderers. Afterward his brother the emperor came and commanded the burghers to give R. Hezekiah ha-Nadiv approximately three hundred talents. May the Lord comfort us twofold by consoling Zion and Jerusalem. Amen.

THE MUNICIPALITY OF BOURGES, 1251

IN 1248, *King Louis IX of France set forth on one of the greatest of the crusading expeditions. Quickly the hopes and expectations of Christendom were crushed, as the pious monarch was captured and his army destroyed. Upon his release, Louis nonetheless proceeded to the Holy Land and remained there a number of years, attempting to aid in strengthening the spiritual and temporal fortifications of Outremer. As so often, an official Crusade sparked a mass movement. In this case, there was a special sense that the poor and humble might be able to achieve what the mighty had failed to accomplish.*

Once more, however, popular crusading achieved nothing but internal upheaval within Christendom. Led by popular preachers, this Crusade of the peasants and the shepherds terrorized northern France, particularly its clergy and its Jews. Favored briefly by the regent, in hopes that it might extend some aid to her son, the shepherd army soon revealed itself as hopelessly dangerous and destructive. One particular group, led by the so-called Master of Hungary, invaded and destroyed the synagogue of Bourges. In the wake of this assault, the citizenry of Bourges armed itself, pursued the Crusaders, and dealt them a fatal blow. This response was partially in redress for the attack on the local synagogue and partially an act of self-defense against the spread of unwarranted violence.

The incident reflects the relationship between Jewish well-being and the general security and tranquillity of society. Where Jews could be attacked with impunity, no one was safe. Efforts to protect the Jews and to punish their persecutors were essential steps in securing the general peace and welfare of European civilization.

THE YEAR 1251. The terrible incident of the shepherds who claimed that they were journeying to the Holy Land took place. There were leaders among them who gave the cross to the rest. They falsely claimed to produce signs and wonders. These brigand chieftains, in order to deceive the simple, suggested that they had seen a vision of angels and that the Holy Virgin Mary had appeared to them and commanded that they gather an army of shepherds and simple folk, whom God had chosen, in order to aid the Holy Land and King Louis who was tarrying there. They depicted that vision on a standard which they bore before them. Then the aforesaid brigands traversed cities and countryside throughout Flanders and Picardy. They seduced by false exhortations the shepherds and the simple folk. When they reached France, they already appeared as a military force reaching one hundred thousand. When they moved through the countryside, the shepherds left their animals without permission. Moving through towns and cities, they gathered swords and axes and other weapons, so that they were feared by the populace and by the authorities. They reached such a state of error that they officiated at weddings, gave the sign of the cross, and absolved from sin. They deceived the populace to such an extent that many believed that bread and other victuals placed before them were not diminished by being eaten and drunk, but were instead increased. Since the clergy wished to correct this error, it incurred great hatred, to the extent that they killed many clerics found in the fields. They were permitted to traverse the city of Paris without hindrance by Queen Blanche, the royal regent, who hoped to provide aid through them for her son King Louis in the Holy Land. As a result the audacity of their errors increased. When plundering and pillaging they reached the city of Orléans, they began a battle with the clergy and killed many, although many of them were also killed. Then they came to the city of Bourges and their leader, whom they called "the Master of Hungary," entered the synagogue of the Jews and destroyed their books and ravaged their goods. But when he left the city with his forces, the people of Bourges, armed and prepared, followed them vigorously and killed the aforesaid master with many of his associates and caused a great slaughter . . . After the aforesaid slaughter, they were dispersed widely. Some of them were killed or hanged for their crimes; others fled by ship; others returned home. Thus the whole affair came to naught.

PART FOUR

ECCLESIASTICAL LIMITATION

INTRODUCTION

THE PREVIOUS SECTION focused on the positive and protective elements in the relationship of the medieval Church and State to the Jews. There were, at the same time, forces exerting strong pressure for limiting the position of the Jews, chief among them the Church itself. Church doctrine, as noted in Part One, emphasized a dual policy of protection and limitation. Where the texts in Part Three show the Church making an effort to provide the stipulated protection, the sources in this section highlight Church efforts to restrict.

Ultimately the execution of the restrictive policies initiated by the Church depended on the cooperation of the secular authorities. The effort to enlist governmental support for Church policies did not always proceed smoothly; in fact, there was often strong resistance to ecclesiastical pressure. Sometimes this reluctance stemmed from a practical conflict of interests, in other cases it simply represented an assertion that the government would not tolerate undue ecclesiastical interference in the affairs of its Jews. Still, several major rulers of western Christendom were indeed willing to enact a broad set of stipulations, expressing old and new Church demands in regard to the Jews.

The concluding chapters of this section focus on two important instances of Church initiative and governmental response. The first involves ecclesiastical demands concerning a central facet of Jewish economic life, moneylending. As a result of its efforts during the twelfth century to eradicate the sin of usury from Christian society, the Church in effect opened the way for extensive moneylending by the Jews. By the late twelfth and early thirteenth centuries, ecclesiastical reformers were concerned with what their efforts had produced and were suggesting a new look at Jewish usury. Some called for restrictions which would abolish the pernicious abuses related to Jewish usury. The prohibition of "heavy and immoderate usury" enacted at the Fourth Lateran Council represents one such reform. More radical voices, however, called for an outright prohibition of Jewish usury. Again, execution of the Church's policies required the acquiescence of the Jews' overlords. The slow enactment of anti-Jewish legislation in France reveals the steady success of the Church in its campaign and the resultant constriction of Jewish economic life.

A second issue on which the Church exerted increasingly successful pressure involves allegations of blasphemy in Talmudic literature. Down to the mid-thirteenth century, Christian Europe knew very little of post-biblical Jewish literature. When converts from Judaism to Christianity began to provide information on the Talmud, it was found to include a variety of materials offensive to Christian readers. The result was a papal call, in the late 1230s, to examine Talmudic literature and take the necessary steps to deal with such offensive material. At the outset, this call was largely disregarded by the rulers of western Europe. The pious king of France, however, responded affirmatively and supported a campaign which ended in mass burnings of rabbinic literature. The sources reveal once more a major instance of Church-State cooperation, out of which Jewish life—in this case, Jewish spiritual life—was decisively circumscribed.

POPE INNOCENT III TO KING
PHILIP AUGUSTUS OF FRANCE, 1205

INNOCENT III *was one of the most powerful and influential popes of the Middle Ages. He labored both to formulate ecclesiastical policy and to urge its implementation. The vigor and impact of Innocent III can be readily noted in the area of Jewish affairs as well. He was extremely active in defining and executing Church programs in regard to the Jews.*

The first of the letters of Innocent presented here is addressed to Philip Augustus, king of France. The pope begins with a traditional justification for Jewish presence in Christendom, the notion that Jews must be preserved "until such time as their remnant shall be saved." At the same time Innocent expresses concern over reports regarding some aspects of Jewish behavior and over evidence that these Jewish practices are receiving governmental support. The issues raised by the pontiff are many and varied, some general and some specific. Essentially, Innocent appeals for governmental aid in limiting offensive Jewish abuses.

TO THE KING OF FRANCE:

It does not displease God, but is even acceptable to Him, that the Jewish dispersion should live and serve under Catholic kings and Christian princes until such time as their remnant shall be saved, in those days when "Judah will be saved and Israel will dwell securely." Nevertheless, such princes are exceedingly offensive to the sight of the Divine Majesty who prefer the sons of the crucifiers, against whom to this day the blood cries to the Father's ears, to the heirs of the crucified Christ, and who prefer the Jewish slavery to the freedom of those whom the Son freed, as though the son of a servant could and ought to be an heir along with the son of the free woman.

Know then that news has reached us to the effect that in the French kingdom the Jews have become so insolent that by means of their vicious usury, through which they extort not only usury but even usury on usury, they appropriate ecclesiastical goods and Christian possessions. There seems to be fulfilled among the Christians that which the prophet bewailed in the case of Jews, saying: "Our heritage has been turned over to strangers, our houses to outsiders."

Moreover, although it was enacted in the Lateran Council that Jews are not permitted to have Christian servants in their homes, neither under pretext of rearing their children nor for domestic service nor for any other reason whatever, but that those who presume to live with them shall be excommunicate, yet they do not hesitate to have Christian servants and nurses, with whom, at times, they work such abominations as are more fitting that you should punish than proper that we should specify.

Moreover, although the same council decided to admit Christian evidence against Jews in lawsuits that arise between the two since they use Jewish witnesses against Christians, and although it decreed that whoever preferred the Jews to the Christians in this matter should be anathematized, yet they have to this day been given the preference in the French realm to such an extent that Christian witnesses are not believed against them, while they are admitted to testimony against Christians. Thus, if the Christians to whom they have loaned money on usury bring Christian witnesses about the facts in the case, the Jews are given more credence because of the document which the indiscreet debtor left with them through negligence or carelessness, than are the Christians through the witnesses produced. Nay, more, in complaints of this nature witnesses are not received against them at all.

By this time, and it is with shame that we repeat it, they have become so insolent that at Sens they have built a new synagogue near an old church, a good deal higher that the church. There they celebrate the Jewish rites, not in a low tone, as they used to before they were expelled from the kingdom, but, in accordance with their custom, with great shouting. Thus they do not hesitate to hinder divine services in that church.

What is even worse, blaspheming against God's name, they publicly insult Christians by saying that Christians believe in a peasant who had been hung by the Jewish people. Indeed, we do not doubt that He was hung for us, since He carried our sins in His body on the Cross, but we do not admit that He was a peasant either in manners or in race. Forsooth, they themselves cannot deny that physically He was descended from priestly and royal stock and that His manners were distinguished and proper. Also on Good Friday the Jews, contrary to old custom, publicly run to and fro over the towns and streets and everywhere laugh at the Christians because they adore the Crucified One on the Cross and, through their improprieties, attempt to dissuade them from their worship.

The doors of the Jews are also open to thieves half the night, and, if any stolen goods be found with them, none can obtain justice from them. The Jews likewise abuse the royal patience, and, when they remain living among the Christians, they take advantage of every wicked opportunity to kill in secret their Christian hosts. Thus, it has recently been reported that a certain poor scholar had been found murdered in their latrine.

Wherefore, lest through them the name of God be blasphemed and Christian liberty become less than Jewish servitude, we warn, and in the name of God exhort Your Serene Majesty—and we join thereto a remission of sins—that you restrain the Jews from their presumptions in these and similar matters and that you try to remove from the French kingdom abuses of this sort for you seem to have the proper zeal of God and knowledge of Him. Moreover, since secular laws should be directed with greater severity against those who profane the name of God, you should so turn against these blasphemers that the punishment of some should be a source of fear to all and that ease of obtaining forgiveness serve not as an incentive to evil doers. You should bestir yourself, moreover, to remove heretics from the French kingdom, nor should your Royal Highness permit wolves who hide in sheep's clothes in order to destroy the ewes to wander in your realm, but rather by persecuting them Your Highness should display the same zeal with which he follows the Christian faith.

Given in Rome, at Saint Peter's, January 16,
in the seventh year [1205].

POPE INNOCENT III TO
THE COUNT OF NEVERS, 1208

THE SECOND *of Innocent's letters presented here is addressed to a leading secular authority of northern France. Again the Pope notes the fundamental Church doctrine of toleration of the Jews, with the concomitant notion that the Jews should exhibit their gratitude by refraining from behavior offensive to the ruling faith. Instead, the papal court continues to receive reports of a variety of abuses committed by the Jews. Some of these offenses bring actual harm to the Christian population; others demean the honor of Christianity. In any case, a Christian prince responsible for the well-being of his realm should be sensitive to such abuses and control the offensive behavior of his Jewish subjects. According to Innocent, however, not only have the count and his peers been lax in this regard, they have gone so far as to persecute Church dignitaries attempting to rectify such errors. The pope both entreats and warns the count to correct these misdeeds.*

TO THE COUNT of Nevers:

The Lord made Cain a wanderer and a fugitive over the earth, but set a mark upon him, making his head to shake, lest any finding him should slay him. Thus the Jews, against whom the blood of Jesus Christ calls out, although they ought not be killed, lest the Christian people forget the divine law, yet as wanderers ought they to remain upon the earth, until their countenance be filled with shame and they seek the name of Jesus Christ, the Lord. That is why blasphemers of the Christian name ought not to be aided by Christian princes to oppress the servants of the Lord, but ought rather be forced into the servitude of which they made themselves deserving when they raised sacrilegious hands against Him Who had come to confer true liberty upon them, thus calling down His blood upon themselves and upon their children.

But it has been brought to our notice that certain princes do not have their eyes upon the Lord, before whom all things lie clear and open. While they themselves are ashamed to exact usury, they receive Jews into their villages and towns and appoint them their agents for the collection of usury. They are not afraid to afflict the churches of God and oppress the poor of Christ. Moreover, when the Christians, who had taken a loan from the Jews, have paid them back the principal and more besides, it often happens that these appointees of the princes and the servants of their power, after seizing the pledges and casting these Christians into prison, compel them to pay most exorbitant usury. Thus are widows and orphans robbed of their inheritance, and churches defrauded of their tithes and other regular sources of income, since the Jews maintain themselves in seized castles and villas and utterly refuse to reply to prelates of the churches in accordance with parochial law.

Another scandal of no mean consequence is created by them in that, while they themselves shrink from eating, as unclean, the meat of animals killed by Christians, yet they obtain it as a privilege from the favor of the princes to give the slaughtering of the animal over to those who cut the animals according to the Jewish rite. They then take of these animals as much as they desire and offer the leavings to the Christians. Similar to this is what the Jewish women do with the milk which is publicly sold for the nourishment of children. There is also another thing, no less detestable to the Christians, that they presume to do. At the vintage season the Jew, shod in linen boots, treads the wine, and, having extracted the purer wine in accordance with the Jewish rite, they retain some for their own pleasure. The rest, which is abominable to them, they leave to the faithful Christians, and with this, now and again, the sacrament of the blood of Christ is performed.

Moreover, secure in the favor of the mighty, they do not at all admit against themselves any Christian witness, no matter how good in character and no matter in what respect superior.

Indeed, not long ago our venerable brother, the bishop of Auxerre, in order to remove such an abomination from his diocese, consulted men of prudence and, under the threat of interdict, forbade such occurrences in the said land, in solemn synod enjoining the clergy that stood around him to prohibit such practices under pain of excommunication in their churches. To him the greater part of the faithful fathers devoutly promised to abstain from the above-mentioned abominations, but certain nobles and princes and their ministers, with their eye to the Jewish gifts that had corrupted their hearts, have tried to terrify by threats and influence by shame those of the faithful who, for the sake of obedience and the fear of the sentence promulgated, had decided to abstain from such actions. Some of these later were captured, and the princes compelled them to redeem themselves and refused to set them free unless it pleased the Jews. These nobles, in order that they may not be checked by personal excommunication and an interdict against their lands, try to guard themselves by setting up as an obstacle an appeal to the Apostolic Throne, thereby evading Church discipline. The Jews, however, rejoice if, because of this, a sentence of excommunication or interdict be pronounced against some Christians, for thus, on their account, the instruments of the churches are hung on the willow trees of Babylon, and the priests are despoiled of their livelihood.

Certainly you, who are, as we have heard, a religious man and a servant of Jesus Christ, ought to keep away from the Jewish superstitions because of your reverence for Him, lest the enemies of the Cross exult among themselves over the servants of Him Who was crucified. Yet you, above all, favor them, and in the aforementioned excesses they have in you a particular defender. Would not your wrath be kindled against a subject of yours if he proved to be of help to your enemy? How much more, therefore, should you dread divine anger because you are not afraid to show favor to those who dared to nail to the Cross the only-begotten Son of God and to this moment have not ceased to blaspheme against Him. Wishing, therefore, that the scandal arising among the people as a result of this should be removed from their midst, and that such unbridled presumption which you are said to be committing against Christ and His Church should be discontinued, we, by apostolic letters sent to you, ask, warn, and urge Your Highness in the name of the Lord, that you yourself so correct the above and refrain from similar crimes of any other kind, as to show that you possess the zeal of the orthodox faith, and so that we should not be forced to lend our hand to correct the state of affairs. For we must promptly punish all disobedience to the successor of the Apostle, since we have for this purpose been appointed by God, that we might uproot that which is to be uprooted and plant that which is to be planted.

Given at Saint Peter's, January 17,
in the tenth year [1208].

POPE ALEXANDER IV TO
    THE DUKE OF BURGUNDY, 1257

DURING THE FIRST HALF *of the thirteenth century, a series of new ecclesiastical demands concerning the Jews appeared in western Christendom. In the accompanying letter, Pope Alexander IV urges the duke of Burgundy to enforce these new regulations in his domain. Jews are not to hold public office; they are to wear special clothing by means of which they may be readily identified; the Talmud, which by this time was condemned, should be confiscated. Once more we see the ruling class under pressure to execute the programs of the Church.*

To THE NOBLE DUKE of Burgundy:

In the sacred general assembly, through careful deliberations, it was decreed that the Jews be distinguished from Christians by the quality of their garb, lest those of the former might be damnably confused with those of the latter. In the same council it was also decreed that Jews not be preferred for public office, since under such pretext they are often dangerous to Christians. However, as we understand, the Jews of your land do not observe this edict, as a result of which an excess of damnable confusion can be presumed under the guise of error. Also the same Jews are preferred for offices contrary to that edict. Since it is fitting that you provide properly for these matters, we request and exhort your nobility, through apostolic writs addressed to you, ordering that, since power has been transmitted to you by God, you compel the aforesaid Jews to wear a badge by means of which they can be distinguished from Christians by the quality of their garb and that they not be preferred for the aforesaid offices. Moreover, you must cause those books which are popularly called Talmud, in which are contained errors against the Catholic faith and horrible and intolerable blasphemies against our Lord Jesus Christ and the Holy Virgin Mary, His mother, to be surrendered by all the Jews of the aforesaid land. Your sincerity should provide in these matters in such a way that the mercy of the eternal King manifest for you that which it bestows for pious acts and that we extend for this full appreciation to your devotions.

Given at Viterbo, September 3, in the fourth year of our pontificate [1257].

12 GOVERNMENTAL REJECTION OF CHURCH PRESSURE

KING FERDINAND III OF CASTILE, 1219

CHURCH INITIATIVES *were not always enthusiastically received by governmental authorities. In the next letter, we see evidence of friction over the introduction of a radical ecclesiastical innovation, the Jewish badge. Enforcement of the badge in Castile caused serious problems. In view of a precipitous loss of royal income, the king of Castile and the archbishop of Toledo earnestly entreated Pope Honorius III for permission to relax the new measures. In this particular instance, the pontiff was responsive to this display of governmental opposition and granted the request.*

TO THE ARCHBISHOP of Toledo:

On behalf of our dearest son in Christ, Ferdinand, the illustrious king of Castile, as well as on behalf of yourself, we have been informed that the Jews who reside in the kingdom of Castile are so seriously wrought up over that which was decided with regard to them in the General Council in the matter of wearing a sign, that some of them choose rather to flee to the Moors than to be burdened with such a sign. Others conspire because of this and make secret agreements. As a result, the king, whose income in large measure derives from these very Jews, can hardly raise his expenses, and serious misfortune may befall the kingdom. Wherefore we have been humbly petitioned both on behalf of this king as well as yourself, that our permission be given you to set aside the execution of this edict, since you cannot proceed to its enforcement without great trouble.

Therefore, since in our paternal solitude we desire to assure the peace of this king and his kingdom, we, by these letters, give you authority to suspend the execution of the said decree for as long as you may think fit, unless you receive a special apostolic mandate with regard to it in the future. Other letters notwithstanding, you shall ask the Apostolic Throne with regard to anything about which this letter is silent.

Given at the Lateran, March 20,
in the third year [1219].

COUNTESS BLANCHE OF CHAMPAGNE, 1219

An EXAMPLE OF THE TENSION *which arose over special Crusader privileges is found in the following letter from Pope Honorius III to three ranking ecclesiastics in the county of Champagne. The countess had lodged a complaint concerning the issue of usury owed by Crusaders. She argued that certain prelates had gone far beyond the official Church position as stipulated in the decrees of the Fourth Lateran Council. Again, the pope proved responsive to these protestations, ordering three select churchmen to investigate the matter and, where necessary, prohibit these prelates from exceeding their proper authority.*

To THE ABBOT of Saint Jean de Vignes of Soissons and the abbot of Valsecret and the dean of Soissons:
Our dear daughter in Christ, the noblewoman Blanche, countess of Champagne, proved to us that, while it was specifically decreed in the

General Council that Jews should be compelled by secular lords to return usury to Crusaders, nevertheless, certain archbishops and other prelates of the Church, usurping undue jurisdiction over the Jews in the lands of the said countess, by new devices and under pretext of ecclesiastical freedom, not content with the decrees promulgated by this council, greatly harass and disturb the land of this countess and her Jews, beyond the decrees of the council mentioned above. Wanting, therefore, to preserve the complete rights of this countess, we, through apostolic letters, order you that by our authority you shall expressly prohibit these archbishops and other prelates from exceeding the regulation of the said council with regard to the above-named matters. If any should disobey, you shall restore to its proper status whatever you find to have been done in these matters contrary to the regulation of the said council. If there are any opponents or rebels, after giving them warning, you will restrain them by whatever punishment is proper, without appeal, etc.

Given at Reate, June 21, in the third year [1219].

KING PHILIP IV OF FRANCE, 1293

As THE THIRTEENTH CENTURY *progressed, a new source of friction developed between Church and State. With the burgeoning importance of the newly founded ecclesiastical orders, especially the Dominicans and the Franciscans, the ire of secular authorities was increasingly aroused by what they regarded as undue interference in their affairs. In France, which had traditionally been a strong supporter of the papacy and the Church, this irritation came to a head during the reign of Philip IV. Concerned with fiscal problems in general and exploitation of his Jews in particular, Philip enacted a decree in 1293, sharply limiting the independent prerogatives of the friars. These papal representatives are henceforth to arrest no Jew, without the knowledge and consent of the responsible royal officials; they are to produce copies of the papal documents upon which their authority is based and sound evidence of the charge upon which the Jew is to be seized. Philip indicates rather explicitly that his concern is primarily fiscal. It seems evident that there was also general resentment of growing Church interference in the affairs of state, resentment which led in the early fourteenth century to a major Church-State confrontation.*

1.   It is ordained that the Jews of the kingdom of France—either one or several of them—shall not, in a case in which they are ordered seized, be seized or imprisoned at the command or demand of any friars of any order or of others who discharge their office, unless with the prior knowledge of our bailiff or seneschal under whose jurisdiction they would normally be seized and unless the cause for which some or any one of them should be seized be clear and unless it is clear by apostolic mandate who bears the right to seize them.

2.   We command that all our seneschals, bailiffs, and other officials possess a copy of that apostolic mandate. Our aforesaid officials may not be excused through ignorance from requiring the aforesaid apostolic mandate.

3.   If there be any doubt or obscurity concerning such a case, these officials shall not seize any of the Jews, unless first the court of the lord king be consulted as well as the masters appointed for that purpose by royal order, recently ordained by his letter to us.

4.   We strictly order and command you that you cause these orders, sealed with the seal of the lord dean of the Church of Saint Quentin in Normandy and sent out to us recently, to be scrupulously upheld and observed.

5.   You must defend those Jews living in our jurisdictions, as well as others who will happen to come to live in our jurisdictions, from unjust extortion, injuries, and violence. You must cause the aforesaid orders to be observed so that the Jews suffer no loss in property or person in these matters, which would lead to our loss. You may permit no undue innovations to be instituted against them through which the payment of their tallage may be in any way impeded.

6.   You shall not permit any Jew or Jews subject to us to be seized or imprisoned at the demand or command of any friar of any order or of those who discharge their office, unless according to royal mandate and the aforesaid order, and unless we or you have been informed of the cause for which they are ordered to be seized, and unless this cause is a clear one with good proof on the basis of which they ought to be seized, and unless it is clear by apostolic mandate who bears the right to seize them.

Given at Carcassonne, Monday before the Feast of Saint Vincent
[January 19] 1293 A.D.

KING PHILIP IV OF FRANCE, 1302

NINE YEARS AFTER *the previous pronouncement, as tension between Philip the Fair and the papacy mounted again, the monarch issued a second edict concerning the inquisition and his Jews. This time the formulation is briefer and sharper. Instead of defining the limits of aid royal officials might lend the friars, Philip here simply declares Jewish affairs outside the jurisdiction of inquisitors. He orders his royal officials to extend no help whatsoever, a step which reflects both the deepening tension and the increasingly radical position of the king.*

PHILIP, to all the seneschals, bailiffs, provosts, and other officials whom the present letter reaches, greetings:

We have the concerns of the Catholic faith at heart above all other concerns and wish to promote effectively that which we intend, by affording to the inquisition of heretical depravity counsel and aid in the affairs of that faith. We wish, however, that these inquisitors be satisfied within their own bounds and that they not exceed the limits of the power accorded to them—to the detriment of temporal jurisdiction and at the expense of our subordinates. Therefore, we strictly order you all and each of you individually that, if the aforementioned inquisitors involve themselves or attempt in any way to involve themselves against the Jews of our kingdom in questions of usury, blasphemy, or other issues which do not pertain to these inquisitors by virtue of their role of inquisitor, you shall at their insistence or request seize no Jew nor cause him to be seized or molested in any way on the aforesaid charges, nor shall you extend aid or favor in connection with these Jews to these inquisitors.

Given at Vincennes on the Saturday after the Feast of the Apostles Saint Peter and Paul [June 30], 1302.

13 GOVERNMENTAL ACCEPTANCE OF CHURCH INITIATIVES

KING PHILIP III OF FRANCE, 1283

WHILE GOVERNMENTS *often rejected ecclesiastical pressures, more frequently they were fully sympathetic to the Church and its programs. Sometimes such programs served the secular authorities' purposes; acceptance of Church demands was a method of ingratiating rulers with large and influential segments of their populace. Often such demands were accepted because the ruling class was truly committed to furthering the ideals of Christian living as defined and formulated by the Church.*

The European monarchy traditionally most committed to cooperation with the Church was that of France. As loyal supporters of the Church and the papacy, the Capetian kings of France attempted to carry out the Church's programs in regard to the Jews. An example of broad royal legislation which reflects Church initiatives is Philip III's edict of 1283.

While Philip III was hardly as pious as his distinguished father, Saint Louis, he was committed to fostering ecclesiastical programs. Philip III's edict of 1283 is his major statement concerning the Jews. The monarch claims in his preamble that the motivating factor was piety—"since nothing reflects more glory on a prince than zeal for the faith." The items enumerated, enhanced segregation of the Jews and continued vigilance against Talmudic literature, constitute a continuation of some of Saint Louis' main efforts. It is striking that a statement on usury is not included in this edict. We know from other sources that Philip was in fact growing lax in this area.

PHILIP, by the grace of God, king of the French, to his beloved and faithful dukes, counts, barons, bailiffs, castellans, provosts, towns, and to all others exercising authority in our kingdom, whom the present letter reaches, greetings and love:

1.   Since nothing reflects more glory on a ruler than zeal for the faith, increasingly devoted to the promotion and exaltation of the Christian faith, we order you and strictly require—in accordance with the statute already enacted—that the Jews bear a badge of felt on their chests and add a second between their shoulders, so that they may be distinguishable from Christians.

2.   Also in accordance with a prohibition already enacted by me, they may not have Christian nurses, maidservants, or male servants in their homes.

3.   Also, they may not build or construct new cemeteries or new synagogues, nor may they replace old ones, nor may they chant loudly. Where the contrary be found, it must be corrected.

4.   Also, in our kingdom, they may not live or dwell in small towns, among the rustics, for a ten year period; rather, they must reside in large towns and well-known places, where they have been accustomed to dwell of yore.

5.   Also, these Jews may not have the Talmud or other books condemned in France; rather, they must be publicly burned in your territories and in the jurisdictions committed to you.

You shall see that there is firm adherence on the above written and on any other matters pertaining to the promotion and defense of the faith, both against heretics and against perfidious Jews. You shall extend aid and support to the inquisitors in our kingdom who present this letter. All this shall be done in such a way that, in the sight of God and in our sight, you need not be reproved for negligence, but rather be recommended for the promptness of your obedience.

Enacted at Corbeil, on the morrow of the
Resurrection of the Lord [March 30], 1293.

KING PHILIP IV OF FRANCE, 1299

PHILIP IV, *the third great French monarch of the thirteenth century, represents a reversal of the pious orientation of his grandfather Saint Louis in favor of the worldly policies of his great-great-grandfather Philip Augustus. As already noted, Philip IV's edicts concerning the Jews reflect substantial tension between the monarch and the Church which eventually led to major confrontations. This tension, discernible early in Philip's reign, abated somewhat toward the end of the 1290s. At this time there were considerable efforts toward rapprochement, with the Church beatifying Philip's grandfather and Philip expressing support for many of the Church's traditional policies. It is from this period of cooperation that we have Philip's major statement of support for ecclesiastical programs concerning the Jews.*

PHILIP, by the grace of God king of the French, to all the officials of his kingdom whom the present letter reaches, greetings:

We understand that the Jews in diverse parts of the kingdom solicit Christians on behalf of heresy and ensnare many with their wiles and with their promises and bribes. In this way they receive from many and dare to handle wretchedly the most holy body of Christ and blaspheme the other sacraments of our faith. They seduce many simple folk and circumcise those whom they have seduced. They receive and conceal fugitive heretics. To the scandal of our faith, they build new synagogues, chanting in a loud voice as though they were officiating in a Church service. They multiply copies of the condemned books called Talmud, containing innumerable blasphemies concerning the most glorious Virgin Mary, and teach an immoderate disparagement of the Christian faith. Thus, through the aforesaid and in many other ways, they are so able to influence the Christian populace that all the ears of the faithful should ring in horror.

In order that such reprehensible misdeeds not go unpunished and in order that the enemies of our faith not be able during our times to gain advantage for their perfidy, we order all of you and each of you that, at the order of the inquisitors of heretical depravity who show the present letter, you seize suspects, imprison them, transfer them from prison to prison, and punish them according to the tenor of the canons of the Apostolic Throne enacted concerning this matter, whenever you are so requested by the aforesaid inquisitors. You should so behave in this regard that, zealous for the Catholic faith, you will be able to be commended properly for diligence and, both by God and by us, minimally reproved.

Enacted at Melun, on the Saturday prior to Pentecost
[June 5], 1294 A.D.

KING HENRY III OF ENGLAND, 1253

DURING THE TWELFTH *and the thirteenth centuries the relationship between the English monarchy and the papacy was at times antagonistic. The English kings were often lax in enforcing ecclesiastical policies concerning the Jews, particularly when such enforcement meant serious financial loss. As the thirteenth century progressed, however, Jewish fiscal usefulness waned and Church pressures intensified. Thus, in 1253, King Henry III issued an important edict ordering enforcement of a series of traditional ecclesiastical demands.*

THE KING has provided and ordained etc:

1. That no Jew remain in England unless he do the king service, and that from the hour of birth every Jew, whether male or female, serve us in some way.

2. That there be no synagogues of the Jews in England, save in those places in which such synagogues were in the time of King John, the king's father.

3.   That in their synagogues the Jews, one and all, subdue their voices in performing their ritual offices, that Christians may not hear them.

4.   That all Jews answer to the rector of the church of the parish in which they dwell touching all parochial dues relating to their houses.

5.   That no Christian man or woman serve any Jew or Jewess or eat with them or tarry in their houses.

6.   That no Jew or Jewess eat or buy meat during Lent.

7.   That no Jew disparage the Christian faith or publicly dispute concerning the same.

8.   That no Jew have secret familiar intercourse with any Christian woman, and no Christian man with a Jewess.

9.   That every Jew wear his badge conspicuously on his breast.

10.   That no Jew enter any church or chapel save for purpose of transit or linger in them in dishonor of Christ.

11.   That no Jew place any hindrance in the way of another Jew desirous of turning to the Christian faith.

12.   That no Jew be received in any town but by special license of the king, save only in those towns in which Jews have been wont to dwell.

The justices assigned to the custody of the Jews are commanded that they cause these provisions to be carried into effect and rigorously observed on pain of forfeiture of the chattels of the said Jews.

Witness the king at Westminster,
on the 31st day of January. By king and council.

৪৩

KING ALFONSO X OF CASTILE, 1260S

AS CHRISTIAN RULE *spread throughout Spain, there developed a concern with improvements in many areas, including legal codification. A major thrust in this direction was initiated by King Ferdinand III and brought to fruition by King Alfonso X. Of the codes completed during this period, the most complete and the most lasting in its influence was* Las Siete Partidas. *Designed to serve as a comprehensive guide to legal norms, the manual included an extensive section on the Jews. Based heavily on Church attitudes and demands, the statement represents perhaps the most striking example of governmental acceptance of Church pressures. It is not clear, however, how real this acceptance was.* Las Siete Partidas *remained for a long time merely a theoretical statement of law, with little actual impact on the life of Spanish society. For the Jews, this obviously represented a great benefit.*

৪৩

Title XXIV   Concerning the Jews.

ALTHOUGH THE JEWS are a people who do not believe in the religion of Our Lord Jesus Christ, the great Christian sovereigns have always permitted them to live among them. Wherefore, since in the preceding title we spoke of diviners and other men who allege that they know things that are to come, which is a kind of contempt of God, since they desire to make themselves equal to Him by learning His acts and His secrets, we intend to speak here of the Jews, who insult His name and deny the marvelous and holy acts which He performed when He sent His Son, Our Lord Jesus Christ, into the world to save sinners. We shall explain what the word Jew means; whence this name derived; for what reasons the Church and the great Christian world permitted the Jews to live among them; in what way Jews should pass their lives among Christians; what things they should not use or do, according to our religion; and which Jews can be subjected to force on account of the wicked acts that they have performed or the debt which they owe. Also why Jews who become Christians should not be subject to compulsion; what advantage a Jew, by becoming a Christian, obtains over other Jews who do not; what penalty those deserve who cause him injury or dishonor;

and to what punishment Christians who become Jews and also Jews who force their Moorish slaves to embrace their religion are liable.

> *Law I   What the word Jew means, and whence this term is derived.*

A party who believes in and adheres to the law of Moses is called a Jew, according to the strict signification of the term, as well as one who is circumcised and observes the other precepts commanded by his religion. This name is derived from the tribe of Judah which was nobler and more powerful than the others and also possessed another advantage, because the king of the Jews had to be selected from that tribe and its members always received the first wounds in battle. The reason that the Church, emperors, kings, and princes permitted the Jews to dwell among them and with Christians is because they always lived, as it were, in captivity, as it was constantly in the minds of men that they were descended from those who crucified Our Lord Jesus Christ.

> *Law II   In what way Jews should pass their lives among Christians; what things they should not make use of or practice, according to our religion; and what penalty those deserve who act contrary to its ordinances.*

Jews should pass their lives among Christians quietly and without disorder, practicing their own religious rites and not speaking ill of the faith of Our Lord Jesus Christ, which Christians acknowledge. Moreover, a Jew should be very careful to avoid preaching to or converting any Christian, to the end that he may become a Jew, by exalting his own belief and disparaging ours. Whoever violates this law shall be put to death and lose all his property. We have heard it said that in some places Jews celebrated and still celebrate Good Friday, which commemorates the Passion of Our Lord Jesus Christ, by way of contempt, stealing children and fastening them to crosses and making images of wax and crucifying them, when they cannot obtain children. We order that, hereafter, if in any part of our dominions anything like this is done and can be proved, all persons who were present when the act was committed shall be seized, arrested, and brought before the king. After the king ascertains that they are guilty, he shall cause them to be put to death in a disgraceful manner, no matter how many there may be.

We also forbid any Jew to dare to leave his house or his quarter on Good Friday. They must all remain shut up until Saturday morning. If they violate this regulation, we decree that they shall not be entitled to reparation for any injury or dishonor inflicted upon them by Christians.

Law III   No Jew can hold any office or employment by which he may be able to oppress Christians.

Jews were formerly highly honored and enjoyed privileges above all other races, for they alone were called the people of God. But they disowned Him Who had honored them and given them privileges. Instead of showing Him reverence, they humiliated Him, by shamefully putting Him to death on the Cross. It was therefore proper and just that, on account of the great crime and wickedness which they committed, they should forfeit the honors and privileges which they enjoyed. Thus from the day when they crucified Our Lord Jesus Christ they never had either king or priests among themselves, as they formerly did. The emperors, who in former times were lords of all the world, considered it fitting and right that, on account of the treason which they committed in killing their Lord, they should lose all said honors and privileges, so that no Jew could ever afterwards hold an honorable position or a public office by means of which he might, in any way, oppress a Christian.

Law IV   How Jews can have a synagogue among Christians.

A synagogue is a place where the Jews pray, and a new building of this kind cannot be erected in any part of our dominions, except by our order. Where, however, those which formerly existed there are torn down, they can be built in the same spot where they originally stood; but they cannot be made any larger or raised to any great height or be painted. A synagogue constructed in any other manner shall be lost by the Jews and shall belong to the principal church of the locality where it is built. And for the reason that a synagogue is a place where the name of God is praised, we forbid any Christian to deface it, or remove anything from it, or take anything out of it by force, except where some malefactor takes refuge there. Then they have a right to remove him by force in order to bring him before the judge. Moreover, we forbid Christians to put any animal into a synagogue, or loiter in it, or place any hindrance in the way of the Jews while they are there performing their devotions according to their religion.

Law V   No compulsion shall be brought to bear upon the Jews on Saturday, and what Jews can be subject to compulsion.

Saturday is the day on which Jews perform their devotions and remain quiet in their lodgings and do not make contracts or transact any business. Since they are obliged by their religion to keep it, no one should on that day summon them or bring them into court. Wherefore we order that no judge shall employ force or any constraint upon Jews on Saturday, in order to bring them into court on account of their debts, or arrest them, or cause them any other annoyance. The remaining days of the week are sufficient for the purpose of employing compulsion against them, according to law. Jews are not bound to obey a summons served upon them on that day. Moreover, we decree that any decision rendered against them on Saturday shall not be valid. But if a Jew should wound, kill, rob, steal, or commit any other offense like these, for which he can be punished in person or property, then the judge can arrest him on Saturday.

We also decree that all claims that Christians have against Jews and Jews against Christians shall be decided and determined by our judges in the district where they reside, and not by their old men. And as we forbid Christians to bring Jews into court or annoy them on Saturday, so we also decree that Jews, neither in person nor by their attorneys, shall have the right to bring Christians into court or annoy them on this day. In addition to this, we forbid any Christian, on his own responsibility, to arrest or wrong any Jew either in his person or property, but where he has any complaint against him he must bring it before our judges. If anyone should be so bold as to use violence against the Jews or rob them of anything, he shall return them double the value of the same.

> *Law VI   Jews who become Christians shall not be subject to compulsion; what advantage a Jew has who becomes a Christian; and what penalty other Jews deserve who do him harm.*

No force or compulsion shall be employed in any way against a Jew to induce him to become a Christian. Christians should convert him to the faith of Our Lord Jesus Christ by means of the texts of the Holy Scriptures and by kind words, for no one can love or appreciate a service which is done him by compulsion. We also decree that, if any Jew or Jewess should voluntarily desire to become a Christian, the other Jews shall not interfere with this in any way. If they stone, wound, or kill any such person, because they wish to become Christians or after they have been baptized, and this can be proved, we order that all the murderers or the abettors of said murder or attack shall be burned. But where the party was not killed, but wounded or dishonored, we order that the judges of the neighborhood where this took place shall compel those guilty of the attack or those who caused the dishonor to make amends to him for the same. Also they must be punished for the offense which they committed as they think they deserve. We also order that, after any Jews become Christians, all persons in our dominions shall honor them. No one shall dare to reproach them or their descendants, by way of insult, with having been Jews. They shall possess all their property, sharing the same with their brothers and inheriting it from their fathers and mothers and other relatives, just as if they were Jews. They can hold all offices and dignities which other Christians can.

Law VII   What penalty a Christian deserves who becomes a Jew.

Where a Christian is so unfortunate as to become a Jew, we order that he shall be put to death just as if he had become a heretic. We decree that his property shall be disposed of in the same way that we stated should be done with that of heretics.

Law VIII   No Christian, man or woman, shall live with a Jew.

We forbid any Jew to keep Christian men or women in his house or to be served by them, although he may have them to cultivate and take care of his lands or protect him on the way when he is compelled to go to some dangerous place. Moreover, we forbid any Christian man or woman to invite a Jew or a Jewess, or to accept an invitation from them, to eat or drink together or to drink any wine made by their hands. We also order that no Jews shall dare to bathe in company with Christians and that no Christian shall take any medicine or cathartic made by a Jew. He can take it by the advice of some intelligent person, only where it is made by a Christian, who knows and is familiar with its ingredients.

Law IX   What penalty a Jew deserves who has intercourse with a Christian woman.

Jews who live with Christian women are guilty of great insolence and boldness, for which reason we decree that all Jews who, hereafter, may be convicted of having done such a thing shall be put to death. For if Christians who commit adultery with married women deserve death on that account, much more do Jews who have sexual intercourse with Christian women, who are spiritually the wives of Our Lord Jesus Christ because of the faith and the baptism which they receive in His name. Nor do we consider it proper that a Christian woman who commits an offense of this kind shall escape without punishment. Wherefore we order that, whether she be a virgin, a married woman, a widow, or a common prostitute who gives herself to all men, she shall suffer the same penalty, which we mentioned in the last law in the title concerning the Moors, to which a Christian woman is liable who has carnal intercourse with a Moor.

Law X What penalty Jews deserve who hold Christians as slaves.

A Jew shall not purchase or keep as a slave a Christian man or woman. If anyone violates this law, the Christian shall be restored to freedom and shall not pay any portion of the price given for him, although the Jew may not have been aware when he bought him that he was a Christian. But if he knew that he was such when he purchased him and makes use of him afterwards as a slave, he shall be put to death for doing so. Moreover, we forbid any Jew to convert a captive to his religion, even though said captive may be a Moor or belong to some other barbarous race. If anyone violates this law, we order that the said slave who has become a Jew shall be set at liberty and removed from the control of the party to whom he or she belonged. If any Moors who are the captives of Jews become Christians, they shall at once be freed, as is explained in the fourth section of this book, in the title concerning liberty, in the laws which treat of this subject.

Law XI Jews shall bear certain marks in order that they may be known.

Many crimes and outrageous things occur between Christians and Jews because they live together in cities and dress alike. In order to avoid the offenses and evils which take place for this reason, we deem it proper and we order that all Jews male and female living in our dominions shall bear some distinguishing mark upon their heads so that people may plainly recognize a Jew or a Jewess. Any Jew who does not bear such a mark shall pay for each time he is found without it ten maravedis of gold. If he has not the means to do this, he shall publicly receive ten lashes for his offense.

14 JEWISH USURY:
ECCLESIASTICAL VIEWS

FOURTH LATERAN COUNCIL, 1215

AS THE JEWS OF WESTERN EUROPE *came to specialize more heavily in moneylending, it increasingly came to be felt that the basic thrust of Jewish economic life was pernicious, both to the Church and to the Christian populace at large. The culmination of the agitation against Jewish usury occurred at the critical Fourth Lateran Council. The issue, as noted already, was the damage Jewish moneylenders inflicted upon Christian society. The assembled prelates noted the ironical fact that it was precisely Church efforts to eradicate Christian usury that had opened the way for Jewish moneylending and its deleterious impact: "The more the Christian religion refrains from the exaction of usury, the more does the Jewish perfidy become used to this practice." Moved by their desire to protect Christians from the oppression of Jewish creditors, the prelates ordered that Jews be forbidden to extort "heavy and immoderate usury." The concern was a pragmatic one and the response was pragmatic as well. While Jewish usury itself was not outlawed, excessive interest, which would inflict the greatest damage on the debtor class, was prohibited.*

This decree was clearly not an easy one to enforce. In the first place, the offense to be eliminated was couched in vague terms. What precisely was "heavy and immoderate usury"? Moreover, the ecclesiastical dignitaries seemed to be aware that the temporal authorities who benefited from the profits of Jewish usury would be loathe to support legislation which would directly diminish their income. The mode for enforcing the decree was thus to force Christians to abstain from all contact with

Jews who controverted the new edict. This was not a highly effective technique. The temporal rulers were mildly asked not to be aroused against those observing the law. In every respect, the decree must be seen as tentative and weak. Nonetheless it represents a major turning point in the struggle against Jewish usury. By putting the Church on record against abuses associated with Jewish usury, the Fourth Lateran Council laid the foundation for far more forceful actions, which would eventually undermine much of Jewish economic life in western Christendom.

THE MORE the Christian religion refrains from the exaction of usury, the more does the Jewish perfidy become used to this practice, so that in a short time the Jews exhaust the financial strength of Christians. Therefore, in our desire to protect Christians in this matter, that they should not be excessively oppressed by the Jews, we order by a decree of this synod that, if henceforth a Jew, under any pretext, extort heavy and immoderate usury from a Christian, all relationship with Christians shall be denied him until he shall have made sufficient amends for his exorbitant exactions. The Christians, if need be, shall be compelled by ecclesiastical punishment without appeal to abstain from such commerce. We also order the princes not to be aroused against the Christians because of this, but rather to try to keep the Jews from this practice.

A JEWISH CRITIQUE, MID-1250S

THE JEWS *were painfully aware of the accusation that their moneylending was harmful to the interests of Christian society, and sought to rebut the allegation. An example of the Jewish counterargument occurs in a letter purportedly addressed to King Louis IX. The Jewish author attempts to prove that the king's program is based on a theoretical misunderstanding of the issue of Jewish usury. In addition, he claims that Jewish usury is not harmful at all; it is in fact useful. It is simply impossible, the Jew contends, for any society to exist without a flow of capital. The king himself is the best proof of this. Despite his enormous wealth, he is constantly in need of fresh capital. If this is true for the king, all the more is it true for those less fortunate. Men of lesser means have to borrow in order to carry on their business affairs. In moments of crisis, they must borrow in order to sustain their families, until the crisis passes. Moreover, argues the Jew, if one examines the realities of moneylending carefully, one finds that Jewish creditors are actually more benign than their Christian counterparts. This then is the twofold contention: Moneylending is indispensable, and Jewish moneylenders are the least exploitative.*

IT WOULD BE BETTER for the king to suffer the sin of usury on the part of the Jews, who are not of his faith and whom he has no obligation to force into his faith, than to bring death to men of his faith by causing them to transgress in public. For, if he were to order an investigation throughout his kingdom, he would find that from the time that he forbade usury to the Jews there have multiplied among the members of his faith, the Christians, usurers far harsher than the Jews. Also, many circumvent the prohibition through business dealings, by selling at one-half or one-third higher than value as recompense for extending the time of payment. In that way the lender loses more than he would give to the Jews as usury for the entire year. Thus you see that the king preserves from sin those who are not members of his faith and leads to sin those who are. For it is impossible for society to exist without lending. Indeed the king himself, whose wealth is very great, has been forced to borrow at high interest a number of times. Likewise his officials borrowed many times for the purpose of protecting his land while he himself was in Paris or the royal domain, until he sent the funds for paying his officers and servants, the guardians of his fortifications. Since society cannot exist without lending, it would be better for the salvation of his soul that he permit the Jews to lend at usury, since they are not members of his faith and he has no obligation to force them to adhere to his belief, rather than causing Christians to transgress their faith since they are members of his faith and the sins which they commit because of him are attached to his soul.

THOMAS AQUINAS, MID-THIRTEENTH CENTURY

SAINT THOMAS AQUINAS *wrote a significant statement on Jewish usury in reply to an inquiry by the duchess of Brabant. The inquiry involved governmental utilization of funds taken from the Jews, funds whose original source lay in usury.*

The essence of the query is that "the Jews . . . appear to possess nothing but what they have acquired by the evil practice of usury." The position of Saint Thomas is clear—"the Jews have no right to retain the money they have extorted from others by usury; neither have you any right to retain it if you take it back from the Jews." The view espoused here is a much more radical one than in the previous documents. The issue is not the abuses flowing from Jewish usury, but Jewish usury itself, which Thomas declares improper. The Jews, in his eyes, have no right to lend money at interest to Christians and no right to retain the profits accruing from such lending.

❧❦❧

To the Duchess of Brabant:

I have received your letter and fully understand from it your pious solicitude for the government of your subjects and the devout affection you bear toward the brothers of our order. I thank God who has moved your heart to such great virtue. In truth, I find myself in some difficulty in meeting your request for advice on certain points, partly because I am fully occupied in lecturing and partly because I would have preferred that you had addressed your questions on these matters to others, more versed in them than I. It would be illbefitting of me, however, and a poor requital of your affection, should I fail to give you what help I can in your difficulties. Thus I have attempted, in what follows, to answer the questions you have raised, but without prejudice to any better opinion.

In the first place, then, you asked, "whether at any time, and if so when, it is permissible to exact tribute of the Jews." To such a question, put thus in general terms, one may reply that it is true, as the law declares, that Jews, in consequence of their sins, are or were destined to perpetual slavery, so that sovereigns of states may treat their goods as their own property, with the sole proviso that they do not deprive them of all that is necessary to sustain life. But because we must bear ourselves honestly, even to those who are outcasts, lest the name of Christ be blasphemed (as the Apostle warns us by his own example, to give no offense either to Jews or to Gentiles or to the Church of God), it would seem more correct to forego what is permitted by the law and to abstain from forced loans which it has not been the custom to exact in the past; for what is unaccustomed always rankles more deeply in men's minds. According to this opinion, therefore, you may exact tribute of the Jews according to the custom established by your predecessors, and where there are no other considerations to be taken into account.

But, from what I have been able to conjecture, it would seem that your doubts upon this point are heightened by the question you proceed to ask: by the fact, that is, that the Jews in your country appear to possess nothing but what they have acquired by the evil practice of usury. You ask whether it is right to exact from them monies, which in any case should be restored, owing to the way in which they were extorted. The reply to this question would seem to be that, although the Jews have no right to retain the money they have extorted from others by usury, neither have you any right to retain it if you take it back from the Jews; except, perhaps, in the case of goods they may have extorted from you yourself or from your predecessors. If they possess goods which they have extorted from others, it is your duty to restore them to those persons to whom the Jews are obliged to make restitution. So if you can find with certainty those of whom usury was extorted, you must make restitution to them. Otherwise, such money must be put to pious use, according to the advice of diocesan bishops and of other upright men, or used for the public benefit of your kingdom, to relieve want or serve the interest of the community. Nor will you be doing wrong by exacting such goods back from the Jews, providing always that you observe the customs of your predecessors and have the intention of using them in the manner prescribed.

THE ARCHBISHOP OF NARBONNE AND
A JEWISH SPOKESMAN, MID-THIRTEENTH CENTURY

THE DRIVE AGAINST JEWISH USURY *was predicated in part on the notion that the Jews were causing irreparable damages to Christian society through their moneylending. But there was another foundation as well to the anti-usury campaign. As the thirteenth century progressed, a number of voices within the Church began to suggest that the issue was not a pragmatic one at all but one of principle; they asserted that usury from Christians was prohibited to the Jews. We have noted one such view in the writings of Saint Thomas Aquinas.*

The Jews were fully aware of such objection in principle and elaborated arguments against it. The following selection illustrates one set of claims and counterclaims. It is part of a lengthy debate on Jewish moneylending held between the archbishop of Narbonne and one of his Jewish subjects. The archbishop's open-

ing statement is a general one. While he protests his concern for the Jews, he indicates clearly that he can no longer tolerate Jewish moneylending. Specifically this means that loans at interest are no longer to be contracted and that usury still owed is to be forgiven. The Jewish response is likewise general, claiming that repudiation of oaths is a serious sin while neither payment nor acceptance of usury involves any religious trespass.

All this amounts to little more than preliminary sparring. The real issue is joined when the archbishop challenges the Jew's claim that lending at interest to Christians is permitted. In his statement, the prelate presents the most common thirteenth-century theoretical argument against Jewish usury. He claims that the mistaken case for the permissibility of Jewish usury rests on the famous verse in Deuteronomy: "You may charge interest on a loan to a foreigner but not on a loan to a fellow-countryman." The Jews understand this to mean that lending at interest to Christians is permitted, but this, says the archbishop, is not so at all. While others had proposed a variety of reasons for showing why Christians should not be seen technically as "foreigners" by the Jews, the archbishop argues from immediate personal experience. He claims that his own behavior and that of his fellow Christians involve a graciousness and brotherliness that necessarily remove them from the category of foreigners. Since this is so, the Jews are obviously prohibited from taking usury from Christians, just as from their fellow Jews.

Many Jews had denied the contention that Christians did not fall into the category of foreigners, and tried to prove it by adducing biblical verses. The Jewish spokesman in Narbonne, however, is in a ticklish position. The archbishop had not analyzed Christian-Jewish relations in theoretical terms, but had appealed to the protections which he himself had extended. The Jews could hardly afford to deny this. Thus, in this particular exchange, the Jew uses a different tactic. He agrees that Christians and Jews are not foreigners to one another, but contends that this is not the issue. The essential distinction in usury is not between fellow countrymen and foreigners but between rich and poor. The Bible merely outlawed one special kind of usury, from the poor. This was done as a special kindness to be extended to indigent Jews. From this special case nothing can be learned in a general way. Usury, then, is basically permissible, between Jew and Jew and between Jew and Christian, with an exception made only for poor Jews.

THE BEGINNING of the archbishop's remarks were in the presence of our sages and leaders and the community of Capestang, indicating that we had already witnessed his intentions to do well by us by guarding our persons and our property. He noted that we had seen him stand in the breach on our behalf and for our benefit before the castellan and all the other officials. However, in the matter of usury, since it is clearly sinful, he knew that his soul and the soul of all those who tried to promote it would be punished on the day of judgment before the Lord, at the hands of the king of France, whose knowledge of their faith exceeds the archbishop's, and at the hands of the rest of their leaders. Indeed, even though that king must accumulate silver and gold to pay his warriors, nonetheless he removes usury from his land and does not seek silver and gold through it. Indeed what could we ourselves answer on the day of judgment against the king. "Therefore know that my proper advice is that you no longer lend at interest from this day forth. For debts already contracted, they shall pay you the principal, but all the interest included in those obligations shall be totally annulled, since the punishment for that sin is great. Behold, all the land lies before you. Live and trade in it, but remove the sin of usury from your souls . . ."

These are my replies to his words. I said to him: "Behold it is known and agreeable to the intellect that, where there are two ways, one difficult and one easy, it is fitting to choose the better of the two and to abandon the worse. In this matter, there are two paths. One is good and includes nothing forbidden; the other involves a serious prohibition and severe punishment. Therefore every intelligent and pious man should reject the evil path and choose the good. The evil path which should be rejected involves the annulment of an oath and its transgression . . . The good path involves fulfillment of the oath. Indeed the giving of usury is not forbidden, for you will find no warning in the Torah except for the lender. Thus the Christian does nothing prohibited in paying usury; rather he performs a commandment by fulfilling his vow. Likewise the Jew does nothing prohibited, according to his religion and faith, when taking usury from the foreigner. Indeed you are commanded to protect us and not to force us to accept the commandments according to your understanding of them . . ."

The archbishop replied: "It is true. As you say, so it is. The power of an oath is great, for we find, concerning the daughter of Jephthah, that they permitted her death but did not wish to relax the vow of her father. However, in regard to your statement that the Jew does nothing prohibited, according to his religion and faith, when taking usury from the foreigner, it is obviously and clearly an error. Indeed I have known for some time from your sages the well-known error upon which you depend. It is said in your Torah: 'You may charge interest on a loan to a foreigner, but not on a loan to a fellow countryman.' Now you consider us foreigners, but you should consider us brethren and friends. For we preserve you and your money from the violence of the barons. You should remember the saying of the wise Solomon who said: 'A neighbor at hand is better than a brother far away.' Now consider—do you have a brother or sister among the members of your faith who could save you from the violence of the castellan and the seneschal who sought this year to drive you out of your fine houses and to send you forth naked into the cold and to bind your wealthy Jews in prison until they redeem themselves? . . . Therefore you should explain 'You may charge interest on a loan to a foreigner, but not on a loan to a fellow countryman' as referring to the Muslims who do not live among you and do not protect you or as referring to someone else. Thus your mistake is clear and your sin is great. One must not protect you in this matter; one must rather object strongly and forcefully as is proper. How much better if you understand this matter. It will be righteousness on your part, and you will reap blessings from the Lord.''

I said to him: "No, my lord. Listen to me. Indeed it is as you say. You have surely been a faithful father to us, and all the Christians have been brothers and friends to us. But the reason for the permission to take interest from Christians is not quite as you have said. Know well that in all the Torah of Moses, in the statements made directly by the Divine, you will not find Him forbidding the taking of interest except from the poor. Thus it is written in the pericope *Mishpatim*: 'If you advance money to any poor man among My people, you shall not act like a moneylender; you must not exact interest from him.' And in the pericope *Be-Har Sinai*: 'When your brother Israelite is reduced to poverty and cannot support himself in the community . . . you shall not charge him interest on a loan, either by deducting it in advance from the capital sum, or by adding it on repayment. You shall fear your God, and your brother shall live with you. You shall not deduct interest when advancing him money nor add interest to the payment due for food supplied on credit.' Thus He did not forbid the taking of interest except from the poor. The basis for this is the concept of charitable behavior, just as He commanded to return the poor man's pledge at night on the basis of the concept of charitable behavior. It is certainly not fitting to say that he must return a pledge to a wealthy man. Therefore there is in the Torah no prohibition of usury from the wealthy at all.''

15 JEWISH USURY: GOVERNMENTAL REACTIONS

KING PHILIP AUGUSTUS OF FRANCE AND COUNTESS BLANCHE OF CHAMPAGNE, 1206

THE STATE *during the thirteenth century generally most responsive to Church demands was Capetian France. This was particularly true during the middle decades of the century, when the kingdom was ruled by the saintly Louis IX and his pious mother. A series of important texts allows us to follow in some detail the unfolding royal restrictions on Jewish lending, which led eventually to a total prohibition of Jewish usury.*

The first major legislation was jointly adapted by Philip Augustus and two other key barons of northern France. In all likelihood, the decision to enact jointly such an edict limiting Jewish moneylending was an effort to ensure that the Jews not respond by simply leaving one domain for another. The central innovation in this edict was a twofold restriction on the rate of interest to be charged. The first was the stipulation that Jewish usury not exceed two pennies per pound per week, an annual rate of 43 percent. Equally important was a limitation on the compounding of interest; henceforth interest was not to be compounded until after a full year had elapsed. Other substantive issues addressed concern interest owed by Crusaders, which was frozen at the standard rate of two pennies per pound per week, and utilization of Church vessels as pledges, which was prohibited.

PHILIP, by the grace of God, king of the French, let all whom the present letter reaches know that this is the ordinance which we have instituted concerning the Jews, with the assent and will of our beloved and faithful Blanche, countess of Troyes, and Guy of Dampierre, on the first day of September, viz., on the Feast of Saint Egidius:

1.   No Jew shall lend at a rate higher than two pennies per pound per week. The Jew may not reckon with his debtor within a year, unless the debtor wishes to reckon and repay within a year. Whenever the debtor wishes to reckon and repay, the Jew may not deny him this right. All this will be in effect after a certain day to be established by our bailiffs.

2.   The Jews shall have all their debts sealed with new seals. If, after the ordered date, these debts will not be so sealed, from then on nothing which the Jews demand on the basis of the old seals will be returned to them.

3.   If anyone be a fugitive or detained on a pilgrimage, his debts shall be halted and from then on shall not accumulate usury, except for two pennies per pound per week.

4.   The Jews shall lend nothing on any ecclesiastical vessel or ornaments nor upon bloody or recently washed garments nor upon Church lands which are under our jurisdiction—except through our permission—nor upon Church lands of the countess of Troyes or other barons—except through their permission. If they be convicted of doing this, they shall lose their loan and he to whom the pledge belongs shall regain it.

5.   When the debtor accepts his loan from the Jew, both the Jew and the debtor shall swear that the debtor received exactly what was indicated in the writ of agreement and that the debtor gave and will give to the Jew nothing except that which was set in the contract. If either of them be convicted thereafter, the Jew shall lose his debt and the debtor shall remain in the disfavor of the lord king.

6.   Moreover, if a Jew lends anything without a seal, he will not be repaid hereafter, unless he has a pledge of gold or silver or garments or livestock.

7.   Two of the most upstanding men of every town shall have charge of the Jews' seal—one of the seal and the other of the disk. They shall swear on the saints that they will never place it upon a contract for any debt of which they do not have good information, either directly or through another. In every town there shall be only one scribe for Jewish documents. He shall give security that he will write properly and fulfill that office properly.

This ordinance will last until we and the countess of Troyes and Guy of Dampierre—who have established it—shall modify it, by our authority and by the authority of those of our barons whom we shall wish to call for that purpose.

In order that this remain firm, we have strengthened the present charter with the authority of our seal.

Enacted in Paris, 1206 A.D., in the month of September.

KING PHILIP AUGUSTUS OF FRANCE, 1206-19

SOME TIME BETWEEN *the preceding edict of 1206 and the next dated ordinance of early 1219, Philip Augustus enacted another decree concerning Jewish usury. Its major innovation was a further limitation on compound interest. Loans left for a period of years, with interest compounded, resulted in enormous debts. The edict of 1206 had forbidden compounding of interest within the first year of the loan. Now in this second pronouncement, the king orders that no interest accrue after the first year has elapsed. In this way, the problem of compound interest was totally eliminated, a great benefit for the debtor class and a serious loss for the Jewish creditors. It is interesting that Philip ends the decree with an order to royal officials to enforce Jewish loans. This became critical to the Jewish lenders, since beyond the first year an unpaid loan simply became profitless and a serious drain on the Jews' resources.*

To ALL AUTHORITIES established throughout France and Normandy:

1.   We order you that you choose two proper men in each town, who by their oath will faithfully take charge of the Jews' seal. With this seal they shall seal, with the assent of each party, the contracts concerning agreements which will be made between Christians and Jews from sixty shillings and above. These foresworn officials shall retain copies of these contracts for our use.

2.   This is the form of the contract: If by the first term stipulated in the charter, the Christian does not repay his debt to the Jew, from then on—after the term has passed—the Christian will be obliged to return to the Jew two pennies per pound per week for an entire year.

3.   If, however, the Christian desires to retain the debt and the Jew wishes to allow him to do so, then beyond that year the Jew will not be able to exact usury from the Christian by virtue of that debt, since beyond a year that debt cannot accrue usury.

4.   Moreover, we wish and command that, for proving debts of Christians against Jews or Jews against Christians, neither Christian nor Jew will be admitted in testimony, except in that way which has been established of old. In that way witnesses concerning these matters should be admitted.

5.   Moreover, we command you that, unless you shall be requested by the Jews, you shall cause their debts to be repaid to them without delay throughout your bailliages. This should be done in such a way that we henceforth have no complaints.

❦❧❨

KING PHILIP AUGUSTUS OF FRANCE, 1219

In 1219, *Philip again promulgated a broad general ordinance concerning Jewish usury. In this edict, the king repeats the two major innovations previously introduced, the limitation on the rate of interest and the elimination of compound interest.*

At this point, royal concern has shifted from controlling excessive Jewish profits to protecting certain classes of French society and restricting the range of pledges and guarantees offered in exchange for loans. Specifically, Jews are enjoined from lending to poorer elements in society and to members of the clergy. The primary factor underlying this new restriction appears to have been a concern for those who borrowed but were incapable of repaying. For the upper classes, to whom loans can still be extended, new stipulations are made concerning modes of repayment. Foreclosure on lands, which was both common and widely criticized, is now outlawed. In the loan agreement, a source of income from which the Jews can be repaid is to be specified. The Jew is to be aided in collecting these funds, but lands are not to pass out of the hands of their rightful owners. Once again Philip is responding to serious complaints about abuses stemming from Jewish moneylending, a stance unquestionably welcomed by many segments of Christian society and resented by the Jews.

THIS IS THE ORDINANCE which the lord king made concerning the Jews of his domain in 1219 A.D., in the month of February:

1.   No Jew, from the octave of the Purification of Holy Mary [February 9] on, shall extend a loan to any Christian who labors by hand, such as a farmer, a cobbler, a carriage maker, and so forth, who lack inherited property or movable goods by means of which they can be sustained, but who labor only by their own hands.

2.   The debts shall not run beyond a year from the time the loan was made.

3.   It shall not accrue interest beyond two pennies per pound per week.

4.   Also, no Jew may extend a loan to a monk or a canon regular, except with the assent of his abbot or chapter through letter patent, or to any cleric, except with the assent of his superior through letter patent.

5.   Also, no Jew may accept as a pledge a Church ornament or bloody or wet clothes or the implements of a coach or the beasts of a coach or unwinnowed grain.

6.   Also, if any Jew lends money to a knight or a burgher or a merchant, he shall accept for his debt from his debtor an assigned income of inherited property or of tenured property or of rights, with the assent of the lord from whom the debtor holds it. If the debtor shall do violence in regard to the assigned income, then interest will accrue after the Jew's complaint, so long as the violence lasts. He who does the violence shall pay a fine to the lord king. From the time that the assigned income be given over, however, the debt shall not accrue interest, unless violence be done, as has been stated.

7.   Also, the Jews of Normandy shall, before their bailiff in assize where records are kept or before their bailiff in the presence of ten knights, make a record of the debt—the sum of the debt and the assigned income—so that there shall be enrolled both the debt and the assigned income. If, however, in the absence of the bailiff the assigned income be made, and if the debtor does not wish to come before the bailiff and ten knights or in the assize, as has been indicated, and if the Jew proves this by proper Christian witnesses, then the bailiff shall compel the debtor and the stipulated guarantor to make a record and enroll both the debtor and the assigned income before himself and ten knights or in assize.

8.   If a knight or anyone else, whoever it might be, wishes to place in pledge his horse or his garments or any other valuable goods, whatever they might be, the Jew shall be permitted to accept. The lord king shall not interfere in this matter.

9.   Concerning debts extended prior to the Purification of Holy Mary, the debtor and his guarantor shall not be compelled to sell their inherited property or their income, nor on that account should they be seized. Rather, two-thirds of their inherited property or of their income —both of the debtor and of the guarantor—shall be assigned to the Jew and from the third part shall they sustain themselves. On this account the coach animals of the debtor or his mattress or other household utensils may not be seized.

10.   All debtors, both of France and Normandy, who lack inherited property or valuable goods by means of which they might sustain themselves, but who rather labor by their hands, shall have a moratorium of three years for paying their debts. They must make security for returning one-third each year.

KING LOUIS VIII OF FRANCE, 1223

ON JULY 14, 1223, *Philip Augustus died and his son Louis succeeded to the throne. Shortly thereafter, a radical step was taken by the Capetian monarchy. The focus of royal concern shifted from the abuses deriving from Jewish moneylending to the removal of the government from any moral stigma attached to Jewish usury. Clearly the more extreme Church positions were beginning to influence the kings of France.*

A new ordinance was enacted in an assembly of barons, held on November 8, 1223. Included in the ordinance is an agreement that none of these barons hold the Jews of another. This was motivated by a desire to forestall any significant population movement in the wake of the deleterious new legislation.

The key provision in the edict is the first clause, in which the assembled barons agree that none of them will henceforth enforce Jewish usury. This is not a total withdrawal of support from Jewish business affairs, and it is certainly not a prohibition of Jewish moneylending. Nevertheless, it is unquestionably a disastrous turn of events for the Jews of France, who had depended heavily on the government to back their financial affairs.

In this edict, arrangements are also specified for terminating those obligations already owed. A period of three years is stipulated, with three payments to be made per year.

LOUIS, by the grace of God king of the French, to all whom the present letter reaches, greetings:

Know that with the will and assent of the archbishops, bishops, counts, barons, and knights of the kingdom of France—those who have Jews and those who do not—we have made an ordinance concerning the Jews which those whose names are written below have sworn to observe: William, bishop of Châlons and count of Perche; Philip, count of Boulogne; the duchess of Burgundy; the countess of Nevers; Walter, count of Blois; John, count of Chartres; Robert, count of Dreux, for himself and for his brother the count of Brittany; Guy, count of Saint

Paul; Hugo of Châtillon and his brother; the count of Namur; the count of Grandpré; the count of Vendôme; Robert of Courtenay, the butler of France; Matthew of Montmorency, the constable of France; Archembaud of Bourbon; William of Dampierre; Enguerrand of Coucy; Amaury, seneschal of Anjou; Dreux of Mello; the viscount of Beaumont; Henry of Sully; William of Chauvigny; Gaucher of Joigny; John of Viévi; William of Saillé. The ordinance is as follows:

1.   No Jews' debt shall accumulate interest from the octave of All Saints' Day [November 8] onward. Neither we nor our barons shall henceforth cause to be repaid to the Jews usury which accumulates from this November 8 onward.

2.   All debts which are owed to the Jews shall be terminated in nine payments within three years by being repaid to the lords to whom the Jews are subject, in each year a third part of the debt in three terms, viz., a third on the coming Feast of the Purification of Holy Mary [February 2], a third on Ascension Day, and a third on the subsequent All Saints' Day [November 1] and likewise for the following two years.

3.   It is to be known that we and our barons have decreed and ordained concerning the status of the Jews that none of us may receive or retain the Jews of another. This is to be understood both for those who have sworn to the ordinance as well as those who have not.

4.   The Jews shall henceforth not have seals for sealing their debts.

5.   The Jews must have enrolled, by the authority of the lords to whom they are subject, all debts prior to the coming Feast of the Purification of Holy Mary. Debts not then enrolled as stipulated shall not henceforth be repaid to the Jews nor returned to them.

6.   If the Jews exhibit loan documents more than five years old, we order that they be considered invalid and that the loans contained therein need not be repaid.

In testimony and confirmation of this matter, we had our seal appended to the present charter, and the counts, barons, and other forenamed dignitaries have had their seals appended.

Enacted in Paris, 1223 A.D., Tuesday,
the octave of All Saints' Day [November 8].

KING LOUIS IX OF FRANCE, 1230

THE EDICT OF 1230 *represents a watershed in Capetian legislation concerning the Jews and Jewish usury. As had been the case in 1223, this ordinance was enacted in an assembly of important northern-French barons. Once more the intention is to preclude the possibility of wide-ranging demographic upheaval in the wake of binding new restrictions. In this case, however, the formulation of baronial rights over the Jews is radical: "Wherever anyone shall find his Jew, he may legally seize him as his serf." The introduction of the terminology of serfdom in French legislation concerning the Jews is one of the key innovations in this ordinance.*

A second innovation lies in the relation of the government to Jewish lending. In the texts presented thus far, we have seen, first, the correction of certain significant abuses, followed in 1223 by the effort to extricate the government from its involvement with Jewish usury. Seemingly convinced that Jewish loans supported by governmental authority will inevitably include interest, the king and his court now take the extreme step of breaking all ties with Jewish business affairs. For the Jews this was a catastrophic turn of affairs and would seriously limit their business opportunities.

Finally, this legislation is a milestone in French legal history, with the monarchy asserting its right to issue an edict binding both upon those agreeing to it and those dissenting from it.

LOUIS, by the grace of God king of France. Let all know, present and future alike, that we, for the salvation of our soul and that of our father, King Louis of glorious memory and of our ancestors, thinking also of the needs of all our kingdom, with our sincere will and the common advice of our barons, order:

1.   That we and our barons shall henceforth cause no contracted debts to be repaid to the Jews.

2.   Nor shall anyone in all our kingdom be permitted to retain the Jew of another lord. Wherever anyone shall find his Jew, he may

legally seize him as his serf, whatever the custom which the Jew may enjoy under the rule of another or in another kingdom.

3.   Debts which up to this point are owed to the Jews shall be paid in three terms, viz., a third part on the present November 1; a third part on the following November 1; and on the subsequent November 1 the remaining third part.

4.   Concerning Christians we order that neither we nor our barons cause them to have usury from debts contracted. We understand usury to be anything which is beyond the principal.

5.   We shall observe these statutes and cause them to be observed in our domain and our barons shall do likewise in their domains. If any barons do not wish to observe them, we shall compel them; for the purpose of which other barons will be obliged to aid us in good faith and by force. If others in the domains of the barons be found rebellious, we and our other barons have sworn to compel the rebels to observe the aforesaid statutes. We wish these things to be observed perpetually and undiminished by us and by our barons. Our barons similarly conceded that they and their heirs will observe them forever.

- I Philip, count of Bologne, have desired, resolved, and sworn to those items which have been presented.

- I Theobald, count of Champagne, have desired, resolved, and sworn to these same things.

- I Hugh, count of La Marche, have desired, resolved, and sworn to these same things.

- I Amaury, count of Montfort and constable of France, have desired, resolved, and sworn to these same things.

- I Robert of Courtenay, butler of France, have desired, resolved, and sworn to these same things.

- I Henry, count of Bar, have desired, resolved, and sworn to these same things.

- I Hugh, count of Saint Paul, have desired, resolved, and sworn to these same things.

- I Ralph, count of Auge, have desired, resolved, and sworn to these same things.

- I John, count of Châlon, have desired, resolved, and sworn to these same things.

- I William, viscount of Lignieres, have desired, resolved, and sworn to these same things.

- I Enguerrand of Coucy have desired, resolved, and sworn to these same things.

- I Archembaud of Bourbon have desired, resolved, and sworn to these same things.

- I William of Dampierre have desired, resolved, and sworn to these same things.

- I Guy of Dampierre have desired, resolved, and sworn to these same things.

- I John of Nesle have desired, resolved, and sworn to these same things.

- I William of Vergy have desired, resolved, and sworn to these same things.

We also have desired, resolved, and sworn to these things for the salvation of our souls and those of our ancestors.

6.   It has been added, moreover, that all Jewish letters, which they have concerning their debts, they shall show to their lords before the coming November 1. Otherwise, these letters shall not be of value, nor shall the Jews from then on be able to use them for demanding their debts. We moreover, in order that all the foregoing remain firm and understood forever, have caused our seals to be placed on the present document as a memorial and testimony.

*Enacted at Melun, 1230 A.D., in the
month of December.*

KING LOUIS IX OF FRANCE, 1235

BY 1235 *there remained only one major step yet to be taken in France. The government had totally withdrawn from involvement in Jewish business affairs; while*

Jewish lending against pawns could continue, it was now subjected to governmental scrutiny. All that was missing was outright prohibition of Jewish moneylending. This was remedied by King Louis in 1235 when he ordered his Jews to cease all lending. While the king did not yet specify sanctions, as he would later do, this total prohibition represents the final step in a process of constriction which had begun in 1206.

THE NEW LAW made by the lord king concerning the Jews:

1.   That they live by their own labor or by trade, but without usury.

2.   That they must give up Christian prostitutes and nurses.

3.   That they shall not be received in taverns except as transients.

4.   Concerning Christian servants of the Jews, who have been excommunicated, that the Jews dismiss them.

KING LOUIS IX OF FRANCE,
      MID-THIRTEENTH CENTURY

IN THE EDICT OF 1235, *Saint Louis made no stipulations for the enforcement of his ban on Jewish usury. By the late 1240s he became convinced that the Jews had continued to take interest, and he confiscated their property, using the funds thus realized to repay Christian lenders from whom usury had been exacted. In 1253 he repeated his prohibition of usury, stipulating that those Jews unwilling to abide by his decree must leave France. The following passage by one of the monarch's biographers reveals the king's stern anti-usury sentiment and the radical steps to which it led.*

THE JEWS, odious to God and men, he detested so much that he was unable to look upon them. He wished that none of their goods be transformed for his use, claiming that he did not wish to retain their poison. He wished that they not practice usury, but rather that they earn their food by labor or by proper commerce, as used to be done in other areas. Many of his counselors advised him to the contrary, claiming that, without lending, the populace could not exist nor the land be cultivated nor labor and commerce be pursued. They said that it was better and more tolerable that the Jews, who were damned already, exercise this function of damnation, rather than Christians, who under these circumstances oppress the populace with heavier usury. This good Catholic responded to these contentions: "The matter of Christian usurers and their usury seems to pertain to the prelates of the Church. The matter of the Jews, who are subjected to me by the yoke of servitude, pertains to me, lest they oppress Christians by their usury and lest, under the shelter of my protection, they be permitted to do this and to infect my land with their poison. Let those prelates do what devolves upon them concerning their subject Christians. I wish to do what pertains to me concerning the Jews. Let them abandon usury, or let them leave my land completely, lest it be further defiled by their filth." He had their goods seized along with them, not with the intention of retaining these goods, but so that through proper proof they might be restored to those from whom they had been extorted by usurious depravity. He appointed to this task diligent and prudent inquisitors, placing in their hands those goods, so that they themselves might freely return them. If there remained some concerning which it could not be proved or established to whom they should be returned, he allocated them, with ecclesiastical permission, for pious purposes and for churches.

A JEWISH COMPLAINT,
MID-THIRTEENTH CENTURY

THE CAMPAIGN AGAINST *Jewish usury has been viewed thus far through the series of laws and regulations promulgated by the French government. Evidence also remains of the anguished Jewish response to this progressive strangulation of Jewish moneylending. Sometime during the 1250s, shortly after the* anti-usury legislation had been harshly and abruptly introduced into southern France, a Jewish leader in Narbonne penned a vigorous complaint to King Louis. While this Hebrew epistle was never translated into Latin and never reached the royal court, it reveals to us some of the suffering which the new edicts entailed and some of the outrage felt by the Jews.

BEHOLD our lord the king has turned against us and decreed against our fellow Jews under his rule edicts and laws that are unjust according to the Torah and the Prophets as we properly understand them.

The first. He enacted an edict against our fellow Jews that a Jew not leave one ruler to transfer to another ruler. Now see how burdensome this decree is, for by this edict he has handed us over to the barons for daily destruction, death, and decimation . . . Often the barons think that the Jew has much more than he really has and they torture the body with harsh and painful afflictions until the Jew redeems himself if he can find enough for redemption or until he dies of his afflictions in great pain. Who then caused the Jew's death? Surely the king by his edict. Or if a Jew sees that he cannot live with his family in a certain place and hopes to profit more under the rule of a different baron either by teaching the Jews there or in some other way, he will be unable to change his residence and will die there of hunger—he and his family and his little ones. If he flees for his life, the baron whom he deserted will seize him and place him in chains, and the Jew will die of his afflictions.

Who can say that this edict is proper before the Creator, Who created our bodies and blew in our nostrils an intelligent soul and the wisdom to declare His unity in fear and trepidation and to accept the yoke of His commandments and His Torah as we have received them from the early saints and prophets. Indeed this law contravenes the Torah which said concerning a Jew who sells himself into slavery: "He shall be your slave for six years, but in the seventh year he shall go free and pay nothing." And it is said: "For it is to Me that the Israelites are slaves, My slaves whom I brought out of Egypt, they shall not be sold as slaves are sold." It is further said in Jeremiah: "My people were lost sheep, whose shepherds let them stray and run wild on the mountains; they went from mountain to hill and forgot their fold. Whoever found them devoured them, and their enemies said, 'We incur no guilt,

because they have sinned against the Lord, the Lord Who is the true goal
and the hope of all their fathers.''' In this regard it is further said: ''The
Lord of Hosts has said this: 'The peoples of Israel and Judah together
are oppressed; their captors hold them firmly and refuse to release them.
But they have a powerful advocate, whose name is the Lord of Hosts;
He Himself will plead their cause, bringing distress on the earth and tur-
moil on the people of the world.''' It is further said: ''A king seated on
the judgment throne has an eye to repel all that is evil.'' This means that
if the king administers his affairs lawfully, he will repel diligently every
evil man and every enemy, so that they will be unable to stand up
against him. This implies that, if he does not sit on the judgment throne,
enacting his edicts and laws justly and properly, then every evil man will
stand up against him and the king will be unable to repel them and to
drive them from his presence.

The second edict. He stole our debts and money, so that we are unable
to support ourselves and our little ones. How much worse off are our
poor and indigent, many of whom die of hunger.

The third. He continued our tolls in force and did not annul them.
He should have commanded throughout all his kingdom that tolls not be
collected from any Jews since he had confiscated their money. Thus, if
they go forth in exile from town to town, the toll collector demands a toll
from them. They, however, have no money even to buy necessities for
themselves and their families, and they go about naked and shoeless.
Even when they have among themselves those who attempt to elude the
tolls, the officials pursue them, seizing all they wish and placing them in
iron chains until they pay a fine of sixty pennies—while all they possess
including their clothes is not worth ten pennies. As a result of all this
their cry grows greatly and their plea ascends to God concerning these
harsh decrees. If your servants say: ''The Lord does not see, the God of
Jacob pays no heed,'' indeed He shall uncover all this. For He knows the
secrets of the heart—things revealed before all men are surely revealed
before Him.

The fourth. He has commanded his officers, even though they do not
agree, that they and their subordinates not enforce Jewish debts owed by
Christians, neither the principal nor the interest.

The fifth. If a Jew owes a Christian, they are to force the Jew to pay
his debt to the Christian.

The sixth. We are not to lend at interest at all, even in circumstances
permitted to us by the Torah according to the views of our predecessors.
In this way he steals the sustenance of our poor and indigent, who cannot find any means of support.

The seventh. He confiscates the large houses owned by wealthy Jews subjected to him, saying that small houses worth forty or fifty pounds should suffice for them. But if the man had two or three heirs or more, that house will not suffice for them and their descendants.

POPE GREGORY IX, 1239

DOWN THROUGH THE MID-THIRTEENTH CENTURY, *the Church knew little of post-biblical Judaism. Its suspicions concerning possible Jewish blasphemy were drawn largely from hearsay and when it engaged in polemics against Judaism, its arguments bore little relationship to the views held by the Jews themselves. This began to change radically during the 1230s, when the Church began to interest itself much more intensely in the realities of Jewish and Muslim practice and belief. The possibility of gaining firsthand knowledge of rabbinic Judaism was much enhanced by the appearance of relatively knowledgeable converts to Christianity. These converts brought with them substantial knowledge of the classical texts of Jewish religion and of the realities of Jewish practice.*

The first of these noteworthy converts from Judaism to Christianity was Nicholas Donin. According to Donin, the long-held Christian suspicions of Jewish malevolence and blasphemy were in fact correct. The Jewish faith was heavily dependent upon the post-biblical teachings of the Rabbis, formulated in binding form in the Talmud, and in this collection of laws and homilies, Donin reported, there was repeated vilification of the Christian faith and of the Christian people. Aroused by these allegations, Pope Gregory IX embarked on a program to investigate the charges and to take the necessary steps to correct the evils.

The pope sent Donin to Paris with a series of letters addressed to the prelates and the temporal rulers of western Christendom. In these letters, he delineated the new allegations. The Jewish dependence upon the Talmud, according to Gregory, is in itself an affront to the sanctity of the Bible. In addition, the specific contents of the Talmud are problematic. This lengthy work is filled with "matter so abusive and so unspeakable that it arouses shame in those who mention it and horror in those who hear it." The pope calls for action on a number of fronts. He orders the archbishops of western Christendom to have the books of the Jews seized, invoking if necessary the aid of the temporal authorities. He also addresses the kings of western Christendom with the same request, and orders them, like the archbishops, to turn the sequestered volumes over to the Dominicans and Franciscans. Finally, the Dominicans and Franciscans of Paris are charged with responsibility for investigating the volumes which have been turned over to them and for carrying out the necessary punishment— burning.

Letter to the Archbishops of France

TO THE ARCHBISHOPS throughout the kingdom of France whom these letters may reach:

If what is said about the Jews of France and of the other lands is true, no punishment would be sufficiently great or sufficiently worthy of their crime. For they, so we have heard, are not content with the old law which God set forth in writing through Moses; they even ignore it completely and affirm that God set forth another law which is called "Talmud," that is "Teaching," handed down to Moses orally. Falsely they allege that it was implanted within their minds and, unwritten, was there preserved until certain men came, whom they call "Sages" and "Scribes." Fearing that this law might be lost from the minds of men through forgetfulness, they reduced it to writing, and the volume of this by far exceeds the text of the Bible. In this is contained matter so abusive and so unspeakable that it arouses shame in those who mention it and horror in those who hear it.

Wherefore, since this is said to be the chief cause that holds the Jews obstinate in their perfidy, we have had you warned and urged and herewith order you by apostolic letters that on the first Saturday of the Lent to come, in the morning, while the Jews are gathered in the synagogues, you shall, by our authority, have all the books of the Jews who live in your districts seized and carefully guarded in the possession of the Dominican and Franciscan friars. For this purpose you may invoke, if need be, the help of the secular arm. You may also promulgate the sentence of excommunication against all those subject to your jurisdiction, whether clergy or laity, who refuse to give up Hebrew books which they have in their possession, despite your warning given generally in the churches and individually.

Given at the Lateran, on the ninth of June,
in the thirteenth year [1239].

Letter to the King of France

TO THE KING of France:
If what is said about the Jews of France and of other lands is true, no punishment would be sufficiently great or sufficiently worthy of their crime. For they, so we have heard, are not content with the old law which God set forth in writing through Moses; they even ignore it completely and affirm that God set forth another law which is called "Talmud," that is "Teaching," handed down to Moses orally. Falsely they allege that it was implanted within their minds and, unwritten, was there preserved until certain men came, whom they call "Sages" and "Scribes." Fearing that this law might be lost from the minds of men through forgetfulness, they reduced it to writing, and the volume of this by far exceeds the text of the Bible. In this is contained matter so abusive and so unspeakable that it arouses shame in those who mention it and horror in those who hear it.

Wherefore, since this is said to be the chief cause that holds the Jews obstinate in their perfidy, we earnestly warn and urge your Royal Serenity that on the first Saturday of the Lent to come, in the morning, while the Jews are gathered in the synagogues, you, by our authority, shall have all the books of the Jews of your kingdom seized, both of those Jews subject to your authority as well as those subject to the authority of your vassals, the nobles of the said kingdom. You shall have these books guarded in the possession of our dear sons, the Dominican and Franciscan friars.

Given at the Lateran, on the twentieth of June,
in the thirteenth year [1239].

Letter to the Dominicans and Franciscans of Paris

TO THE BISHOP and the prior of the Dominicans and the minister of the Franciscans in Paris:
If what is said about the Jews of France and of the other lands is true, no

punishment would be sufficiently great or sufficiently worthy of their crime. For they, so we have heard, are not content with the old law which God set forth in writing through Moses; they even ignore it completely and affirm that God set forth another law which is called "Talmud," that is "Teaching," handed down by Moses orally. Falsely they allege that it was implanted within their minds and, unwritten, was there preserved until certain men came, whom they call "Sages" and "Scribes." Fearing that this law might be lost from the minds of men through forgetfulness, they reduced it to writing, and the volume of this by far exceeds the text of the Bible. In this is contained matter so abusive and so unspeakable that it arouses shame in those who mention it and horror in those who hear it.

Wherefore, since this is said to be the chief cause that holds the Jews obstinate in their perfidy, we, through apostolic letters, order you to have the Jews who live in the kingdoms of France, England, Aragon, Navarre, Castile, Leon and Portugal forced by the secular arm to give up their books. Those books in which you will find errors of this sort you shall cause to be burned at the stake. You will silence all opponents through use of ecclesiastical censure without right of appeal. You will also report to us faithfully what you have done in the matter. But, should all of you be unable to be present at the fulfillment of these instructions, someone of you, nonetheless, shall carry out its execution.

Given at the Lateran, on the twentieth of June,
in the thirteenth year [1239].

NICHOLAS DONIN, 1240

AS POPE GREGORY IX *appeared to anticipate, the only political figure in western Europe to respond to his demands was the pious Louis IX of France. The French Jews were arrested in their synagogues, and their books were confiscated. These volumes were then turned over to the Dominicans and Franciscans so that they could be fully examined. The examination involved study of the books and questioning of a number of distinguished French rabbis.*

Two contrasting records of this trial remain. The longer of the two is a Hebrew account, portraying the efforts of Rabbi Yehiel of Paris, the foremost Jewish spokesman, to counter Donin's allegations. The Hebrew narrative reveals the fear and anguish of the Jews and indicates the pressures exerted upon Rabbi Yehiel. At the same time, it portrays Rabbi Yehiel as a clever debater, fully capable of ridiculing Donin and refuting his charges. In the opening sections quoted below, Rabbi Yehiel asserts that the entire examination is ludicrous. Since for many centuries the Church has known of the Talmud and approved of its use, the campaign launched at the initiative of Donin is clearly unacceptable.

The second source is a brief Latin document entitled "The Confessions of Rabbi Yehiel." It omits all the drama of the Hebrew narrative, confining itself to an enumeration of the admissions of Rabbi Yehiel, adding at times the suggestion that some of his statements are lies. In this text are reflected the major charges hinted at in the letters of Pope Gregory IX. Rabbi Yehiel is said to have admitted that the power of rabbis is in effect greater than the power of Scriptures—"the rabbis could revoke the commandment of God"—and that Talmudic knowledge takes precedence over knowledge of the Bible—"one who knows the Bible even by heart is not called rabbi unless he knows Talmud." A second issue is blasphemy against Christianity and Christians. Here the Latin text dutifully notes the denials of Rabbi Yehiel. While admitting derogatory Talmudic references to a certain Jesus, the Jewish spokesman denies that these applied to the Christian messiah. Likewise Rabbi Yehiel acknowledges negative statements about the Gentile world, but claims that these do not apply to Christians. The Christian author dismisses these denials outright.

Precisely what took place during the encounter in Paris is not altogether clear. A series of charges were levelled against the Talmud, and Rabbi Yehiel and his colleagues attempted to rebut them. Whatever the effectiveness of their presentation, it did not convince the ecclesiastical judges. The Talmud was condemned by the tribunal and shortly thereafter quantities of Talmud texts were consigned to the flames.

⚜

A Hebrew Report

AT THE END, since he joined himself to the Gentiles, he was called Nicholas the Heretic—may he weaken and die! At the beginning his name was Donin—may he go childless and may the name of the wicked rot! He gathered items embarrassing to us and brought slanders concerning us to the king and to the Dominicans and to the bishops and to all the leading churchmen in the city of Paris.

On Monday of the week of the reading of *Balak*, in the king's palace, the idolators gathered, and he intended to cast down the glory of Israel, the Torah of the true God. The heretic attempted to destroy all the Jews, to bind up the law, to cut off all which is inscribed in the words of the scholars, and to undo the enigmas of the sages. He intended to present a volume of four columns, written with the guile of a serpent. He intended to reveal all its secrets and its power and its wisdom, with the aid of the idolatrous Dominicans. Four upright Jews were forced to undertake battle on behalf of God, to fight for their lives, and to be zealous for God's Torah with the Lord's aid. These were Rabbi Judah ben Rabbi David, Rabbi Samuel ben Solomon, the great emissary Rabbi Yehiel, and Rabbi Moses of Coucy. They arrived at the king's gate agitated and upset, rebuked improperly before the judges. The community of Israel was like a flock without its shepherd. The wicked one ordered them to call one of the four, for he planned evil against us.

He first called Rabbi Yehiel alone. When he stood in judgment before them, our God was zealous for His Torah and had mercy on the remnant of His people out of His righteousness. He thus sent His word through His servant, and His spirit appeared to him. He put answers in his heart, with which to refute vain allegations by means of the truth. All the Jews stepped back. Sorrow and sighs overtook them, and pain and mourning were spread over the multitude. By words and by alms they called out to the Heavenly One: "Behold those slaughtered by the sword are more fortunate than those who live in desolation without the Torah."

The faithful emissary girded himself with courage and said to the heretic: "On what grounds do you contend against me, and what do you ask?" The heretic then replied: "I ask you about an old matter. For I do not deny that the Talmud is four hundred years old." The rabbi replied: "It is more than fifteen hundred years old." He then said to the queen: "Please, my lady! Do not compel me to answer his charges, since he admits that the Talmud is very old and thus far no charges have been brought against it. Indeed Jerome knew the Talmud, as is recognized by all the churchmen. If there is wrong in it, it would not have been left unscathed till now. Were there not before now churchmen and converts as capable as these? Yet no allegations have been brought throughout these fifteen hundred years. What have you now found against us to put us in this situation, to defend our very lives and to do battle on behalf of our Torah against this sinner who has denied the teaching of our sages for the past fifteen years, believing only in that written in the Torah of Moses without any rabbinic explanation? But you know that every text needs explanation. Therefore, we excommunicated him. From then on, he has planned evil against us, to uproot everything. But he strives in vain. We shall die for our Torah. Anyone who touches it touches the core of our being. If you bring wrath upon us, are we not dispersed to the ends of the earth? This Torah of ours is in Babylonia, Media, Greece, the Arab worlds, and the seventy peoples beyond the river Cush. Thus our bodies lie in your power, but not our souls.''

Then one courtier replied: ''No one will harm you.'' The emissary said: ''You will not be able to protect us—you and the people.'' Then the queen was angry over these words and said to him: ''Do not say such things! It is our intention to protect you and all your possessions. It shall be counted a sin and a transgression for all who do evil to you. Thus we have found in our books, and thus the pope has indicated. Now, answer the charges of this Christian and do not hold back.'' The rabbi said: ''Who can force me to do this, to cause harm to all the Jews, even before being called to judgment before the pope?'' Then the clerics said: ''Speak! Answer! If you do not, we will know what to do. We shall see who will help you and who will save you.'' He said: ''I shall speak my part. If I err, then the Jews have not sent me.''

Then the insect arose—the ignorant heretic—and spread forth lies and asked the wise rabbi: ''Do you believe this book of four columns?'' The sage counselor replied: ''I believe in all the laws and statutes written therein . . . There are, in addition, homilies to attract the human heart to understand parables, as is written: 'To understand proverbs and parables.' There are also wondrous tales, to test the skeptic and the heretic. In regard to these, I need not answer. If one wishes to believe them, he may. If one does not wish to believe them, he need not. For laws are not decided through them. Indeed I know that the sages of the Talmud wrote nothing but words of truth, which are wondrous to those who hear them. There are many such instances in the Bible also . . .''

A Latin Report

THE CONFESSION of Rabbi Yehiel

1.   The aforesaid Rabbi Yehiel wished under no circumstances to take an oath.

2.   He said that the Talmud never lies.

3.   He said that Jesus Nosri is Jesus the Nazarene, son of Mary, who was crucified on the eve of Passover. Concerning this Jesus, he confessed that he was born out of adultery and that he is punished in hell in boiling excrement and that he lived at the time of Titus. Then he says that this Jesus is different from our Jesus. However, he is unable to say who he was, whence it is clear that he lied.

4.   He also said that, in their schools, they study the Talmud more regularly than the Bible and that one who knows the Bible even by heart is not called rabbi unless he knows Talmud.

5.-6.   He also said that the rabbis could revoke the commandment of God to blow the ram's horn on the first day of the seventh month and to carry the palm branch on the fifteenth day of that month and that they would revoke them if those days fell on the Sabbath, lest it happen that the ram's horn or the palm branch be carried on that day.

7.-9.   He also said that it is written in the Talmud that those who did not stand on Mount Sinai and did not receive the Torah are polluted with that impurity which the serpent forced upon Eve when he cohabited with her. He said that the Talmud says of these people that animals should not be left with them, because they prefer Jews' animals to their own wives. Then Rabbi Yehiel said that he did not understand this to be the case with Christians. Let anyone who wished believe him. He lied.

10.   He acknowledged that Adam cohabited with all the animals in paradise.

11.   He also said that it indicates in the Talmud that Adam, after he sinned and 130 years before he sired Seth, sired demons with bodies from his seed, which a spirit seized.

12.   He also said that the entire Talmud—laws, judgments, arguments, and exegesis—was given to Moses on Sinai, unwritten but verbally in his heart. . .

A JEWISH LAMENT, 1242

IN 1242, *as a result of the sentence passed against the Talmud, wagonloads of Hebrew books were brought to Paris and burned. For French Jewry, and indeed for all northern-European Jewry, the conflagration was a tragic event and threatened profoundly the flourishing intellectual tradition which these Jews had painstakingly created. An elegy over the burned tomes was penned by the young Meir of Rothenburg, then a student in Paris and destined to become one of the foremost authorities of German Jewry. While revealing few specific details of the tragedy, the poem conveys the deep sense of Jewish shock and loss.*

O THOU CONSUMED BY FIRE — seek out the welfare of those who mourn thee,
Who desire desperately to dwell in your courtyards;
Those who yearn for the soil of the one true land,
Who suffer in astonishment over the scorching of your parchment pages;
Those who walk in dark despair without illumination,
Who hope daily for a light that will burst forth upon them and upon you.

Seek out the welfare of a shattered man who cries out with a broken heart,
Who mourns incessantly over your pain,
Who howls like a jackal and an ostrich,
Who offers a bitter eulogy over you.

How were you given over to a consuming fire?
How were you devoured by man-made flames and the oppressors not scathed
by your coals?
How long, O lovely one, will you lie quietly,
While my young ones bear your shame?

You must rather sit in grandeur, judging even the heavenly beings,
Bringing all cases before your tribunal.
You shall yet decree the burning of the religion of fire;
Blessed is He Who shall award you your due.

Did our Redeemer give you to us in a pillar of fire,
So that ultimately your pages would be consigned to the flames?

Was it for this, Sinai, that God chose you,
Rejecting greater mountains and shining forth upon you?
Was it to serve as a beacon for a failing faith, one whose glory declines?
I must offer a fitting parable:
You are, Sinai, like a king crying at his son's banquet,
Knowing that the lad is to die—thus do you weep over the Torah.
Instead of your normal covering, O Sinai, you must don sackcloth,
You must put on the garb of widows, you must exchange your raiments.

I shall pour forth my tears until they become a stream,
Until they reach the graves of your two great ministers,
Moses and Aaron, buried there in the hills.
Then shall I ask—Is there a new Torah,
Thus permitting the burning of your pages?
The third month ended, and the fourth began,
A time for destroying your delight and all your beauty.
He smashed the tablets of law
And then repeated the calamity by burning it—is this your recompense?

I am stunned—how can eating be pleasurable
After I have seen how they gathered your booty?
Gathered it throughout your isolated quarter,
Then burned the holy booty, so that you are unable to join your people.
I know not how to find a straight path,
So burdened with mourning are your paths of righteousness.
To brew a cup of tears would be sweeter to me than honey;
O that my legs might be chained in your irons.
To draw the waters of my tears would be sweet to my eye,
So they might be exhausted for all those who hold fast to your cloak.
But those tears dry up as they drop on my cheeks,
For my pity has been aroused by the departure of your master.
He has taken his gold and gone off afar,
And with him have departed your shadows.
And I bereft and abandoned remain alone,
Like a standard at the top of your fortress.
No longer shall I hear the voice of the singers,
For the strings of your lyre have been snapped.
I shall put on sackcloth, for the souls of your deceased,
As many as the sands, were so very dear.
I am shocked by the sun, which shines for all,
But remains dark for me and for you.
My cry to the Lord is bitter, over your decline and your doom—
May He recall the love of your youth!
Put on sackcloth yourself over the conflagration
That broke forth and consumed your peaks.

May the Lord comfort you in accord with your suffering;
May He return the tribes of Jeshurun and raise you from lowliness.
You shall yet bedeck yourself with scarlet and take up the drum,
Going forth in dance and exulting.
My heart also shall be uplifted when my Lord shines forth upon you,
Lighting your shadows and illuminating your darkness.

POPE INNOCENT IV, 1244

FIVE YEARS AFTER *the campaign against the Talmud was inaugurated and two years after the burnings at Paris, Pope Gregory's successor took up the issue once more with the king of France, the only major secular supporter of this new Church initiative. The charges are essentially a repetition of the prior ones: (1) The Jews abandon the revealed truth of the Bible in favor of their tradition. (2) These traditions are in addition blasphemous in their contents, ridiculing Christianity and abusing Christians. Pope Innocent notes the trial and burning of the Talmud in Paris and urges King Louis to broaden the effort.*

TO THE KING of France:
The wicked perfidy of the Jews, from whose hearts our Redeemer has not removed the veil of blindness because of the enormity of their crime, but has so far permitted to remain in blindness such as in a measure covers Israel, does not heed, as it should, the fact that Christian piety received them and patiently allows them to live among them through pity only. Instead, it commits enormities that arouse shock in those who hear them and horror in those who mention them. For, ungrateful to the Lord Jesus Christ Who, in the abundance of His kindness, patiently expects their conversion, they, displaying no shame for their guilt nor reverence for the honor of the Christian faith, throw away and despise the law of Moses and the prophets and follow certain traditions of their elders. On account of these same traditions, the Lord reproves them in the Gospel saying: "Why do you trangress God's com-

mandment and render it void in the interest of your traditions, teaching doctrines and commands of men?'' In traditions of this sort they rear and nurture their children. These traditions are called ''Talmud'' in Hebrew. It is a large book, exceeding in size the text of the Bible. In it are often found blasphemies against God and His Christ, obviously entangled fables about the Blessed Virgin, abusive errors, and unheard of follies. But of the laws and the doctrine of the prophets they make their children altogether ignorant. They fear that, if the truth which is found in the law and the prophets, indicating clearly that the only begotten Son of God is to appear in the flesh, be furnished, these children would be converted to the Christian faith and humbly return to their Redeemer.

Not content with these things, they make Christian women nurses for their children, in insult to the Christian faith, and with these women they commit many shameful actions. On account of this, the faithful must beware lest they incur divine indignation, since they shamefully suffer them to do things which bring confusion upon our faith.

Indeed our beloved son the chancellor of Paris and the doctors, the regents of Paris, after having at the command of our predecessor, Pope Gregory of blessed memory, as expressed in a decree, read the above-named book of abuse and others, along with all their glosses, taken from them by force, and after having examined them, consigned them to the flames, in the presence of clergy and laity, to the confusion of the perfidy of the Jews, as we have seen in their letters. You, also, Catholic king and most Christian prince, have given fitting help in these matters and extended your favor, and on account of this we recommend the Royal Excellency with fitting praise to God and bestow our gratitude upon you. Nevertheless, because the blasphemous abuse of these Jews has not yet ceased, nor their troubles as yet given them understanding, we ask your Royal Highness and we beseech you in the name of the Lord Jesus Christ to strike down with merited severity all the detestable and heinous excesses of this sort which they have committed in insult of the Creator and to the injury of the Christian name and which you have with laudable piety begun to prosecute. You should order that the above-mentioned abusive books, condemned by these doctors, as well as all the commentaries which have been examined and condemned by them, be burned in fire wherever they can be found throughout your kingdom. You should stringently forbid them hereafter to have any Christian nurses or other Christian servants, lest the children of the freeborn serve the children of the maidservants. As slaves reproved by the Lord, whose death they sinfully plotted, they must acknowledge themselves, as a result of this act, as slaves of those whom the death of Christ set free, while condemning them to slavery. Thus henceforth we may with fitting praise be able to commend to God the zeal of your sincerity.

Given at the Lateran, on the ninth of May,
in the first year [1244].

POPE INNOCENT IV, 1247

IN 1247, *Pope Innocent IV surprisingly reversed his position on the Talmud. In his letter of 1244, he had cited Jewish complaints and exulted over the discomfort of the Jews. Three years later, he again indicates Jewish opposition to the anti-Talmud campaign and this time responds positively. The Jewish contention was that Judaism had always been permitted under Christian rule, that the Talmud was essential to Jewish life and practice, and that prohibition of the Talmud was thus in effect an improper attack on Judaism itself. In a certain sense, popes Gregory IX and Innocent IV had earlier recognized the central role of the Talmud in Jewish affairs — "since this [the Talmud] is said to be the most important reason why the Jews remain obstinate in their perfidy." Now, however, the pope accepts the Jewish view that, precisely because the Talmud is so crucial, it cannot be outlawed.*

Since the charges against the Talmud included blasphemy and anti-Christian slander, the books could obviously not be permitted in their entirety. Hence, the new papal order calls for an investigation of the Talmudic books, with suppression of offensive material and return of whatever may be safely permitted. It is a gauge of prior royal involvement and an indication of the need for future royal cooperation that this letter was dispatched to Louis, explaining the new papal policy and soliciting royal support. Unfortunately for the Jews, the ecclesiastical leadership of northern France did not accept the new papal proposal. The churchmen of northern France reiterated their condemnation of the Talmud, and the French monarchs continued to uphold their harsher line.

TO THE MOST illustrious king of France:
Like the animals which John saw in the apocalypse, which were covered with eyes both front and rear, so the Supreme Pontiff, many

eyed, looks all about him. Debtor alike of wise and foolish, he must harm no one unjustly, but is bound to exact what is just and to render to each his due. When, therefore, the Jewish masters of your kingdom recently asserted before us and our brothers that, without that book which in Hebrew is called "Talmud," they cannot understand the Bible and their other statutes and laws in accordance with their faith, we then, bound as we are by the divine command to tolerate them in their law, thought fit to have the answer given them that we do not want to deprive them of their books if as a result we should be depriving them of their law.

Whereupon we directed our letters to our venerable brother, the bishop of Tusculum, legate of the Apostolic Throne, ordering him to cause the Talmud as well as other books to be shown to him and to be inspected. After inspecting them carefully, he should tolerate such as he will find may be tolerated, in accordance with divine command, without injury to the Christian faith, and he shall restore them to the Jewish masters, doing so by quieting their opponents through ecclesiastial censure without appeal. Wherefore we have caused Your Royal Serenity to be asked and urged to find favorable and acceptable whatever will be done in this matter by the said legate. You shall cause it to be carefully observed.

Given at Lyons, on the twelfth of August,
in the fifth year [1247].

৯◆৩

PAPAL LEGATE IN FRANCE, 1247-48

IN HIS LETTER TO KING LOUIS IX, *Pope Innocent IV indicated that he had sent a letter to the papal legate in France, ordering him to have the Jewish books inspected and to return those volumes which might be properly tolerated. This papal letter to the legate Odo, bishop of Tusculum, has been lost. Odo's response, however, has survived. It reflects grudging assent, tinged with strong disapproval of the shift in papal policy.*

Odo opens by reviewing the main events in the anti-Talmud effort: the revelations of Nicholas Donin, the letters of Pope Gregory IX, the examination of the Jewish volumes, the confessions of the Jewish leaders, and the burning of the Jewish books. The legate then argues that the papal shift is unwarranted. Firstly, it repre-

sents a repudiation of decisions made by Pope Gregory IX and by the distinguished prelates who had been involved in the examination and sentencing of the Jewish books in Paris. Secondly, Odo argues, there is a substantive error involved. The papal order to tolerate that which might be tolerable introduces an unacceptable distinction. The Church has always taken the position that a measure of heresy warrants the total rejection of the heretic or his writings. Thus, claims Odo, there should be no partial acceptance of the Talmud. Because of perverse elements, it had been condemned in toto and so it should remain. Having said all this, the papal legate then meekly indicates that he has proceeded according to papal command, has sequestered Jewish books, and will have them examined.

TO THE MOST HOLY FATHER and lord Innocent, by the grace of God Supreme Pontiff, from Odo, by divine goodness bishop of Tusculum, legate of the Apostolic Throne:

Recently it pleased Your Holiness to order me to have the Talmud and other books of the Jews displayed before me and inspected and, after having inspected them, to show tolerance with regard to those books which may seem worthy of tolerance because they are not injurious to the Christian faith and to return these to the Jewish masters. In order that the proceedings which at one time took place about the said books may not be hidden from Your Holiness and that no one be fooled in this affair by the shrewdness and falsehoods of the Jews, let Your Holiness know that at the time of the lord Pope Gregory of happy memory, a certain convert, by the name of Nicholas, related to the said Supreme Pontiff that the Jews, not satisfied with the ancient law which God set forth in writing through Moses and even completely ignoring it, assert that a different law, which is called "Talmud," that is "Teaching," had been set forth by God, handed down to Moses verbally and implanted in their minds. They said that it was thus preserved unwritten until certain men came whom they call "Sages" and "Scribes." Lest this law disappear from the minds of men through forgetfulness, they reduced it to writing the size of which by far exceeds the text of the Bible. In this are contained so many unspeakable insults that it arouses shame in those who read it and horror in those who hear it. This too is the chief cause that holds the Jews obstinate in their perfidy. When he heard of these things, the Supreme Pontiff saw fit to write to all the archbishops of the kingdom of France, as follows . . .

All books that had been sequestered were put under stamp and seal, and many terrible things were found in the said books in the presence of Walter, archbishop of Sens of happy memory, of the venerable fathers of Paris, of the bishop of Senlis, of the friar Godfried de Blevel, your chaplain, then regent of Paris, and of other masters of theology, and even of Jewish masters who, in the presence of these men, confessed that the above-named things were contained in their books. A careful examination having afterwards been made, it was discovered that the said books were full of errors and that the veil covers the heart of these people to such a degree, that these books turn the Jews away not only from an understanding of the spirit, but even of the letter and incline them to fables and lies. From this it is clear that the Jewish masters of the kingdom of France uttered a falsehood to Your Holiness and to the sacred fathers, the lord cardinals, when they said that without these books, which in Hebrew are called "Talmud," they cannot understand the Bible and the other precepts of their laws in accordance with their faith. After the said examination had been made and the advice of all the masters of theology and canon law and of many others had been taken, all the said books which could then be seized were consigned to the flames in accordance with the apostolic decree.

It would therefore be most disgraceful, and a cause of shame for the Apostolic Throne, if books that had been so solemnly and so justly burned in the presence of all the scholars and clergy and populace of Paris were to be tolerated by apostolic order and given back to the masters of the Jews. For such tolerance would seem to mean approval. Saint Jerome, speaking of the lepers whom the Lord cured, says that there is no perverse doctrine that does not contain some truth, and so likewise no heretics are to be found who do not think well of some one article of the faith. Since certain books contained errors, they were condemned by the authority of the councils, although they contained much good and truth; in the same way diverse heretics are condemned although they do not err in everything. Thus, although these books contain some good things, though not many, nevertheless they deserve condemnation. This is the very teaching of which Saint Jerome made mention in regard to the Gospel of Matthew, that it makes errors into commands of God, as the Lord Himself bore witness.

All this have I recounted to Your Holiness in this letter in order that the whole truth about the said books may be revealed to Your Holiness. I have moreover asked the Jewish masters to show me the Talmud and all their other books. They have exhibited to me five most vile volumes which I shall have carefully examined in accordance with your command.

PAPAL LEGATE IN FRANCE, 1248

POPE INNOCENT IV *had ordered the papal legate in France to reexamine the Jewish books and to return to the Jews whatever might be tolerated. In his reply to the papal order, the legate Odo respectfully disagreed with the papal willingness to return some of the condemned material, but grudgingly agreed to do his duty. He did in fact gather the Jewish books and have them scrutinized by experts. The conclusion is formulated in this edict of May 1248. Odo and his experts decided that nothing might be tolerated and returned to the Jews. In a formal sense, the papal legate had complied with the papal injunction. In fact, however, by deciding that nothing might be tolerated, he contravened Pope Innocent's order. In any case, the kings of France accepted the findings of the bishop of Tusculum and his experts, continuing to prohibit the Talmud on numerous occasions after 1248. For the Jews of northern France, the hopes aroused by the shift in papal policy failed to materialize, and thus a great center of Jewish learning fell into decline.*

ODO, by divine goodness bishop of Tusculum and legate of the Apostolic Throne, to all who will read the present letter, greetings in the Lord.

Know all that in Paris, on the sixteenth of May, in the year of our Lord 1248, we pronounced definite judgment on certain Jewish books called Talmud, in the presence of the Jewish masters called for this purpose, as follows:

In the name of the Father, the Son, and the Holy Ghost, amen. By apostolic authority, certain books by the name of Talmud have been presented by the Jewish masters to us. We have examined these books and have caused them to be carefully examined by men of discretion, expert in these matters, God-fearing, and zealous for the Christian faith. We found that these books were full of innumerable errors, abuses, blasphemies and wickedness such as arouse shame in those who speak of them and horrify the hearer to such an extent that these books cannot be tolerated in the name of God without injury to the Christian faith. Therefore, with the advice of those pious men whom we caused to be gathered especially for that purpose, we pronounce that the said books are unworthy of tolerance and that they are not to be restored to the Jewish masters; we decisively condemn them. We are also possessed of full knowledge as to the place and time of other books not shown to us by the Jewish masters nor by us examined, although we have often made demands for them; and we shall do what there is to be done with regard to them . . .

Given in the year of our Lord 1248,
in the month of May.

PART FIVE

MISSIONIZING
AMONG THE JEWS

INTRODUCTION

THE CHURCH was always anxious to bring new adherents into its fold. During the early centuries of the Middle Ages, ecclesiastical circles devoted little effort to formulating new arguments to convince the Jews of the truth of Christianity, tending instead to rely on the arguments advanced in former periods of Christian-Jewish polemic. Exhibiting little understanding of the practices and beliefs of post-biblical Judaism, or of the classics of rabbinic literature, these appeals largely failed to influence the Jews. The first section of this chapter presents examples of these early and relatively ineffectual Church appeals to the Jews and Jewish counterarguments.

As with other issues, the thirteenth century represents a major turning point in this regard as well. A variety of factors now combined to heighten interest in spreading the truth of Christianity by reason and persuasion. In the first place, the Christian world was beset by internal heresy. This was a vexing issue, especially in southern France, and called for a campaign to propagate the proper version of Christian doctrine and efface the pernicious errors of the heretics. In addition, by this time, hopes for a military victory over the forces of Islam had all but dissipated. Particularly after the stunning defeat suffered by King Louis IX of France, little hope was held for spreading the faith through crusading. If King Louis, who was the paragon of royal virtue and piety and who had carefully assembled a large military force, had failed ignominiously, who might yet hope to succeed? As disillusionment with crusading developed, disseminating the truth of Christianity by preaching gained prominence as an alternative.

These tendencies were strongly reinforced by the impressive achievements of thirteenth-century Christian theology. The majestic *summae* of the theologians convinced the ecclesiastical leadership of western Christendom of the innate rationality of Christianity. Church leaders were certain that, if heretics and non-believers could only be brought to ignore their prejudices and examine philosophically the foundations of religious belief, they would emerge convinced of the truth of Christianity. Propelled by the desire to appeal to the intellect and by the conviction that their faith would inevitably triumph in a tournament of reason, the leaders of the Church set out to realize their goals. New orders in the Church were created with the professed goal of spreading Christian truth, first among the disaffected within the Christian fold, then among those outside the Christian camp. Opportunities for studying the languages and literature of the non-Christian faiths were established, and manuals of argumentation were drawn up. The effort to proselytize shifted from the sporadic and incidental to a well-organized campaign.

To be sure, the Jews represented but a minor issue in this broad campaign. They constituted only a small group, and their long history of perseverance could have aroused little hope of any significant breakthrough. Nonetheless, precisely this record of relative failure inspired some churchmen to make the effort. Success in converting Jews would be especially sweet because the Jews had traditionally proven so recalcitrant. One group in particular was especially committed to missionizing among the Jews—these were the recent converts from Judaism to Christianity. It is of course quite common for new adherents to a faith to be particularly zealous in spreading their new credo, particularly among those whom they had rejected. This affords a way both of proving one's loyalty to the new group and of stilling residual doubts which might remain. From the second half of the thirteenth century on, western-European Jewry became the object of intensive conversionist efforts on the part of a series of capable new converts.

These new adherents of Christianity brought with them more than zeal. They opened to the Church new avenues of information on the realities of Jewish ritual and belief, and afforded ready access to the language and literature of their former faith. While these insights were first utilized by the Church to attack and expurgate rabbinic literature, more positive uses quickly developed. New converts, beginning with Friar Paul Christian in the 1250s and 1260s, built upon their knowledge of Jewish belief a new set of arguments designed to convince the Jews of the emptiness of their faith and of the truth of Christianity. We shall, in the second and third sections of this chapter, examine examples of this new argumentation, based on awareness of the realities of contemporary Jewish belief and ritual and rooted in the conviction of the overwhelming rationality of the Christian faith.

The new missionizing zeal of the thirteenth century involved more than simply the amassing of more convincing arguments; it involved also the development of new techniques for penetrating into the circles of heretics and non-believers and confronting them with the falsity of their faith and the truth of Christianity. In this regard, Jews were a particularly easy target. Unlike the heretics within medieval Christian society, the Jews were readily identifiable. As we have seen, they were at precisely this time being forced into ever-deepening isolation from their Christian peers. In addition, the small and weak Jewish minority in western Christendom could be easily forced, with the help of the secular authorities, into gathering for a public sermon or a public debate. The techniques of the forced sermon or the forced debate and the development of more convincing arguments represent the two major innovations in the new and more intense efforts at proselytizing among the Jews.

Forced by their overlords to present themselves before churchmen, often converts, who were now armed with up-to-date and accurate information on post-biblical Judaism, the Jews of western Jewry rightly felt themselves deeply threatened. At the same time that they were being pressured by powerful ecclesiastical demands for heightened segregation and economic limitation, the Jews were exposed to a systematic effort to pry them from their ancestral faith.

17 TRADITIONAL CONVERSIONARY LITERATURE

PETER OF BLOIS, LATE TWELFTH CENTURY

AN OUTSTANDING EXAMPLE *of traditional conversionary literature is found in Peter of Blois's* Contra Perfidiam Judaeorum. *Peter's concern was to compose a manual which would prove the basic tenets of Christianity from the Hebrew Bible. Since the Jews accept the divine origins of Scriptures, ecclesiastics like Peter believed that they need only convey to the Jews a proper understanding of the text in order to persuade them of the truths of Christianity. Of course these hopes were far too optimistic. The Jews had a long tradition of biblical exegesis and held their own views as to the meaning of critical verses. One often feels, in reading this traditional material, that the true purpose was more to reaffirm the faith of Christians than to change the faith of Jews.*

![decorative ornament]

AGAINST THE PERFIDY OF THE JEWS

> *Chapter I   A preface in which he indicates that disputation with Jews and heretics is arduous and dangerous.*

You have composed a long and anxious complaint in your letter, indicating that, surrounded by Jews and heretics, you are constantly beseiged by them and that you do not have at hand the authoritative texts of Sacred Scriptures by means of which you could rebut their calumnies and respond to their deceitful wiles.

Indeed, according to the Apostle, "dissensions are necessary if only to show which members are sound." Therefore life is granted today to the Jews—since they are our slaves—because they bear the Mosaic law and the prophets which attest to our faith. Not only in their books but in their appearance we see the Passion of Christ. Thus, in Psalms, Truth speaks out concerning the Father, saying: "God will raise me over my enemies; do not kill them, lest my people forget."

Would that one who lacks trained views not dispute with a heretic or a Jew. For as a result of illicit and improvident disputations, a virulent crop of heresies grows all around. For those who are ignorant and err, wishing to close the mouth of those who speak iniquities, make light darkness and make darkness light. Thus, because they wish to save others from their errors, they rush headlong into worse sins . . .

Chapter II   Testimonies of the law and the prophets concerning trinity and unity in God.

It is not our intention to compose a tract concerning the sacred trinity and the indivisible unity of God, but simply those pronouncements and authoritative statements of the law and the prophets, by means of which the opponents of the orthodox faith may be confuted, a tower of David may be built, and the ramparts of salvation may be erected. Since therefore the trinity in one God and unity in three beings excites scandal and horror in the Jews, let us prove, with God's help, by irrefutable arguments that God is one and three. The legislator of the Jews says: "Hear, O Israel, the Lord is our God, the Lord is one." And the Lord Himself said: "I the Lord created the skies. I God stretched out the sky and fashioned the earth." And in Isaiah: "I the Lord stretched out the skies, alone I hammered out the earth." Likewise Moses in Deuteronomy: "This day, then, be sure and take to heart that the Lord is God in heaven above and on earth below; there is no other." And in the same: "The Lord alone led him, no alien god at his side." Thus also is the testimony of Saint Hilary, God is one, but not solitary. For unity does not preclude trinity, nor does solitude in any way preclude the trinity. Surely God in Sacred Scriptures is said to be, to speak, and to create in such a way that sometimes one, sometimes two, and sometimes three beings are designated. Behold one being: "I am the Lord God Who has filled heaven and earth and all things which are in them."

Behold the Father in Jeremiah speaking of the Son: "If they have stood in My council, let them proclaim My words to My people and turn them from their evil course and their evil doing. Am I a god only near at hand, not far away? Can a man hide in any secret place and I not see him?" Concerning this word, the prophet David testifies: "The good word stirs my heart." And John the Evangelist: "When all things began, the word already was." God has the power to say and to do, as is written: "He spoke the word and they were created, He established them for ever and ever." The Son is the word of God, the power of God, the wisdom of God. In Him, as in His wisdom and His initiation of all, God created all, as is written: "In the beginning, God made heaven and earth." This is the wisdom of God which in the book bearing its name bears witness to its eternal provenance and says: "I am the word which was spoken by the Most High . . . Before time began He created me." Likewise: "The Lord created me the beginning of His works, before all else that He made, long ago."

Since nothing which was not God existed prior to the creation of the world, how then was this wisdom already created? How were all things created by it? Thus the Jew must confess that this wisdom is God and is created by God and thus is the Son or he must indicate that Sacred Scriptures contain falsehood. A Christian acknowledges that the wisdom of God, through which He created all things, is the Son of God. Nor is it absurd that God the Son is born of God the Father, as light is generated by the sun. Anyone who fails to believe in the eternal generation of the Son from the Father and the temporal generation from the mother incurs the sentence of prophetic curse. For the word of the prophet is: "Ho! you that say to the father, 'What are you begetting?' or to the mother, 'What are you bringing to birth?' " . . .

Chapter VII   Testimonies of the prophets that the Son was sent by the Father.

That God is the Son of God, who was sent by God the Father for our salvation, is most clearly manifest in three verses which can be carefully read in our books and in those of the Jews. For in that authoritative text which we have presented, where the wisdom of God testifies that it was created before all things, it concludes at the end, saying: "My delight is in mankind." For He especially delights in that love which He manifests toward us, that, made human, He redeems man. Concerning this, the prophet Jeremiah says the following: "There is one God; there is none to compare with Him. The whole way of knowledge He found out and gave to Jacob His servant.'' He adds: ''Thereupon wisdom appeared on earth and lived among men.''

> *Chapter VIII   Testimonies that Christ came in the flesh.*

That Christ was born of the seed of Abraham the Lord made clear in Genesis, saying to Abraham: ''All nations shall be blessed through your seed.''

What people of blessings were in Isaac? The Jews? Are they not cursed and damned by God beyond all other people? Seek another of the seed of Abraham in whom all people are blessed and you will find only Christ. ''He gave him the blessing of all mankind.'' All men are blessed with that benediction by the Lord Who made heaven and earth. Concerning this seed Isaiah says: ''If the Lord of Hosts had not left us this seed, we should have been like Sodom, no better than Gomorrah.'' . . .

❦❧

A JEWISH MANUAL,
      MID-THIRTEENTH CENTURY

THE JEWS WERE AWARE *of Christian utilization of significant biblical verses. Full responses to Christian claims were widely circulated and broadly known throughout medieval Jewry. These responses are often embedded in traditional biblical commentaries or at times special tracts are devoted to them. The work quoted below is one such polemical treatise, composed during the middle decades of the thirteenth century but incorporating much older materials. The organizational structure of this work is simple—the author proceeds from book to book of the Bible, isolates significant verses, presents Christian exegesis, and then provides rebuttal. In the selections quoted, all taken from the book of Genesis, the issues are the unity of God and the prophecy of Jacob concerning the future of Judah.*

❦❧

BEHOLD I have entitled this treatise, *Yosef ha-Mekane.* Behold my witnesses are in the heavens that my heart has not moved me to compose this treatise for pride's sake. Rather I have done so for two reasons. First, because I am zealous on behalf of the God of Israel, as I see renegades abandoning the source of living waters and inclining in the direction of vanity. They attempt to appropriate the prophets of truth in order to substantiate Jesus, depending on lies. The omniscient God shall silence them each morning; with the help of God I shall reveal their wickedness. Secondly, I am writing because I have aged and forgetfulness overtakes me and I cannot remove its power over me. Thus I have decided to compose a treatise for those who observe divine commandments, to serve me as a sign and a reminder and to destroy our enemies and despoilers . . .

"In the beginning God created heaven and earth." The term for God—"Elohim"—is plural. However, the rebuttal lies in the adjacent word. "Created" is written in the singular and not in the plural. Thus they have falsified by saying that the term for God indicates two . . .

"Let us make man in our image." The unbelievers claim that the divine is plural. The answer lies in the adjacent verse: "And God created man in His own image." The word "created" is not in the plural.

"Let us make man in our image and likeness." They claim that the Creator has a human form. They bring proof from the fact that we find verses which mention organs in regard to the Creator: "The helmet of salvation on His head." "The mouth of the Lord has spoken." "My eyes will set aside the most loyal for My companions." "His ears are open to their cries." "The hand of the Lord will strike your graying heads." "On that day His feet will stand on the Mount of Olives." "The Lord said within His heart." The confused say: "What is lacking to prove that He is human?" Behold I shall answer them from what I have found in the name of R. Saadia, R. Nissim, ibn Gabirol, ibn Ezra; they all follow the same path with regard to human likeness. How is it possible to say "What likeness will you find for God?" Indeed the simple meaning of the text can be explained in a number of ways. "In our image"—the image of the angels who are called "Elohim," and they are in the form of men, as is written "Behold three men were standing in front of him." R. Saadia gave another explanation: Image and likeness are meant allegorically. For just as David said, "The earth is the Lord's and all that is in it," so it is said with respect to man, "Thou hast made him little less than a god." Likewise it is said, "Man has become like one of us." . . .

"The sceptre shall not pass from Judah, nor the staff from his descendants, until Shiloh comes"—meaning the messiah. They used the translation which translates "until the messiah comes" and they call Jesus the messiah, indicating that after he appeared the Jews no longer had an anointed king. They have descended into deep waters and brought forth nothing. For after Nebuchadnezzar, king of Babylonia, exiled Zedakiah, king of Judah, we no longer had a king anointed with oil, and this was more than two hundred years prior to the appearance of the Nazarene.

Ibn Ezra explained "the sceptre shall not pass from Judah" in the following way. From the day that Judah was blessed, he enjoyed blessing and power, as is written in Chronicles: "He [Reuben] was, in fact, the first son born, but because he had committed incest with a wife of his father, the rank of the eldest was transferred to Joseph, and Judah held the leading place among his brothers." Judah was first in carrying the banners and in dedicating the altar. In Judges it is said: " 'Which tribe should attack first?' The Lord answered, 'Judah shall attack.' " Likewise during the kingship of Saul, David was the commander. After Saul he became king. This then is the meaning of "the sceptre shall not pass": Judah shall not become the reigning and powerful king until he assumes the kingship . . . Psalms 78 lends support to this explanation. "He forsook his house at Shiloh, . . . he despised the clan of Joseph; . . . he chose David to be his servant." This is the meaning of "until Shiloh comes," that the sanctuary at Shiloh declined and was destroyed. As soon as Saul, who was of the tribe of Ephraim the son of Joseph, was killed, then "the obedience of the people was his." For all Israel gathered to acknowledge David, as is written in the Book of Samuel: "Then David inquired of the Lord, 'Shall I go up into one of the cities of Judah?' . . . The men of Judah came, and there they anointed David king over the house of Judah." After the incident with Abner, "all the tribes of Israel came to David at Hebron . . . and anointed David king over Israel." His kingship lasted until the exile of Zedakiah.

Another explanation. "The sceptre shall not depart from Judah"—the persecutor and oppressor shall depart from Judah, meaning that kingship shall not be total in Judah . . . and that evil shall rear up against Judah "until Shiloh comes," that is, the messiah, concerning whom it is said: "His resting place shall be glorious." "The obedience of the nations shall be his"—as is written: "On that day a scion from the root of Jesse shall be set up as a signal to the peoples; the nations shall rally to it."

JOSEPH KIMHI, MID-TWELFTH CENTURY

THE NEXT SECTION *introduces both a new form of polemical literature and a new set of arguments. R. Joseph Kimhi's* Sefer ha-Brit *is one of many polemical works presented in dialogue form. Such dialogues afford a useful vehicle for an exchange of views, with the faith of the particular author always emerging victorious. The issue in the following citation is not faith, but moral behavior. Each side attempts to prove that its community has achieved a higher level of ethical goodness, a claim that was often advanced during the Middle Ages. As both the "believer" and the "unbeliever" indicate, the moral argument is not decisive—religious truth must involve a combination of proper faith and good works. Nonetheless it is an important ancillary issue, one which often appears in the polemical treatises of Christians and Jews.*

THE UNBELIEVER SAID: Whoever wishes to have faith should not scrutinize the words of Jesus even though they be acceptable to reason. You have neither faith nor deeds, dominion nor sovereignty, for you have lost all. I have many verses in your Torah which support me in this contention. Now finish your words.

The believer said: Know that all the good which a man achieves in this world is of two kinds: good works and faith. If I can attribute good works and faith to the Jews, then they have everything. I shall begin to tell of those good works which you cannot deny and I shall start with the Ten Commandments: "I am the Lord," etc.—the Jews declare God's unity; "You shall have no other gods beside Me"—the Jews do not make idols; "You shall not take the name of the Lord in vain"—there is no nation in the world which avoids vain oaths as does Israel; "Remember the Sabbath day"—only Israel keeps the Sabbath; "Honor your father," likewise, "You shall not murder" and "You shall not commit adultery"—there are no murderers or adulterers among them. Oppression and theft are not as widespread among Jews as among Christians, who rob people on the highways and hang them and sometimes gouge out their eyes. You cannot establish any of these things with respect to the Jews. These Jews and Jewesses, who are modest in all their deeds, raise their children, from the youngest to the oldest, in the study of the Torah. If they hear a vile word from the mouth of a child, they beat him and chastise him so that he no longer swear with his lips. They train him too to pray every day. If they hear that he has become accustomed to swearing, they will keep him from doing so. Their daughters, with modesty, are not to be seen about nor found wanton like the daughters of the Gentiles who go out everywhere to streetcorners. The Holy One, blessed be He, has prevented all this among the Jews. Are you not then ashamed and embarrassed to say that you are a good people since you regularly and publicly encourage these sins. You are not from a people that will prevent this sort of thing. On the contrary, your children become accustomed to sin. The sins may be light as cobwebs in the windows of a house, yet such cobwebs keep out the light as these sins keep the light from you.

I tell you further that whenever a Jew stops at the home of his fellow for a day or two or even a year, he will take no payment for food from him. This is so with all the Jews in the world who act toward their brethren with compassion. If they see their brother a captive, they ransom him; if naked, they clothe him and do not allow him to go about begging. They send him provisions in secret. You see with your own eyes that the Christian goes out on the highways to meet travellers—not to honor them—but to swindle them and take all their provisions from them. No one can deny that all these good traits which I mentioned are found among the Jews and that their opposites are found among Christians. Further, the Jews keep their Sabbaths and festivals conscientiously, while the Christians do all manner of work and travel about even on Sunday which is their holy day. What more can you ask for in the way of good deeds found among Jews and bad deeds found among Christians?

He answered: You are right in part. Yet what good are their deeds if they have no faith? I shall show you other deeds which you do that are contrary to religion. You lend with usury, although David said: "Who will dwell in your tabernacle? He who has not lent his money with usury." I shall show you other good deeds which Christians do. There are people among them who separate themselves in their way of life from the world and from its pleasures and dwell in forests and deserts in affliction all their days.

The believer said: Usury, to which you refer is mentioned in the Torah of Moses: "You may take usury on loans to foreigners but not on loans to your countrymen." Thus when David said, "He who has not lent his money with usury," he reiterated what had been forbidden them. Do you not see that although Scripture said, "You shall not kill," David killed thousands from among the nations? This is because "you shall not kill" means that you shall not kill one who is innocent. Similarly, "He who has not lent his money with usury" is to be interpreted with reference to what the Torah forbade. There was no need for David to refer to this, since Moses had already stated it. The Jews are indeed scrupulous about usury and the taking of interest from their brethren as the Torah forbade. They are indeed very scrupulous about anything that smacks of usury. A Jew will not lend his brother wheat, wine, or any commodity on a term basis in order to increase his profit, while you, who have disdained usury, sell all commodities to your brethren on a term basis at twice the price. You should be ashamed to say that you do not lend with usury, for this is enormous usury. Furthermore, many Gentiles clearly lend on interest to both Jews and Gentiles, although Jews do not lend to their fellow Jews.

Now with respect to your statement that there are many holy people among the Gentiles who separate themselves from this world in their lifetime, it must be said that they are one in a thousand or ten thousand, while the rest are contaminated by the ways of the world. It is well known that your priests and bishops who do not marry are fornicators. Now when the Jews were in their land, there were a few righteous men among them. Because there were many wicked men, however, Nebuchadnezzar came and exiled and slaughtered them. Thus David said: "O God, Gentiles have invaded your domain. They have given the corpses of your servants to the fowl of heaven for food, the flesh of your righteous ones to the beasts of the earth." What good will it do you then if you have one man in a million who is conscientious about serving his God? Even more so, I do not believe that one who has isolated himself in the forest is perfect in his actions and his belief. Yet if he *is* perfect in his actions, they will do him no good if his faith is not perfect.

KING JAMES I OF ARAGON, 1242

ONE OF THE EARLIEST *western authorities to lend his support to the new missionizing was King James I of Aragon. His royal edict of 1242 deals with aiding the Muslim or Jewish convert to Christianity—he or she is not to be reviled or to lose property rights. The important provision, for our purposes, is the last one, in which the monarch orders his royal officials to force the attendance of Muslims and Jews at conversionary sermons.*

KNOW ALL, that we, James, by the grace of God, king of Aragon, Majorca, and Valencia, count of Barcelona and Urgel, and lord of Montpellier, for the love of our Lord Jesus Christ and the glorious Virgin, His mother, and for the salvation of our soul, decree forever for ourselves and for all our successors in Aragon, Catalonia, Majorca, and Montpellier, in the kingdom of Valencia, and in all the dominions and jurisdictions which we now possess or that we and our successors may with the help of God possess in the future, as follows:

Any Jew or Saracen who, by the grace of the Holy Spirit, may want to accept the orthodox faith and the font of baptismal salvation shall be able to do so freely and without hindrance on the part of anyone. No statute, prohibition, or agreement of our predecessors or of anyone else nor any established custom regarding these matters shall stand in the way. He shall not, on this account, lose any of the movable or immovable property which was his before. On the contrary, he shall have it and hold it and possess it all securely and freely, by our authority, except for the legitimate inheritance of his sons and relatives. The children and relatives of the said convert shall be able to claim nothing of his property while he is alive. After his death they shall be able to claim only that which they would have been able to claim reasonably if he had died a Jew or a pagan. For even as these converts merit divine grace, so shall they be known to have ours, whose duty it is to imitate His will and favor. Likewise, we decree in perpetuity, and we firmly prohibit, under pain of a fine to be imposed at the discretion of a judge, that no one shall dare taunt any convert from Judaism or paganism to our Catholic faith, by labelling or calling him "renegade," or "turncoat," or any other similar name.

Likewise, we desire and we hereby decree that, whenever an archbishop, bishops, or Dominican or Franciscan friars visit a town or a place where Saracens or Jews dwell, and whenever they wish to preach the word of God to the said Jews or Saracens, these shall gather at their call and shall patiently listen to their preaching. Our officers, if they want to attain our favor, shall, heedless of excuse, compel them to do this.

Wherefore, we order the vicars, bailiffs, city elders, as well as all our subjects and officials, present and future, to have all the above instructions everywhere followed and strictly observed, if they rely upon our favor and our love.

Given at Lerida, in the year 1242 A.D.,
on the ninth of March.

A DOMINICAN FRIAR,
MID-THIRTEENTH CENTURY

THE FOLLOWING HEBREW SOURCE *was composed in the wake of a forced sermon, probably in the late 1250s. It purports to be the record of a counter-sermon subsequently preached by the Jewish author. According to the account, the missionizing sermon was delivered by a Dominican friar in the synagogue of Narbonne. Accompanying the friar were "many great and important people," which undoubtedly augmented the force of the friar's message and deepened Jewish anxiety and discomfort. After the conversionary message was completed, the Jewish author delivered a sermon of his own. It is not altogether clear whether the Christian visitor remained for the Jewish sermon or not.*

From the Jewish sermon it is clear that the Dominican had argued forcefully that the promised messiah has already appeared and that the lengthy Jewish exile will be interminable. To this the Jew responds with an extensive commentary on a set of verses in the Song of Songs. He contends that the time for Jewish redemption has not yet arrived. Thus, the key to Jewish fate lies in the resolve to reject all conversionary pressure and to remain faithful to Judaism. If this is done, the inevitable redemption will bring with it untold material and spiritual rewards.

THIS IS THE BEGINNING of the sermon which I preached after the Dominican friar not of our faith made his remarks in the synagogue before the congregation. With him were many great and important people. In this sermon were responses to the remarks which he made against us in that occasion.

It is written, "We have a little sister, who has no breasts; what shall we do for our sister, when she is called for?" This verse was written by the wise King Solomon at the end of one of his books called the Song of Songs. It was written allegorically and requires extensive explanation. If we are a bit lengthy, let it not offend you, even though the time for dining has already come and gone. Indeed it is fitting to tarry and to postpone a bit our eating, which only concerns our transitory physical being, and to hear an explanation of the words of the prophets, which are the words of the Lord uttered with divine spirit and which concern our spiritual being, which is eternal, as well as our physical being . . . With your consent and your permission and with God's aid we shall explain the verse and the section. The Lord from Whom comes the wit of the tongue shall be with us and show us what to say, as we find Him promising to Moses when He sent him to speak before the lords of the land, its wise men, and its officers. Thus it is written: "Go now; I will help your speech and tell you what to say."

This verse with which we began was written at the end of the Song of Songs, after the author told of the love of God for Israel and of Israel for God and the matter of the dispersions which Israel has suffered. All this was done allegorically, in terms of the love of a great and handsome king for his beautiful betrothed. After all these allegorical stories, the

author related what the officers of the king and his grandees say about
the love which they feel for the betrothed, because she behaves as they do
in many matters relating to the love of the king. They therefore call her
their sister in an affectionate way and say: "We have a little sister." The
heavenly hosts say this about Israel who imitate these superior beings in
their love and fear of God and in accepting His Holy Torah. "Small"—
this does not mean that they are small in number, for they are like the
stars of the sky and the sand . . . "Who has no breasts"—this refers to
the pious and the prophets, who by virtue of the prophecies which they
reveal and the wonders which God does through them sustain humanity
in its eternal life, as does the woman who nurses the infant and sustains
it with her breasts and the milk which flows from them. They say that
she does not yet have those prophets, as in the case of the young woman
who until she reaches the age of thirteen or fourteen does not show signs
of maturity in her breasts and limbs. The same is true for us, the
children of Israel. Until the end of days indicated in Daniel arrives, it is
not yet time for prophets and wonders to develop among us—even
though there are among us many pious who are worthy of having divine
spirit descend upon them—since prophets and wonders will occur only
at the end of days, at the time of redemption, as is written: "Your young
men shall see visions."

They say after this: "What shall we do for our sister, when she is
called for?" They say: "How shall we behave with this sister of ours on
the day when she will be spoken of, that is when the king will speak of
her and have her come to him, on the day of redemption when she will
come to the holy city and to the Lord's sanctuary?" They respond to this
among themselves: "If she is a wall": that is, if she stood like a
sturdy wall which is unharmed by stones and likewise if she was unharmed
and was not seduced to idolatry despite continual pressure, then "we
will build upon it a silver parapet": that is, when the time of redemption
arrives, the heavenly hosts will go forth with silver and gold and clothing . . .

⚶

KING JAMES I OF ARAGON AND
        RAYMOND OF PENAFORTE, 1263

ONE OF THE MOST SIGNIFICANT *debates of the thirteenth century, to*
be discussed shortly, took place in Barcelona in 1263, under the patronage of King

James I of Aragon. In the wake of the debate, the king and his entourage visited the
synagogue in order to preach to the Jews. R. Moses ben Nahman (Nahmanides), an
outstanding scholar and leading communal figure in Aragonese Jewry who had been
the Jewish protagonist in the debate, was also the Jewish spokesman in the
synagogue. Our information, which surely represents a one-sided view, comes from
the record of the debate and its aftermath penned by R. Moses himself.

R. Moses reports that there were two Christian speakers; the first was the king
himself. The fears aroused in the Jewish audience must have been profound as the
king of Aragon ascended the pulpit. According to the account, King James argued
forcefully that Jesus was the promised messiah. Rabbi Moses's reply was necessarily
circumspect. The second preacher, Friar Raymond of Penaforte, a major spiritual
leader in western Christendom, spoke on the Trinity. R. Moses felt somewhat freer
to express himself following the friar's sermon. A vigorous exchange took place,
involving also Friar Paul Christian, who had been the Christian spokesman in the
debate. Whatever the reliability of Rabbi Moses's narrative, clearly a distinguished
Christian delegation made its appearance in the synagogue of Barcelona, with the
king and Friar Raymond preaching to the Jews. While the Jews appeared to have
the right to respond, the situation was unquestionably uncomfortable and dangerous.

I HEARD AT COURT that it was the will of the king and of the
Dominicans to come to the synagogue on the Sabbath. I, therefore,
remained in the city eight days. When they came there on the following
Sabbath, I replied to our lord the king as is fitting, for he preached
forcefully, claiming that Jesus was the messiah.

I stood up and said: "The words of our lord the king are in my eyes
princely, superior, and honored, for they come from the mouth of a
prince, a superior man, and an honored leader. However, I cannot laud
these words as true. For I have many clear proofs and illuminating
indications that they are not true. However, it is not fitting to disagree
with the king. Nonetheless I shall say one thing. I am very surprised at
the king. For the claims that he made—that we should believe in Jesus as
the messiah—Jesus himself made to our ancestors. He tried to convince
them, and they rejected him soundly. Surely he should have been able to
prove his case better than the king, since according to their view he is
divine. Now if our ancestors who saw Jesus and knew him did not listen,
how shall we believe the king who has no clear knowledge, but only

information from men who did not know Jesus and were not from his land as were our ancestors?''

Subsequently Friar Raymond of Penaforte arose and preached concerning the Trinity. He said that the Trinity included wisdom, will, and power. He then said in the synagogue: ''Even the rabbi admitted this in Gerona, according to Friar Paul.''

I stood up and said: ''Listen and heed my voice, Jews and Gentiles. Friar Paul asked me in Gerona whether I believe in the Trinity. I asked him what the Trinity is, whether it is three physical entities, like divine bodies. He said no. I then asked whether it is three ethereal entities, like souls or angels. He said no. I then asked whether it is one entity composed of three, like entities composed of the four elements. He said no. I then asked him: 'What then is the Trinity?' He said: 'Wisdom, will, and power.' I then said: 'I acknowledge that God is wise and not foolish, willful and not apathetic, and powerful and not weak. However the term Trinity is a complete error, for wisdom is not an attribute of the Creator. Rather He and wisdom are one; He and His will are one; He and His power are one. Thus wisdom and will and power are all one. Even if these were attributes, it would not mean that there were three divinities. Rather there is one divinity bearing three attributes.' Our lord the king repeated here a metaphor which those who err taught him. He said: 'Wine has three attributes, color, taste, and odor, and yet it is one entity.' But this is a complete error. For redness and taste and odor in wine are separables and may be found one without the other. For there is redness or whiteness or other colors, and likewise with taste and odor. Moreover, the redness is not the wine, nor is the taste, nor is the odor. Rather it is the wine itself which fills the vessel. Thus the wine is an entity which bears three separate attributes and has no unity. If we thus erroneously reckon, we shall inevitably speak of a quadrity. For the entity which is the divinity, his wisdom, his will, and his power must be reckoned, and thus there are four. Indeed you should speak of a quinquity. For he exists, and existence is like wisdom. Thus his definition will be: existence, wisdom, will, power, and divinity itself. All this is clearly erroneous.''

Then Friar Paul stood up and said that he believes in a perfect unity, in which there is nonetheless a trinity. But it is a profound matter, which even the angels and the heavenly hosts do not understand. I then stood and said: ''Clearly one cannot believe what one does not know. Thus the angels do not believe in the Trinity.'' His colleagues then silenced him.

Our lord the king then stood up, and they descended from the pulpit.

❧❦❧

PAUL CHRISTIAN, 1269

FRIAR PAUL CHRISTIAN, *the zealous ex-Jew who had been at the center of missionizing efforts directed at the Jews of Spain in the early 1260s, shifted his field of activity northward at the end of the decade. He arrived in Paris as King Louis IX was completing his preparations for a second ill-fated crusading venture. Friar Paul was warmly received by the pious monarch, anxious to set his affairs straight prior to embarking on the Crusade. It was under the influence of Friar Paul that Louis instituted the Jewish badge. Equally significant, the king empowered the Dominican preacher to initiate a campaign of sermonizing to the Jews. The edict is addressed to the royal officials, ordering them to ensure the presence of Jews at Friar Paul's sermons. It is specifically noted that many of these are to be delivered in synagogues. The Jews are to respond openly to questions which Friar Paul raises and are to present their books as he demands.*

❧❦❧

LOUIS, king of the French, to his bailiffs, viscounts, seneschals, provosts, and others exercising authority through us, greetings:

Since our beloved brother in Christ, Paul Christian of the Order of Preaching Brethren, the bearer of the present letter, wishes and intends, for the glory of the Divine Name, to preach to the Jews the word of light, in order, we understand, to evangelize for the exaltation of the Christian faith, we order you to force those Jews residing in your jurisdiction to present themselves to hear from him without objection the word of the Lord and to present their books as the aforesaid friar shall require. You shall compel the Jews to respond fully, without calumny and subterfuge, on those matters which relate to their law, concerning which the aforesaid friar might interrogate them, whether in sermons in their synagogues or elsewhere. You shall provide, moreover, for the protection and safety of the aforesaid friar as he shall require of you, so that no violence or injury or impediment be inflicted upon him or his circle.

This letter shall be valid for as long as it pleases our will.

Enacted in Paris, July 18, 1269.

PAUL CHRISTIAN, 1269

THE EDICT OF SAINT LOUIS *did not remain a dead letter. Friar Paul immediately embarked on a campaign of forced preaching analogous to that which he had already undertaken in southern France and Spain. A Latin chronicle from Paris shows us the Jews assembled almost immediately to hear Paul's message. A Hebrew record, most of which has unfortunately disappeared, describes a forced confrontation in the early 1270s. In both sources, Paul is depicted as vigorously challenging the Jews and their faith, denigrating their religious heritage, and urging them to accept Christianity.*

A Latin Report

IN THE SAME YEAR, during the period of Pentecost, a certain friar of the Dominican Order, named . . . , from Lombardy, who had been a Jew and was a learned cleric in the Mosaic law and in our law, came and publicly preached to the Jews in the royal court in Paris and in the court of the Dominicans. They came there at the order of the king, and he showed them that their law was null and invalid, that for a long time they had not observed it, and that they have deviated daily from all its articles.

A Hebrew Report

THESE ARE THE REPLIES to the heretic who rose up against us in the year 4032 [1272] and came from Spain to destroy the remnant of Israel. His name was Paul the Dominican . . .

In the year 5033 [1273] the heretic Paul came and assembled all the rabbis. Thus he said to them before the bishop of Paris and the chief clerics who were there: "Listen to me, O house of Jacob and all the families of the house of Israel. Know that, if you do not listen and repent and abandon your faith as a result of the resounding arguments that I shall show you, I shall not leave you without taking vengeance upon you and demanding your blood. I wish to show you that you are a faithless people, a people of *bougres*, and that you are fit for burning. I shall announce your sins. For each one you should be sentenced to death. Now listen carefully and send me all your outstanding leaders and let them answer me immediately. For thus have I been commanded by the king to bring you to your end."

Know that each time we were in the royal court or in the Dominican court—more than a thousand souls pelted with stones. Thank the Lord, not one of us turned to the religion of lies and fancies. When dusk began to descend, we were commanded to go and to return on the morrow . . .

PAUL CHRISTIAN, 1263

THE FORCED SERMON *suffered from one major deficiency: It had little control over internal Jewish responses to Christian claims. A more effective technique for eliciting and then rebutting Jewish counterclaims was the forced disputation. Such debates were intended as extensions of the forced sermon. Jews would be compelled to hear Christian arguments, to respond, and then to hear the Christian rejoinder.*

In a sense, these were not true disputations or debates, since they did not involve equal parties challenging one another. The Christian depiction of the disputation at Barcelona makes this evident. The confrontation was undertaken "not that the faith of the Lord Jesus Christ—which because of its certitude cannot be placed in dispute—be put in the center of attention with the Jews as uncertain, but that the truth of that faith be made manifest by destroying the Jews' errors and in order to shake the confidence of these many Jews." Thus the purpose was not to debate abstractly conflicting religious systems, but rather to bring the message of Christianity to the Jews in a new and particularly compelling way.

One of the most famous of the forced confrontations took place in Barcelona in 1263 under King James I of Aragon. The disputation was sponsored by the Dominicans, who chose as their spokesman Friar Paul Christian, already noted for missionizing among his former coreligionists. The Jewish spokesman was the famed R. Moses ben Nahman. The agenda for the disputation reflects both the new knowledge of rabbinic Judaism which converts like Paul Christian brought with them and the missionizing aim of the debates. In the first item, for example, Friar Paul attempts to prove, using Talmudic sources, that the promised messiah has already come. Whether the messiah has or has not come is not in dispute; his coming is an accepted truth for the Christian world, one about which Rabbi Moses can say nothing. The issue under consideration is only whether Talmudic sources themselves prove this Christian truth.

The disputation is significant for both its intrinsic value and the parallel and conflicting sets of sources we have concerning it. A Christian observer left a brief Latin depiction of the events, which was vouched for by the king himself. Rabbi Moses, the Jewish spokesman, wrote a lengthier first person report in Hebrew. There is a great deal upon which the two accounts agree, but equally noteworthy are the disagreements. According to the Latin record, Rabbi Moses was confused, humbled, vanquished, and forced to flee; according to his own narrative, he responded cleverly and tellingly to each thrust by Friar Paul and was eventually dismissed by the king with warmth and dignity.

The disputation at Barcelona shows the pressures of proselytizing reaching their peak, and the texts concerning the disputation reveal the chasm that separated Christian majority from Jewish minority.

৪৩

A Latin Report

ON JULY 20, 1263, in the presence of the lord king of Aragon and many other barons, prelates, clerics, and knights, in the palace of the lord king at Barcelona, Moses the Jew, called "rabbi," was summoned from Gerona by the lord king, at the request of the Dominicans, and was present there, along with many other Jews who seemed and were reputed among other Jews more learned. Deliberation was undertaken with the lord king and with certain Dominicans and Franciscans who were present, not that the faith of the Lord Jesus Christ—which because of its certitude cannot be placed in dispute—be put in the center of attention with the Jews as uncertain, but that the truth of that faith be made manifest in order to destroy the Jews' errors and to shake the confidence of many Jews. Since they could not defend their errors, these Jews indicated that the said rabbi could sufficiently reply to each and every question which would be placed before them.

Friar Paul proposed to the said rabbi that, with the aid of God, he would prove from writings shared and accepted by the Jews the following contentions, in order: that the messiah, who is called Christ, whom the Jews anticipate, has surely come already; also that the messiah, as prophesied, should be divine and human; also that he suffered and was killed for the salvation of mankind; also that the laws and ceremonials ceased and should have ceased after the advent of the said messiah. When the said Moses was asked whether he wished to respond to these contentions which have been indicated, he said and affirmed that he would and that, if necessary, he would remain at Barcelona for that purpose not only for a day or a week or a month, but even for a year. When it was proved to him that he should not be called "rabbi," because no Jew should be designated by that title from the time of the Passion of Christ, he conceded at least that this was true for the previous eight hundred years.

Then it was indicated to him that when Friar Paul had come to Gerona for the purpose of conferring with him on these matters, which pertain to salvation, and had expostulated carefully concerning the Holy Trinity, both about the unity of the divine essence and about the trinity of beings, the beliefs which Christians hold, he had conceded that, if Christians believed in the manner explained to him, he would believe indeed that so it should be held. When this was repeated before the king, he did not contradict. Rather he was silent, and thus by remaining silent he conceded.

Then in the palace of the lord king, the said Jew was asked whether the messiah, who is called Christ, has come. He responded with the assertion that he has not come. He added that the messiah and Christ are the same and that, if it could be proved to him that the messiah had come, it could be believed to refer to none other than him, namely Jesus Christ, in whom the Christians believe, since no one else has come who has dared to usurp for himself this title nor has there been anyone else who had been believed to be Christ. It was then proved to him clearly, both through authoritative texts of the law and the prophets as well as through the Talmud, that Christ has truly come, as Christians believe and preach. Since he was unable to respond, vanquished by proper proofs and authoritative texts, he conceded that Christ or the messiah had been born in Bethlehem a thousand years ago and had subsequently appeared in Rome to some. When he was asked where that messiah who he said was born and appeared at Rome might be, he replied that he did not know. Subsequently he said that the messiah lives in a terrestrial paradise with Elijah. He also said that, although the messiah has been born, he has still not come, since the messiah may be said to have come when he achieves dominion over the Jews and liberates them and when the Jews follow him. Against this response was adduced the authority of the Talmud, which clearly says that the messiah would come to them daily, if they would hear his voice and not harden their heart, as is said in Psalms: "Today if you will listen to his voice."

It was added that the messiah was born among men, that he came among men, and that he could not otherwise be or be understood. To this he was unable to respond. Also among the proofs presented concerning the advent of the messiah was that from Genesis: "The sceptre shall not pass from Judah, nor the staff from his descendants." Since therefore he must acknowledge that there is neither sceptre nor staff, he acknowledges that the messiah who was to be sent has come. To this he responded that the sceptre has not been removed. It is merely temporarily absent, as happened during the time of the Babylonian captivity. It was proved to him that in Babylonia the Jews had exilarchs with jurisdiction, while after the death of Christ they had neither a staff nor a prince nor exilarchs according to the prophecy of Daniel nor a prophet nor any jurisdiction, as is manifestly obvious every day. It is thus certain that the messiah has come. He then said that he would prove that the Jews had the aforesaid exilarchs after Jesus, but he was able to show nothing in these matters. On the contrary he confessed that they have not had the aforesaid exilarchs for the past 850 years. Therefore it is clear that the messiah has come, since an authoritative text cannot lie.

The said Moses claimed that Jesus Christ should not be called the messiah, since the messiah, he said, should not die, as is said in Psalms: "He asked of thee life and thou didst give it him, length of days for ever and ever." Rather he should live eternally, both he and those whom he would liberate. It was therefore asked of him whether chapter 53 of Isaiah—"Who could have believed what we have heard"—which according to the Jews begins at the end of chapter 52, where it is said: "Behold my servant shall prosper," speaks of the messiah. Although he consistently claimed that this passage in no way speaks of the messiah, it was proved to him through many authoritative texts in the Talmud which speak of the passion and death of Christ, which they prove through the said chapter, that the aforesaid chapter of Isaiah must be understood as related to Christ, in which the death, passion, burial and resurrection of Christ is obviously contained. Indeed forced by authoritative texts, he confessed that this section must be understood and explained as relating to Christ. From this it is clear that the messiah was to suffer.

Since he did not wish to confess the truth unless forced by authoritative texts, when he was unable to explain these authoritative texts, he said publicly that he did not believe these authoritative texts which were adduced against him—although found in ancient and authentic books of the Jews—because they were, he claimed, sermons in which their teachers often lied for the purpose of exhorting the people. As a result he reproved both the teachers and the scriptures of the Jews. Moreover, all these issues, or almost all, which he confessed or which were proved to him, he first negated; then confuted by authoritative texts and confused, he was forced to assent. Moreover, since he was unable to respond and was often publicly confused and since both Jews and Christians insulted him, he persistently claimed before all that he would in no way respond, since the Jews prohibited him and Christians, namely Friar P. de Janua and certain upstanding men of the city, had sent him messages advising that he in no way respond. Concerning this lie he was publicly refuted by the said Friar P. and by these upstanding men. Whence it is clear that he tried to escape the disputation by lies. Moreover, although he promised before the king and many others that before a few he would answer concerning his faith and his law, when the said lord was outside the city, he secretly fled and departed. Whence it is clear that he did not dare nor was he able to defend his erroneous belief.

We James, by the grace of God king of Aragon, Majorca and Valencia, count of Barcelona and Urgel, and lord of Montpellier, confirm and acknowledge that each and every statement and action took place in our presence and in the presence of many others, as contained above in the present letter. In testimony of this we have caused our seal to be appended as a perpetual memorial.

A Hebrew Report

OUR LORD THE KING commanded me to dispute with Friar Paul in his palace before him and his advisors in Barcelona. I replied: "I will do as the king commands, if you permit me to speak freely. I hereby request the permission of the king and the permission of Friar Raymond of Penaforte and his associates who are here." Friar Raymond of Penaforte replied: "So long as you do not utter blasphemies." I said to them: "I wish to observe your law in this regard. But I also wish to speak freely in debate, as you speak freely. I have the wisdom to speak properly in debate as you indicate, but it must be according to my will." They all gave me permission to speak freely.

I then said: "The debate between Christians and Jews concerns many matters of custom which are not essential. In this revered court, I wish to debate only matters that are essential.'' They all said: "You have spoken properly.'' Thus, we agreed to speak first about the messiah —whether he has already come as the Christians believe or if he is yet to come as the Jews believe. Subsequently, we shall discuss whether the messiah is divine or fully human, born of man and woman. Afterward we shall discuss whether the Jews observe the true law or whether the Christians do.

Then Friar Paul began, saying that he would prove from our Talmud that the messiah concerning whom the prophets testify has already come. I replied: "Before we debate this, I ask that he tell me how this is possible. Indeed while he was in Provence and in many other places, I heard that he said this to many Jews. But I am most surprised. Would he answer me in this regard? Does he mean to say that the sages of the Talmud believed in Jesus as the messiah and believed that he is both human and divine, as held by the Christians? However, it is well-known that the incident of Jesus took place during the period of the Second Temple. He was born and killed prior to the destruction of the Temple, while the sages of the Talmud, like R. Akiba and his associates, followed this destruction. Those who compiled the Mishnah, Rabbi and R. Nathan, lived many years after the destruction. All the more so R. Ashi who compiled the Talmud, who lived about four hundred years after the destruction. If these sages believed that Jesus was the messiah and that his faith and religion were true and if they wrote these things from which Friar Paul intends to prove this, then how did they remain in the Jewish faith and in their former practice? For they were Jews, remained in the Jewish faith all their lives, and died Jews—they and their children and their students who heard their teachings. Why did they not convert and turn to the faith of Jesus, as Friar Paul did? He understood from their words that the faith of the Christians is the true faith—Heaven forbid—and he went and converted as a result. But they and their students who learned Torah from them remained and died Jews, as we are this day . . . If these sages believed in Jesus and in his faith, how is it that they did not do as Friar Paul, who understands their teachings better than they themselves do?''

Friar Paul responded: "These are lengthy observations, intended to cancel the debate. Nonetheless, you shall hear what I have to say.'' I said to them: "But this is clear proof that he shall not say anything of substance. However, I shall hear his claims, because our lord the king wishes so.''

He began: "Behold Scriptures say, 'the sceptre shall not pass from Judah, nor the staff from his descendants, until Shiloh comes,' meaning the messiah. Thus the prophet says that Judah shall have power forever, until the coming of the messiah who will descend from Judah. Thus today, when you Jews have neither sceptre nor staff, the messiah has already come, and he is of the seed of Judah, and his is the power.''

I responded and said: ''It was not the prophet's intention to say that the rule of Judah would never be suspended. Rather, he said that it would not pass away and be annulled completely. This means that, so long as there be a monarchy in Israel, it should belong to Judah. If because of their sins it should be suspended, it would ultimately return to Judah. This is proved by the fact that, prior to Jesus, there was a long period during which ruling authority was suspended from Judah but not from Israel and a long period during which rule was suspended both from Israel and Judah. For during the seventy years of exile in Babylonia, neither Judah nor Israel enjoyed ruling authority. During the period of the Second Temple, only Zerubabel and his sons ruled briefly from Judah. There remained, however, 380 years to the destruction, during which priests of the Hasmonean family reigned.''

Friar Paul replied: ''Through all these times, even though the Jews had no kings, they did have authorities. For thus they explained in the Talmud, 'The sceptre shall not pass from Judah'—these are the exilarchs in Babylonia who control the people; 'Nor the staff from his descendants' —these are the offspring of Hillel who teach the Torah publicly. Today, however, you do not have the ordination known in the Talmud. Thus even that authority has been annulled, for there is no one among you worthy of being designated 'rabbi.' That they call you 'magister' is an error, and you use that title deceitfully . . .''

I responded and said: ''I shall show you that it was not the intention of the rabbis to explain this verse other than meaning actual kingship. However, you do not understand law and *halakhah*; you only understand a little *aggadah*, with which you have made yourself familiar. The matter which the sages mentioned concerns the fact that properly no man should judge a case on his own and be free of liability to pay in case of error, unless he receives permission from the patriarch, who is like a king. They said that during the period of exile, since these are those of royal descent who have some authority from the Gentile kings, such as the exilarchs in Babylonia and the patriarchs in Palestine, they have the right to confer permission and ordination. This, however, took place among the sages of the Talmud, more than four hundred years after the death of Jesus. For it was not the view of the sages of the Talmud that this would constitute the sceptre and the staff which come from the seed of Judah. Rather the prophet promised Judah that kingship over Israel would be his. He promised him actual kingship. Nonetheless this promise was suspended for a long period, as I have mentioned. During the period of exile in Babylonia there was no sceptre or staff whatsoever, neither exilarch nor patriarch, for authority was held by the priests, the judges, the officers, or whoever they chose.''

Then Friar Peter of Janua responded: ''This is true. The verse only says that kingship shall not cease entirely, but there might be a suspension . . .''

I said to the king: ''Behold Friar Peter rules according to my view.''

Friar Peter said: ''I have not made a ruling. For the seventy years in Babylonia constitutes a short time. There were still many who remembered the First Temple, as is written in the book of Ezra. This might be called a suspension . . . However now that you have remained more than a thousand years without kingship, that is complete abolition.''

I said: ''Now you change your mind. However, the term 'abolition' cannot be used with a recurring phenomenon. Moreover, there is no distinction in the words of the prophet between a long suspension and a short suspension. Moreover, the period that I mentioned was lengthy. Moreover, our forefather Jacob did not promise Judah that he would hold the sceptre and staff over his tribe only. Rather he accorded Judah kingship over all Israel; as is written: 'Judah, your brothers shall praise you.' It is also written: 'Judah held the leading place among his brothers and fathered their rulers.' However kingship over all Israel was suspended from the time that Solomon died, as is written: 'The tribe of Judah alone followed the house of David.' Thus it is clear that the prophet said only that kingship would not pass completely. The truth is that, during the period of exile, it is not to be called annulment or abolition at all, for it does not involve Judah but the entire nation. For the prophet did not promise Judah that the people of Israel would never go into exile, so that he might be king over them at all times.''

Friar Paul then claimed that in the Talmud it is said that the messiah has already come. He adduced the story in Midrash Lamentations concerning a man who was ploughing and whose ox lowed. An Arab passed and said to him: ''Jew, Jew, unhitch your ox, unhitch your ploughshare, unhitch your plough for the Temple has been destroyed.'' He unhitched his ox, unhitched his ploughshare, and unhitched his plough. The ox lowed a second time. The Arab said to him: ''Hitch up your ox, hitch up your ploughshare, hitch up your plough, for your messiah has been born.''

I responded: ''I do not believe in this story at all, but it is a proof for my view.''

He then cried out: ''Behold he denies their books.''

I said: ''Truly I do not believe that the messiah was born on the day of the destruction of the Temple. Thus this story is not true or else it has another meaning drawn from the secrets of the sages. However I shall accept it at its simple meaning as you claim, for it is a proof for my case. Behold it says that on the day of destruction, after the Temple was destroyed, the messiah was born. Thus Jesus was not the messiah, as you claim. For he was born and killed prior to the destruction of the Temple. In fact he was born about two hundred years prior to the destruction of the Temple. According to your reckoning, he was born seventy-three years prior to the destruction of the Temple.'' Then he was silent.

Master William, the royal judge, then said: ''The dispute does not now concern Jesus. The question is whether the messiah has come or not. You say that he has not come, and this book of yours says that he has come.''

I said to him: ''You choose, as is your custom, to respond craftily. Nonetheless I shall answer you. The sages did not say that the messiah has come. Rather they said that he was born. For on the day that our teacher Moses was born, he did not come and redeem us. However, when he came before Pharaoh at the command of God and said to him: 'These are the words of the Lord—Send forth My people!' then he may be said to have arrived. Likewise the messiah—when he shall come before the pope and shall say to him at God's command: 'Send forth My people,' then he may be said to have come. However, to this day he has not yet come and is in no sense the messiah. For King David on the day that he was born was not the anointed one. Only when Samuel anointed him was he the anointed one. On the day that Elijah will anoint the messiah at God's command may he be called the messiah. On the day that he will subsequently come before the pope to redeem us, then he may be said to have arrived.''

Friar Paul claimed: ''Behold the passage in Isaiah, chapter 53, tells of the death of the messiah and how he was to fall into the hands of his enemies and how he was placed alongside the wicked, as happened to Jesus. Do you believe that this section speaks of the messiah?''

I said to him: "In terms of the true meaning of the section, it speaks only of the people of Israel, which the prophets regularly call 'Israel My servant' or 'Jacob My servant.' "

Friar Paul said: "I shall prove from the words of your sages that it speaks of the messiah."

I said to him: "It is true that the rabbis in the *aggadah* explain it as referring to the messiah. However, they never said that he would be killed at the hands of his enemies. For you will find in no book of the Jews, neither in the Talmud nor in the Midrash, that the messiah, the descendant of David, would be killed or would be turned over to his enemies or would be buried among the wicked. Indeed even the messiah whom you made for yourself was not buried. I shall explain for you this section properly and clearly, if you wish. There is no indication that the messiah would be killed, as happened to your messiah." They, however, did not wish to hear.

Friar Paul then said that, in the Talmud, it is indicated that R. Joshua b. Levi asked Elijah when the messiah would come. He answered him: "Ask the messiah himself." He said "Where is he?" He said: "At the gate of Rome, among the sick." He went there and found him. He asked him . . . Thus the messiah has already come, is in Rome, and is in fact Jesus who rules in Rome.

I said to him: "Isn't it clear from this that he has not come? For he asked Elijah when the messiah would come. Likewise he asked the messiah himself: 'When will you come?' Thus he has not yet come. Rather, according to the simple meaning of these stories, he was born already. But I do not believe this."

Then the king responded: "If he were born on the day of the destruction of the Temple, which was more than a thousand years ago and has not yet arrived, how will he arrive? For it is not human nature to live for a thousand years."

I said to him: "Conditions were set that I not debate with you and that you will not participate in the debate. However, already among early man Adam and Methusaleh lived almost to a thousand years and Elijah and Enoch more than that, since life lies in the hands of God."

He said: "Where is he now?"

I said: "This is not a necessary element in the debate, and I shall not respond. Maybe you can find him at the gates of Toledo, if you send there one of your couriers." I said it jokingly.

They then rose, and the king set a time for resuming the debate, on the following Monday.

On that day the king went to the cloister in the city, where all the men of the city gathered, Gentiles and Jews. The bishop, all the clerics, and the sages of the Franciscans and Dominicans were there. Friar Paul rose to speak. I said to our lord the king: "My lord, hear me." He said to me: "Let him speak first, since he is the interlocutor." I said: "Allow me to clarify my view concerning the messiah. Then he can reply to the clarification."

I rose and said: "Listen all you people. Friar Paul asked me whether the messiah of whom the prophets spoke has come. I said that he has not come. He then cited an *aggadah* which said that, on the very day the Temple was destroyed, the messiah was born. I then said that I do not believe this, although it is a proof for my view. Now I shall explain to you why I said that I do not believe this. Know that we Jews have three types of books. The first is the Bible, and we all believe it completely. The second is called Talmud, and it is a commentary on the commandments of the Torah. For in the Torah there are 613 commandments, and there is not one of them that is not explained in the Talmud. We believe in the Talmud concerning explanation of the commandments. We have yet a third book called Midrash, that is, sermons. This is analogous to the bishop standing and giving a sermon, with one of the listeners deciding to write it. In regard to this book, those who believe it well and good, but those who do not believe it do no harm. We have sages who wrote that the messiah will not be born until close to the time ordained for redeeming us from exile. Therefore I do not believe in this book, where it says that he was born on the day of the destruction of the Temple. We also call this book *aggadah*, that is, stories, meaning that these are only things which one person tells another. However, I shall accept this *aggadah* literally, as you wish, because it is an explicit proof that Jesus is not the messiah, as I said to you, because he was not born on that day. Rather, by that time, everything related to him had already transpired long before.

"Now you, our lord the king, asked and objected properly that it is not human nature to live a thousand years. Now I shall explain to you the answer to your questions. Behold Adam lived a thousand years minus seventy. Moreover, it says explicitly in Scriptures that he died because of his sin; had he not sinned, he would have lived much more or even forever. Both the Gentiles and the Jews agree that the sin and punishment of Adam will be annulled during messianic times. Thus after the messiah comes, it will be annulled from all of us, but with the messiah himself it will be completely annulled. Thus the messiah is capable of living thousands of years or even forever. Thus Psalms says: 'He asked of Thee life, and Thou didst give it him, length of days for ever and ever.' You further asked, our lord the king, where he is now. It is already indicated in Scriptures. For Adam lived in terrestial paradise. When he sinned, it is said: 'So the Lord God drove him out of the Garden of Eden.' Thus, one who is free from the punishment of Adam's sin lives there in paradise. Thus said the sages in the book of *aggadah* which I mentioned.'' The king said: "Did you not say in the same *aggadah* that he was in Rome." I said to him: "I did not say that he lived in Rome, only that he appeared in Rome on a particular day. For Elijah told the sage that he would find him there on that day . . .''

This is the content of the debates. I have not consciously altered a detail. Subsequently, on that same day, I stood before our lord the king and he said: "Let the dispute be suspended. For I have never seen a man whose case is wrong argue it as well as you have done.''

PART SIX

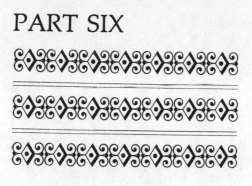

GOVERNMENTAL PERSECUTION

INTRODUCTION

THE ESSENTIAL FRAILTY of Jewish life in medieval Christendom
led the Jews into an ever-deepening alliance with the governmental
authorities. While these authorities repeatedly intervened to protect
their Jews from popular hostility or from ecclesiastical pressure, there
was little Jews could do when the government failed them or turned
against them. In Parts Four and Five, we examined a series of instances
in which the rulers of western Europe vigorously supported Church initiatives against the Jews. Beyond backing ecclesiastical programs, the
governing authorities occasionally undertook directly deleterious actions
in which Jewish property was adversely affected, Jewish life was lost,
and Jewish existence in particular areas was prohibited. Given the traditional cast of medieval European society, however, such programs were
almost always presented in religious terms, justified by an appeal to
ecclesiastical issues or alleged Jewish misdeeds.

Three varieties of governmental actions against the Jews will be
examined in this section. The first is governmental confiscation of
Jewish goods and debts. In periods of crisis, it was always tempting to
view the Jews as a source of substantial and immediate funds. Although
it was generally recognized that, by confiscating Jewish property and
enjoying temporary profit, much might be lost in the long run, this was
sometimes not a strong enough consideration to overcome the prospect
of relief from pressing financial problems. In a number of cases, such as
the confiscations ordered by Saint Louis, it seems quite likely that there
were elements of genuine piety at work as well. Convinced that the Jews
were consistently flaunting his anti-usury legislation, Louis seized
Jewish goods and debts in order to strip the Jews of their ill-gotten gains.

Louis IX, however, was a most unusual ruler, for the Middle Ages
or any other period. Most of the authorities of medieval Christendom
were caught up in far more mundane issues and concerns. While they
never failed to cite pious motives for their actions, we may treat such
protestations with skepticism. Thus, the monkish biographer of Louis'
grandfather, the worldly Philip Augustus, portrays the confiscation of
Jewish goods and later of Jewish debts as motivated by simple concern
over alleged Jewish misdeeds. Yet Philip Augustus was, throughout his
reign, a hesistant and reluctant supporter of the Church, willing on a

number of important occasions to oppose ecclesiastical initiatives damaging to the interests of the State. These confiscations came, moreover, during the most precarious period of Philip's reign, at a time when he was fighting fiercely against a powerful baronial coalition. Desperately in need of resources and allies, the young king gained, through the measures undertaken against the Jews, both substantial revenue and the enthusiastic support of many of his subjects. Pious terminology aside, his moves appear to be the calculated maneuvers of a shrewd and beleaguered young monarch.

On other occasions, governmental actions became, from the Jewish point of view, yet more dangerous and destructive, directed not only against Jewish goods but against Jewish life. Such instances were not commonplace during the Middle Ages, but they did occur—and with disastrous results. The motivations for such assaults were varied and complex. In some cases, attacks seem to have been genuinely inspired by religious motives. In the early eleventh century the primary aim of conversionary efforts in northern Europe was to enforce religious unity. In other cases, persecution reflects simply the sharing of common assumptions about the malevolence and evil of the Jews. The rulers of western Christendom were, after all, not immune to the hatreds and stereotypes that pervaded society as a whole. While they may often have risen above such widespread animus or at least restrained it for practical reasons, under certain circumstances it was bound to burst forth, with destructive consequences. In other instances, there were practical considerations that dictated persecution of the Jews. The simplest of these was to profit from the Jews' goods, but political motives were also occasionally at the root of such attacks.

The final type of anti-Jewish activity presented is expulsion. Since it was the support of the governmental authorities which made Jewish settlement in medieval Christendom possible in the first place, the decision to withdraw this support destroyed any basis for Jewish existence. While there were occasional early expulsions from areas of western Europe, most of them temporary, in the late thirteenth and early fourteenth century a number of banishments occurred, most of which became relatively permanent. With the shattering exodus from Spain in 1492, almost all the western sections of Europe were left bereft of Jews. Once again, it must be noted that, while the terminology of edicts of banishment and chronicle accounts is deeply pious, it seems clear that actual motives varied widely. To cite Saint Louis, when that monarch decided in 1253 to rid his realm of Jewish usurers, the act was one of genuine piety on his part, probably undertaken at some loss to the royal treasury. But again, Saint Louis cannot be taken as a reflection of the norm. Expulsions for the sake of revenue and popular commendation no doubt far outnumbered those undertaken truly for religious motives.

This section, more than any of the preceding, reveals the essential fragility of Jewish existence in medieval Christendom. To take up residence at the behest of rulers and to live under their protection meant ultimately to be totally dependent. When these rulers withdrew their invitation and support, the Jews of western Europe had no choice but to gather up their belongings and seek new havens elsewhere.

KING LOUIS IX OF FRANCE, 1234

ON OCCASION, *confiscation of Jewish goods was motivated by a genuine sense of Jewish wrongdoing. This was particularly true during the reign of Saint Louis. Convinced that Jewish usury was illicit, the pious Louis a number of times seized Jewish goods and loans, intending to strip Jews of property which he saw as deceitfully accumulated and to return usury whenever possible. The first instance of such seizures occurred in the early 1230s. While the edict of confiscation itself has not survived, a related order from 1234 shows the king making every effort to return the usury taken by his Jews. In the case of debts already paid, one-third was to be returned; for debts still owed, one-third was to be forgiven.*

IN 1234 A.D., it was enacted by Louis, son of King Louis:

1.   It is to be known that the lord king of the French, for the salvation of his soul and the soul of his father and of all his ancestors, has acquitted all Christians who were indebted to Jews—when they were recently seized and their debts enrolled—a third part of the entire debt

which they owed the Jews. That is to say, a third part will be returned to those who paid the entire sum. To those who are still indebted a third part will be forgiven. For the two parts remaining they shall have a term for payment, viz., for the first half up to the coming November 1 and for the other half up to the following Feast of the Purification of Holy Mary [February 2].

2.   It is also strictly ordered to all bailiffs that Christians not be seized for Jews' debts and that Christians not be forced on that account to sell their inherited property.

3.   It is moreover ordered that Jews may accept no pledges, except through the testimony of good men, worthy of belief. If any pledges be found with them, for which they lack warranty, they shall lose their capital and the pledges shall legally belong to the Christian.

4.   The bailiffs are also ordered that they presume to take nothing for implementing faithfully the foregoing, for thus they hold dear the lord king and care for his person, his lands, and all his goods. Be strong.

༄

KING LOUIS IX OF FRANCE, 1237

KING LOUIS' CONCERN *with the stigma of usury attached to the funds he had confiscated from the Jews led the monarch in 1234 to return the usury to Christian debtors. One-third of the debts already paid were to be returned and one-third of the sums still owed were forgiven. Still not satisfied, Louis addressed the pope, suggesting that the tainted funds be used for the pious purposes of the Crusade. The papal letter presented here is Pope Gregory IX's affirmative reply.*

༄

TO THE ILLUSTRIOUS king of France:
    On your behalf we have been told that, since you have received no small sum of money from the Jews of your kingdom and from their

Christian debtors and in the latter's name, and since this money acquired by the Jews bears the stigma of usury, you desire to bring satisfaction for the said money, lest the sin of it be imputed to you and you be punished for it. Wherefore you humbly pray us that, in view of the fact that many from whom the said Jews have extorted usury can no longer be discovered and that you want to send the money, which you are bound to restore to them, as a subsidy to the empire of Constantinople, we shall, in the benignity of the Apostolic Throne, take the trouble to grant to Your Serene Highness permission to do this. By doing this, the matter may redound to your salvation in the sight of God, and, because of the great amount of such assistance, you may be free from the obligation of repayment. Therefore, inclined to your prayers, we grant you by these letters the authority requested.

Given at Viterbo, October 6,
in the eleventh year [1237].

KING LOUIS IX OF FRANCE, 1246

DURING THE LATE 1240S, *as Saint Louis prepared for his great crusading venture, he became disturbed with the moral state of his realm. As part of the process of spiritual cleansing, he turned his attention once more to the issue of usury. Convinced that Jewish usury was still rampant, particularly in the newly absorbed southern areas of the kingdom, Louis once again confiscated Jewish funds and loans. The accompanying edict was issued after an initial seizure had already taken place. The king orders the release of Jews belonging to other barons. The king's Jews, however, are to be carefully examined and as much as possible is to be confiscated from them.*

LOUIS, by the grace of God king of the French, to his beloved and faithful J. de Cranis, seneschal of Carcassonne, greetings and best wishes:

1.   We order you to return to those to whom they belong all those Jews held captive who do not belong to us and not to seize anything from them.

2.   However, from those held captive who are our Jews, since we wish to have from them as much as possible, you should seize goods and, indicating to us the sum which you are able to realize therefrom, you should cause that sum to be carefully and safely guarded and preserved.

3.   We further order, concerning captive and other Jews of your seneschalsy or Jews who live in those areas under our jurisdiction, that you cause them to be forbidden by person and goods from henceforth presuming to extort usury. Rather, they should earn their sustenance from another source.

4.   We also order and command you not to compel anyone to repay debts to the Jews and to receive nothing of debts which Christians owe to Jews.

Enacted at Saint-Germain-en-Laye, 1246,
in the month of July.

🙙◈🙚

KING LOUIS IX OF FRANCE, 1257-58

PRIOR TO SETTING OUT ON HIS CRUSADE, *Louis once again issued an edict aimed at returning usury to those who had paid it. Despite this effort, the monarch remained disturbed over the issue. Thus, after returning from the Crusade, the king turned his attention once more to the vexing problem of the money confiscated previously from the Jews. He appointed a distinguished commission charged with the responsibility of exploring every avenue for returning monies illegally extorted by the Jews.*

🙙◈🙚

LOUIS by the grace of God king of the French, to all reading this letter, greetings:

1.   Prior to setting forth on our Crusade, we seized certain goods from the Jews, not indeed with the intention of retaining them.

Subsequently, when we ordered these Jews to be expelled from our land, we seized other goods which they had. Moreover, concerning the goods of certain deceased usurers in Normandy, we discovered that some had been seized. Concerning these matters, we, anxious to provide for the safety of our souls and to remove doubt from our conscience, thus wish and order that, from these goods and other property of the Jews, both movable goods and real estate, usury be returned to those from whom it had been taken or to their heirs, if they can be found. This is to be done by careful men, our beloved and faithful William, bishop of Orléans, B., abbott of Bonneval, and Master Peter, archdeacon of Poissy in the diocese of Chartres, whom we have specially deputized for this purpose and to whom we have extended our authority in this issue.

2.   In regard to these goods of the Jews, wherever they were seized or received by any bailiffs, provosts, or anyone else, and concerning which careful accounting and full satisfaction has not yet been made, we order also that the aforesaid bishop, abbot, and archdeacon demand and receive them from anyone who seized them and retains them and that the aforesaid have them held in the hands of trustworthy men. They may compel those who seized and retain these goods to remit them by our authority, if that be necessary.

3.   Moreover, we accord them full authority to sell houses, rights, and any other Jewish real estate. We wish, however, that old synagogues and those items without which they cannot be used as synagogues and their cemeteries be returned to those Jews.

4.   In order that all the aforesaid be executed both by those appointed and by others whom they deem proper and to whom they delegate responsibility, we wish and order that, if it should happen that we die before all the above be completed, nonetheless the aforesaid bishop, abbot, and archdeacon proceed to complete this task, as execution of our last will in this matter.

❧

KING PHILIP AUGUSTUS OF FRANCE, 1180

SAINT LOUIS' GRANDFATHER, *Philip Augustus, represents a strikingly different image of a medieval monarch. Philip Augustus shared little of his grand-*

son's piety. He was, above all else, a shrewd and calculating politician, determined to perpetuate and expand the power of his dynasty. The successes of his reign were remarkable. He enlarged enormously the boundaries of the royal domain and firmly established royal dominance in northern France. Yet, at the outset of his reign, there had been serious doubt as to the future of the young monarch. Crowned only after his father became seriously ill and challenged by a coalition of puissant barons, Philip had to use every wile simply to survive his initial years on the throne. *Casting about desperately for every available resource, the struggling young king decided to exploit his Jews. He did this in two stages. He first simply seized his Jews and confiscated their wealth. His second move was more clever—he annulled outstanding Jewish loans, retaining only one-fifth for the royal treasury. In this way, he realized a double advantage, both tangible profit and the approbation of substantial sections of the Christian populace. While there can be little serious doubt as to the motives of the young Philip Augustus, his biographer Rigord portrays the monarch as inspired solely by Christian piety. He, therefore, cites a series of misdeeds which allegedly aroused King Philip to initiate his actions.*

♦

PHILIP AUGUSTUS had often heard that the Jews who dwelt in Paris were wont every year on Easter Day, or during the sacred week of our Lord's Passion, to go down secretly into underground vaults and kill a Christian as a sort of sacrifice in contempt of the Christian religion. For a long time they had persisted in this wickedness, inspired by the devil, and in Philip's father's time many of them had been seized and burned with fire. Saint Richard, whose body rests in the Church of the Holy Innocents-in-the-Fields in Paris, was thus put to death and crucified by the Jews and through martyrdom went in blessedness to God. Wherefore many miracles have been wrought by the hand of God through the prayers and intercessions of Saint Richard, to the glory of God, as we have heard.

And because the most Christian King Philip inquired diligently and came to know full well these and many other iniquities of the Jews in his forefathers' days, therefore he burned with zeal, and in the same year in which he was invested at Rheims with the holy governance of the kingdom of the French, upon a Sabbath, the first of March, by his command the Jews throughout all France were seized in their synagogues and then bespoiled of their góld and silver and garments, as the Jews themselves had spoiled the Egyptians at their exodus from Egypt. This was a harbinger of their expulsion, which by God's will soon followed . . .

At this time a great multitude of Jews had been dwelling in France for a long time past, for they had flocked there from diverse parts of the world, because peace abode among the French, and liberality. The Jews had heard how the kings of the French were prompt to act against their enemies and were very merciful toward their subjects. And therefore their elders and men wise in the law of Moses, who were called by the Jews *didascali*, made resolve to come to Paris.

When they had made a long sojourn there, they grew so rich that they claimed as their own almost half of the whole city and had Christians in their houses as menservants and maidservants, who were open backsliders from the faith of Jesus Christ and judaized with the Jews. This was contrary to the decree of God and the law of the Church. And whereas the Lord had said by the mouth of Moses in Deuteronomy, "Thou shalt not lend upon usury to thy brother," but "to a stranger," the Jews in their wickedness understood by "stranger" every Christian, and they took from the Christians their money at usury. So heavily burdened in this wise were citizens and soldiers and peasants in the suburbs and in the various towns and villages, that many of them were constrained to part with their possessions. Others were bound under oath in houses of the Jews in Paris, held as if captives in prison.

The most Christian King Philip heard of these things, and compassion was stirred within him. He took counsel with a certain hermit, Bernard by name, a holy and religious man, who at that time dwelt in the forest of Vincennes, and asked him what he should do. By his advice the king released all Christians of his kingdom from their debts to the Jews and kept a fifth part of the whole amount for himself.

❦

KING PHILIP IV OF FRANCE, 1306

ALMOST EVERY MAJOR EXPULSION *of Jews from areas of medieval Christendom was accompanied by large-scale confiscation. In some instances, expulsions resulted directly from baronial desires for the profits stemming from confiscation, in other cases, profit was simply a useful by-product.*

The specific arrangements of confiscation varied. By and large, governmental concern lay mostly with Jewish real estate and Jewish loans. In the expulsion of

1306, it seems quite clear that the motive was largely economic. More important, evidence abounds for concerted efforts on the government's part to realize as fully as possible the anticipated revenues. In the accompanying document, issued shortly after the Jews had been banished, the king orders the disposal of Jewish real estate. He goes to great length to reserve his rights over hidden treasures, fearful that monies sequestered by the Jew might escape his grasp.

PHILIP, by the grace of God king of the French, to the overseers of Jewish affairs in the bailliage of Orléans and to the bailiff of that area, greetings:

We command you and each of you to have all lands, houses, vineyards, and other possessions, which the Jews of the said bailliage held as their own at the time of their arrest, sold at public auction for a just price on our behalf. This should be done as quickly as possible. Moreover, you must expressly warn the purchasers of these goods and possessions that, if treasures or funds should happen to be found in the aforesaid houses, lands, vines, sites, or possessions either now or subsequently, they must disclose them to you or to our men, under threat of the punishment decreed for those finding treasures in our kingdom and not disclosing them to us. We wish those who find these treasures or funds to incur that penalty, unless, as noted, they reveal them to us or to our men without delay. You should cause all this to be announced throughout the entire bailliage without delay.

Enacted at Paris, Thursday after the Assumption of the Blessed Virgin Mary [August 18], 1306 A.D.

KING PHILIP IV OF FRANCE, 1309

KING PHILIP *was concerned both with the sale of Jewish real estate and with the collection of Jewish loans. The latter represented an especially difficult task. Jewish records had been seized in early 1306, but they were often difficult to decipher. Moreover, the Christian debtors were anxious to avoid payment if at all possible. The royal bureaucracy embarked on an intensive campaign to collect Jewish loans, arousing much animosity in the process. In 1309, complaints were lodged by spokesmen for the debtor class and the king responded with the following edict. While stipulating a series of provisions designed to ease the lot of the debtor, the king in no way renounces his rights. In fact, there is evidence that collection efforts continued unabated. King Philip was even willing to bring some Jews back into the kingdom in order to track down the monies owed him.*

PHILIP, by the grace of God king of the French, to the overseers of Jewish affairs in the seneschalsies and bailliages of N., greetings:

1.   Since the complaint of men of this area and of several other areas of this seneschalsy and bailliage have been heard, we command you and each of you that you not collect old Jewish loans of twenty years or more, since it is not plausible that the Jews granted such a delay to their creditors. You are not to collect such loans, unless it is clear that the said Jews demanded or sought out these old debts prior to their expulsion from the kingdom. You are not to collect such loans provided the debtors swear they gave satisfaction for those debts. However, concerning the loans of the Jews who were totally expelled from the seneschalsies of Saintonge and Poitou about nineteen years ago and who, because of their expulsion and banishment and because of the intervening wars were unable to collect the debts which were owed to them in the kingdom, I order that proceedings against these debtors remain in force, if the debts be good and legitimate, and that these loans now be sought out and collected.

2.   Indeed, when a debtor proves the payment of his debt by showing the document recording the debt which had been returned to him by the Jewish creditor prior to the aforesaid expulsion and by his oath, such proof shall suffice, and you must in no way harass a debtor thus proven and sworn.

3.   Also, if in Jewish cartularies which are not suspect and which were written prior to their arrest, you find a note written by the Jews

indicating that the debtor paid his debt, such proof of payment shall suffice.

4.   Also, when the debtor is of good reputation and the size of the debt is moderate, viz., ten pounds or less, one proper witness along with the oath of the debtor shall suffice for proving the payment of such a debt.

5.   Also, you must never collect interest. Rather you must remain satisfied with the principal only.

6.   Also, you must not imprison Christian debtors who are willing to yield goods when debts are clear, and you must not do violence to them nor cause violence to be done.

7.   Also, you must not imprison or cause to be imprisoned those who lodge claims before you or your associates. Rather you must consider their legitimate claims.

You must care to observe all the aforesaid, so that complaint not be brought to us in this regard if you presume to harass the said Christians in contravention of the aforesaid articles and if you do not observe these articles as we have commanded. We order our seneschals in the said seneschalsies that they compel you to desist from harassing the said Christians in this regard in contravention of the aforesaid articles and to observe all the aforesaid, for the aforesaid reasons.

Enacted in Paris, on January 11, 1309 A.D.

KING ROBERT OF FRANCE, 1007

AS WAS THE CASE WITH CONFISCATION, *overt physical persecution of western-European Jewry stemmed from a variety of motives. One of the earliest recorded persecutions in northern Europe appears to reflect a desire on the part of a number of major rulers to cleanse their realms of heresy and dissidence. Late in the tenth century and early in the eleventh century, the first traces of significant heresy were seen in northern France. Reports of this sectarianism disturbed both ecclesiastical and secular authorities and a program of repression was quickly undertaken. Concern over heresy was transformed into more generalized anxiety over religious dissidence, leading to a questioning of the Jews' rights to live in western Christendom. While the Hebrew source here describes the attack on Jewish life in highly stereotyped terminology taken largely from the biblical book of Esther, a careful comparison with other sources indicates that the assault was in fact based on the charge that "there is one people spread throughout all the provinces, which does not obey us." According to the narrative, although the roots of the assault lay in a conscious royal and baronial decision, once this new stance was announced, it elicited a strong wave of popular animosity and violence against the Jews.*

IT CAME TO PASS in the year 4767 [1007] that the wicked government decreed a forced conversion against the Jews, in the days of Robert, king of France.

The Gentiles murmured and plotted, intending to wipe out, to kill, and to destroy all the Jews in the land. The king and queen then took counsel with his officers and barons within the boundaries of the kingdom. They said to him: "There is one people spread throughout all the provinces, which does not obey us. Its laws and teachings are different from those of all peoples. Now let us go and obliterate them, so that the name of Israel be no longer remembered; for they are a snare before us. Let us announce throughout all your land that whoever does not accede to us, and does not heed our words will die." The king and his officers were in perfect accord and agreed on this plan.

On a certain day the king sent for the Jews who dwelled in his land, and they came before him. He then said to them: "Behold I have sent for you, so that you might reveal your views and not hide anything from me. I took counsel with my officers and servants. My desire is for one unified people. You will be powerful and respected. Turn to our teaching because it is more correct than yours. If you refuse, I shall put you to death by the sword. Now take counsel and answer on this matter."

The Jews took counsel among themselves. They refused to accede, to desecrate the Torah of Moses, and to give up the worship of the Lord. They strengthened their faith in God; in Him they placed their trust. They came before the king and said to him: "Our lord, we shall not accede to you in this matter and deny the Lord. Do with us as seems proper in your eyes." They then extended their necks before the sword in sanctification of the Divine Name and its great unity.

The enemy gathered and killed the pious of the Lord. They spilled their blood like water, giving the Jews over to the sword and confiscating their property. At that time precious women came, holding one another's hands, and said: "Let us go to the river and drown ourselves, so that the name of heaven not be desecrated by us. For the sacred is being trampled in the streets and our precious ones are being given over to the fire. Better death than life." Some fled for their lives. The father did not tarry over his son nor the son over his father, so as not to desecrate the Revered Name. The elderly who lacked the strength to flee the wicked were dragged by their feet through the mud, since they refused to obey.

There was one Jew, Seigneur by name, of the holy ones of the land, wise and discerning. The Gentiles plotted to bring him into their faith. Their faith was despicable in his eyes, and he thus blasphemed their images and ridiculed their idols. Those who heard his words ran him through with their swords and trampled him under the hoofs of their horses.

COUNT HUGH III OF MAINE, 992

OFFICIALLY SANCTIONED *violence against the Jews of western Christendom stemmed less often from concern with religious dissidence than from governmental acceptance of popular slanders or from governmental exploitation of the pervasive popular hostility. A tenth-century Hebrew source from western France shows us an instance of governmental acceptance of popular slander which led to persecution of the Jews.*

The narrative depicts western France as an area of violence and insecurity. The near catastrophe that befell the Jews of Le Mans in one sense derived from special circumstances—a highly unscrupulous ex-Jew and his deliberate plot to incriminate his former coreligionists. In another sense, however, the episode reveals the underlying instability of Jewish life, particularly the willingness of the Christian populace to believe tales of Jewish malevolence and the total reliance of the Jews upon their baronial overlords.

This particular case of governmental violence is perhaps the simplest of all. As far as the Jews who composed this record are concerned, there were no ulterior motives in Count Hugh's behavior; according to the report, the count threatens the Jews because he accepts the slander instigated by the renegade Sehok. When he decides to impose upon them an unusual trial by combat, nothing is left for the Jews but to accede. It should be emphasized that this is, from the Jewish point of view, a story with a happy ending. Although the source breaks off, clearly the opening exultation indicates that somehow the Jewish community was rescued from impending doom. Nonetheless, the near-destruction of the Jewry of Le Mans reveals the dangerous implications of Jewish dependence. When a powerful baron was convinced of Jewish misdeeds, his Jews lay completely at his mercy.

A LETTER written by the Jewish community of Le Mans, a record of the salvation wrought by God, effected for the Jews who preserve His covenant and observe His commandments in the 924th year after the destruction of the Second Temple [992]. This record was written as an everlasting memorial for the Jews, enabling them to tell their descendants, so that they would thus know and appreciate the salvation and power of God, Who did not withhold His loving-kindness from those who truly serve Him. God was merciful to the Jews, providing them a remnant in their dispersion, in order to establish His covenant with Abraham, Isaac, and Jacob.

This then is the content of the full record preserved in this valuable letter:

There arose a wicked shoot, a cunning root, in the city of Blois in France, and his name was Sehok ben Esther Israeli. This man behaved evilly in the sight of the Lord God of Israel, angering Him with his deeds. This Sehok left the Lord's Torah and the law and statutes which He had commanded His servant Moses. Instead he served the Gentiles' god, the idols of the Christians, which neither see nor hear nor eat nor smell. To such gods he clung, serving them and worshiping them. But the Lord our Refuge he no longer acknowledged. He was more fully evil than anyone before him. Subsequently he said to himself: "Let me make a visit to a number of towns; let me investigate a number of communities, different peoples and their gods." He then went forth to towns with Jewish communities. He tricked the Jews, saying: "I am a Hebrew." The Jews had pity upon him and supported him as is their custom, in whatever town he visited. He sinned repeatedly before the Lord; indeed as a result of his plotting and his wickedness the Jews came to hate him. He was an accomplice to robbery and designed snares; he blasphemed and was devious; he despised righteousness. Nonetheless he seemed to prosper. However, finally he was unsuccessful in establishing himself throughout the land, for all who knew and heard his deeds joined together to expel him.

Subsequently he went to the city of Le Mans, a small Jewish community at the edge of France. In this city lived his aunts, one married to a Christian. He visited them and then dwelled with them for some time. He married one of his aunts and became the lord of her household. He then waxed arrogant. His evil tongue did not slacken and his wicked deeds did not cease, until the Lord was angered over the evil which he did—robbing, killing, committing adultery, swearing falsely, and worshiping idolatrously. All this he did and more—perverting justice, stirring up contention, robbing the poor and inferior, burdening the righteous, and aiding the Christian. He was more evil than anyone before him.

Then a quarrel broke out between him and ha-Levi, his neighbor. The wicked one attempted to usurp the latter's property. When Sehok saw that ha-Levi was strong and could not be discomfited by his designs, he became exceedingly disturbed and sought excuses to do him harm.

He then took counsel with twelve Christians from his native city, hiring them to assassinate an innocent man. These killers, armed with swords, then set an ambush for ha-Levi at night, although they bore him no prior grudge. Ha-Levi rose before sunrise, at the time of the morning star, and made his way to the synagogue, as was his daily custom. He did not know that they lay in ambush for him outside his house. As soon as he stepped outside his door, the twelve set upon him and smote him with their swords. He cried out loudly, and the town was aroused by his shouting. Everyone awoke, came, and found him struck by the sword, with his body thrown into the road. They carried him home, while he was yet alive. They asked him, "Who stabbed you?" He told them the names of his attackers.

The assassins were inhabitants of the native city of the persecutor. They were old acquaintances, good friends, his associates. When they fled, they sent messengers to our enemy a number of times, saying: "Thus says so-and-so the assassin—send me the wages agreed upon for killing on your behalf. So much is the sum; so much you must pay. If not, anyone traveling henceforth to Le Mans, carrying books and merchandise, will be attacked and robbed in order to gain our recompense. Why should the city be cut off on your account?" Although the arrogant one was frightened, he was unwilling to pay and gave them no heed. He stopped up his ears so as not to hear and closed his eyes so as not to see. It was God's design to harden his heart. When the assassin heard that he paid no heed, he seized a number of men traveling from the deceased's town. Despite all this, Sehok did not repent of his wicked deeds but continued to sin yet more grievously. He did not abandon his sinful ways or return to God's Torah.

He became a source of trouble for all the Jews and a persecutor. When the elders of the land reproved him, he became their enemy and oppressed them. He was unwilling to heed numerous delegations, refusing even to listen to them. He mocked God's Torah and all of Israel's saintly ones. He wickedly counseled the Christians to attack the Jews, to put those God-fearing ones to destruction, to force them to abandon God's Torah. He suggested burning those Jews, dearer than gold and pure metal; he proposed destroying them totally, without leaving them root or branch. It was not enough for him to assault only the community of Jews in which he dwelt; he wished to destroy, kill, and decimate all the remnant of Israel, from young to old, infants and women, all in one day, with their goods to be despoiled. The rest of his plots are known only to God, Whose covenant he intended to break. A varied band of ruffians attached itself to him.

The cruel oppressor then took counsel and made a waxen image in human form, in order to melt down his soul like wax before a fire. He then came and placed the image in a wooden cabinet in the synagogue, near the pillars, where the Torah was kept. He then went and said to the count: "Do you know what this people has done? They have taken a waxen image made like you and pierce it three times a year to destroy you. Indeed this is what their ancestors did to your deity. Now if you agree, let the matter be investigated. If it be found true, then order that they be destroyed. Their silver and gold will come to your treasury; the spoils will be divided among your servants and the populace. What you have done will be heard by all and they will follow suit. Indeed who is this people that presumes to blaspheme my lord and his faith! Indeed they have always done this. They began to do such evil to the image of your deity. Moreover, they have inscribed letters concerning you and use them to curse your name daily. Now then, let my master go with his servant, and I shall show you in their cabinet this waxen image which they have made. If it is not there, then you may kill me."

When the count heard this, he was enraged and frightened over this matter. He said: "Listen to me. If it turns out as you have said, then I shall consign these Jews to the sword and shall make you second in power in my realm. If not, know that you shall surely die." Sehok responded and said again: "Just as you say, my lord." The count then rose and went with him to the synagogue. When he arrived at the synagogue, on a Sabbath day, the congregation was sitting and singing the songs of King David. The count commanded, and a search was made in the cabinet among the pillars. The waxen image was found in it. This was its appearance: Its hands were on its thighs; there were nails between its knees; and its feet were cut off. When the count saw this, he was outraged and exceedingly angry with the Jews. They, however, knew nothing. Such a thing had never occurred to them, and they were in no way involved in making an image—which in any case the Lord God of Israel despises. It was the oppressor Sehok alone who, with wicked designs, had done this.

The count then said to the Jews: "Listen to me, you sinning people. Why have you done this evil deed, plotting against me?" The entire congregation, aghast, arose as one and answered: "Let our lord not say such a thing. We swear that this evil deed was not our doing. Behold this evil man has sought in his malice to destroy us." Then the evil one responded: "Cease, you wicked people. For your end has come, because of the sins which you have committed, attempting to harm my lord and to plot against him. Now the plot has been discovered. Also the evil letters with which you curse the count—bring them out and reveal your shame.'' They answered: ''Neither the letter nor the image ever occurred to us. God forbid that we make any images, since the Lord our God has commanded us not to do so.'' Sehok then said to them: ''Choose one man and let him do battle against me. If he can smite me and kill me, then you will be innocent. However, if I overcome him and smite him, then your name will be obliterated. For you have sought to destroy my lord and to harm him and his God.'' The count then said: ''Do so quickly. Let your words be tested out as to whether they are true.''

When the Jews heard this, they were very frightened. They said to the count: ''Our lord, do not do this to your servants. For the custom of the Jews is not to do battle, as is the custom of the Gentiles. Behold we have great wealth—silver and gold—take it and do with it as you wish. But do not change our divine laws.'' The count then swore to them as follows: ''Thus may God do to me and thus may He continue to do— you shall go to battle.'' The count was very firm and he forced the Jews to give guarantees that they would come to battle on the appointed day. He also commanded to search for the letters, but they were not found. Those conducting the search took books from some of the Jewish homes on the Sabbath day . . . When they saw that there were no such letters, they returned the books to their owners. Meanwhile the artisan who had prepared the image revealed openly that the oppressor Sehok had ordered him to make it. The Jewish community, cast down before its oppressor, did penitence before God, while the Gentiles took the evil one up to the prince's castle.

On that day the sighing of the Jews grew and their wailing increased. Their hearts melted and the entire community was in consternation. All the Jews said: ''Woe! For the Lord intends to destroy totally the remnant of His people among the nations. Now let all men of understanding and wisdom gather together. Let us pour out our hearts before the Lord in fasting and crying and mourning. Perhaps the Lord God will show favor to the remnant of His people and not destroy them in anger and wrath. For the Lord God is greatly angered by our sins. Who knows— perhaps the Lord God will reconsider and relent from His great anger and we will not perish. For the God of Israel is merciful and kind, relenting in punishment. Who can present before Him proper prayer of supplication? Nothing can help but His great kindness, which He has exhibited bountifully toward us and our ancestors to this very day. In His great mercies He will help us, leaving us a remnant in the land. We for our part must be silent. Let us gather at the synagogue and call forth the community, from small to great.'' On the morrow, all the community gathered early in the synagogue and declared a fast. They put on sackcloth and placed ashes on their head and fasted together, men and children, old and young. For the fear of the Lord had fallen upon them and their anguish was very great.

The voice of the Christian mob swelled up against the Jews. They said: "The time has come to destroy all the Jews and to remove them totally from the land since they have made this waxen image, in addition to the earlier sins which their ancestors have committed for many years. Let the recompense now be made for their wicked deeds and their evil actions. For the days of reckoning have arrived, to destroy them totally from the land." The evil one also exulted, saying: "Behold, at this time tomorrow, I shall come upon them with a bare and cruel arm, against the whole people of Israel." At that point a wicked man, a Christian, tonsured, a cleric, came along and forbade anyone from defending the Jews. He stood before the count and said: "Listen to me, you count and all his men. Be not like your ancestors who did not learn the proper lessons and take vengeance against these people, unfortunate and scattered throughout the earth. Thus these people became a great snare for us and for our ancestors down to this very day. Now they have repeated the sins of their ancestors, making an image of lust to rouse lustful passions. This is what you must do to them—desolation and decimation. You must utterly destroy them from the land, leaving them neither root nor branch. Let us send letters throughout all the distant towns, and let them do likewise to this recalcitrant people, lest they be strengthened and win a reputation and become once more a snare. Heed that which I have said to you and do not leave undone my suggestions."

COUNT THEOBALD OF BLOIS, 1171

DURING THE TWELFTH CENTURY, *in the wake of the hatred and violence stirred up by the First Crusade, damaging anti-Jewish slanders began to circulate throughout western Europe. The kernel of these stereotypes lay in the notion of Jewish malevolence and the Jewish propensity to murder Christians, particularly defenseless and innocent youngsters. In the early instances of such charges, Jewish life was rarely imperiled, and where Jews did suffer, the violence was spontaneous, unsupported by recognized governmental authority. The Blois incident of 1171 was a significant and striking departure.*

The Blois incident was among the least likely to gain governmental backing, as there was never any tangible evidence uncovered of a crime. The whole affair began with an unfortunate meeting at dusk along the banks of the Loire River. A Christian servant's horse bolted at the sight of a freshly slain animal slung over the back of a Jew's horse. Prejudiced by anti-Jewish slanders, the Christian rushed into town and reported having seen a Jew drop a Christian corpse into the rapidly flowing stream. This accusation served the purposes of many in Blois, where an affair between the count and a Jewess had aroused bitter antipathy against the Jews. To this festering hostility was added the inflammatory preaching of a Christian cleric. The result was a monstrous decision on the part of the count of Blois; he decreed a trial by ordeal to decide the guilt or innocence of Blois Jewry. When the Christian witness survived the ordeal, the fate of Blois Jewry was sealed. Over thirty members of the community perished by fire. For the Jews of northern France, it was a shattering blow. On the flimsiest of pretexts, a major baron had signalled his belief in the new slanders, subjecting his Jews to irregular trial and eventually destroying a respected community. It is not surprising that the Jews of northern France should have plunged into a whirlwind of political negotiations in the wake of the catastrophe.

THIS CONCERNS the saintly ones who were burned. It is difficult for the heart to express and the hand to portray the wrath and pain. The people of God cannot contain the anger in its soul. Who can pause to write of this tragedy, without having his heart spill over. Indeed when one hears of it, his ears ring and his spirit departs until he loses consciousness. How much more is this the case for us, afflicted in our hearts. Can a man tell his woes without having his lips tremble; can he write of them without being affected? Yet it is the command of the king and the command of Rabbenu Jacob Tam, and we cannot desist therefrom.

Upon us, the Jewish community of Orléans, has the burden been laid. Behold we groan under it. It is because of our sins and shortcomings that all this has happened. The Lord is sanctified by those closest to Him.

From the time He gave over His people to destruction and set fire to our Temple, holy ones such as these have not been offered up as a sacrifice. These angels of the Lord went up in flame—thirty-one angels, *serafim,* who stand by the Lord. When the oppressor ordered them taken out and burned, his men said: "Let us call them and ask them. Perhaps they will abandon their god." The Jews answered unanimously: "No.

We shall cling to our God, the God of Israel. Him we shall fear with all our hearts and all our souls." The Jews were taken out and the Gentiles watched them closely, perhaps one of them might waver. But the Jews said to one another: "Shall we tremble over this fire? Is not this day for which we were chosen?" Then they said as they went forth: "Take care, lest your heart be seduced. Strengthen yourselves and let us be firm in the fear of our Creator so that our death may serve as atonement for all our sins." Indeed these are the sufferings of the community through which all Israel achieves atonement. For those burned for the sake of the Lord bring offerings for their God and become sanctified. God inhaled this sacred incense on the fourth day of the week, on the twentieth of the month of Sivan in the year 4931 [May 26, 1171]. It is fitting that this day be established as a fast day for all our people. The significance of this fast will exceed that of the feast of Gedaliah b. Ahikam; it is a veritable Day of Atonement.

They were struck and wounded. But the more the enemy tortured them, with wounds and blows, the more these Jews strengthened and steeled their hearts to love the Lord and to remain His sacred ones. Thus they were faithful to the Lord. Woe is us! As the day grew warm, in the morning, the fire was lit. As the flames rose, the Jews sang together; they lifted their voices sweetly. Indeed the Christians came and told us of this, asking: "What is your song that is so sweet? We have never heard such sweetness." For at first the sound was low. But at the end they raised their voices mightily, singing *Aleynu le-shabeah;* at that point the fire blazed forth.

Two *cohanim* were tied to one post. They called out to the servants of the persecutor, Theobald the Wicked, saying: "Behold we are in the midst of the fire, but it does not harm us!" They replied: "Go forth from it." R. Judah b. R. Aaron freed his hands, along with the bonds holding the hands of his friends. They then said: "Let us go forth. If they kill us, we shall die; if they let us live, we shall live." The three of them went forth and the enemy rose against them and smote them mightily. These saintly Jews died there before the Lord, unwilling to utter wickedness. They remained righteous from beginning to end. The Gentiles threw them into the fire and heaped coals upon them—but still their corpses were not burned.

Our townsmen and acquaintances, who were present, told us all these things. But we are not dependent upon them for verification of all these details. For at the time of the burning Baruch b. R. David ha-Cohen was there. With his own eyes he saw and with his own ears heard. Only the burning itself he did not see, lest he be swallowed up by the people gathered there outside the city at the place of the fire. Afterward, when the people calmed down from their wickedness, when the burning ended, he immediately fled and made his way to Orléans.

The reason for the tragedy was as follows. On the fifth day of the week—that accursed day—in the evening, at dusk, R. Isaac b. R. Elazar of Blois went forth and watered his horse in the river. He was carrying fresh hides in his pouch, bringing them from the house of a fur trapper. One of the edges of the hide—which is called "peau"—slipped out and was visible under his cloak. At the same time a servingman came also to water his horse. When he came, the horse of the serving-man saw the whiteness of the hide and jumped back. The servingman was then unable to bring him to the water. The Christian did not call out or say anything until he reached his master. Then he said: "Did you know that I met a certain Jew, dropping in the water the corpse of a youngster. It was dark. My horse fled in fear and carried me off. It would not drink." His master replied: "Be silent! This is the day for which I have hoped. Thus and so has the Jewess planned; thus and so shall I do. As she has harmed me, so shall I harm her."

She was harsh as a rock to her fellow-citizens because of the count's protection. She dealt arrogantly with all who came in contact with her, for the count loved her. She even dealt harshly with the countess and her guardian. When all these saw that she no longer stood with the count as heretofore, her fellow citizens planned to do her evil.

Even though she too was seized, she remained unfettered, for they did not put her in chains. She was, however, restricted to the fortress, along with all the members of the community. Whatever she wished to say she could; only to the count himself was she unable to speak. She remained confident, since she did not believe that the heart of the count had turned against her. For his love for her had been strong for so long—how could it now change?

The count made many plans in order to know what to do. Satan also appeared in their midst—an Augustinian cleric, may his name be blotted out and his memory effaced! He advised bringing the evil servingman who had seen R. Isaac in water, to test him in holy water and to observe. If he would sink, he had not spoken the truth; but if he should float, then he had spoken the truth about the Jews. If this were so, then the count should punish the Jews heavily. They listened to him immediately, and this tragedy transpired as a result of the afore-mentioned cleric.

At the outset the count had begun by discussing money. He com-manded Baruch b. R. David ha-Cohen and R. Isaac b. R. Judah, who had come to talk to him, to speak to the Jews, to ask what they would give. They went and returned the Jews' decision to the count, saying to him: "They will give one hundred pounds. Here is yet another one hundred eighty pounds. That will suffice for you." When the count heard, he was angry and ceased speaking with them. Because of his anger, he did not listen to them. He turned only to the priest and did all that he ordered.

They then brought that unclean one into the water, freeing the guilty and condemning the innocent. They then wickedly burned those most saintly ones, a burning of the soul with the body intact. Even all the Christians testify that these bodies were not burnt. Only those that hated them said that their bodies were burned. It seems that out of their hatred they said this.

Prior to this affliction, the community of Loches reported that it had safely escaped calamity. Only the informer himself was seized. I, Baruch ben R. Meir, will reveal to you what happened. A young lad from Loches desired a girl and asked her hand from her father and her relatives. They replied: "We would sooner drown her than allow a union with you." The lad proceeded deceitfully, betrothing the girl before witnesses. He then came to her father and said: "We have been united against your will." The father responded: "This outrage which you have committed will gain you nothing." Finally, the lad went before the count and slandered these other Jews, and they were arrested. Thank the Lord, these Jews have been released, although the informer has not yet been released. We do not know if, God forbid, this incident had spoiled the Jews' reputation or not.

Those burned at Blois were not accorded burial, as a result of our great sins. But the site of the burning was a low area, and the count ordered that the bodies be covered with dirt and stones. We have heard that the count was angry with those Christians who smote with sticks and staffs those who escaped from the fire and were subsequently killed.

After the completion of our letter, we were reminded of one saintly woman who had been forgotten . . . Fortunate are they, for they were equal to the test.

෨෯෨

KING PHILIP AUGUSTUS OF FRANCE, 1192

IN THE SPRING *of 1192, immediately after his return from the Third Crusade, Philip Augustus led his royal forces over the border into neighboring*

Champagne and destroyed the Jewish community of Bray. A brief Hebrew account of the incident appears to record the legal justification for the attack. According to this source Philip behaved as an aggrieved overlord, determined to avenge the death of a vassal for which the Jews were partially responsible. A Christian report of the same incident presents a remarkably different picture. Philip's biographer Rigord depicts the king's actions as yet another royal response to the Jewish sin of ritualized murder. The monk describes the death of the Christian in Champagne as a case of Jewish reenactment of the crucifixion. The king, Rigord maintains, set forth not as an aggrieved overlord, but rather as "the most Christian king," determined to punish the appalling wickedness of the Jews.

It is likely that neither the Jewish nor the Christian presentation tells the whole story. King Philip Augustus was committed to a policy of expansion and was especially covetous of the lands of Champagne. The absence of Count Henry II on the Crusade and the weak regency of Countess Mary made a move against Champagne particularly appealing. The death of a royal vassal probably provided just the rationale which the king desired, allowing him to initiate a murderous assault on ostensibly acceptable grounds. This incident thus provides us with an instance of governmental exploitation of anti-Jewish animosity for specific political gains.

The Report of Ephraim of Bonn

REMEMBER O LORD what befell us, for we have gone from calamity to calamity. We have become weary, without finding respite.

A wicked Christian killed a Jew in the city of Bray in France. The Jew's relatives came and cried out before the countess, although the murderer was a serf of the king of France, and gave her a bribe to hang this murderer. They hung him on the day of Purim.

The king of France heard this—that wicked king who had previously expelled all the Jews of his land in the year 4846 [1186] and taken all their money—that king steadfast in his wickedness from beginning to end. He came to the city of Bray and commenced to burn the Jews—some of them very wealthy and as important as barons—some of them great rabbis and some of them advanced students. These Jews refused to sully themselves by denying the one Lord and were burned in sanctification of the unity of their Creator.

The lads under the age of thirteen the king commanded to leave alive, that they might flee.

All this I have seen in my days of vanity; my soul has despised this life. Our Creator shall exhibit vengeance on our behalf and shall bring speedily our messiah. Amen. So may it be His will.

The Report of Rigord

WHEN SEVERAL MONTHS HAD ELAPSED, on March 12, 1192, King Philip, resting at Saint-Germain-en-Laye, heard of the ignominious death of a certain Christian perpetrated by the Jews. Feeling compassion for the Christian faith and religion, he suddenly departed, without his associates knowing whence he proceeded. With greatest haste, he quickly reached the town called Bray. When guards had been posted at the gates of that town and when the Jews had been seized, he caused eighty or more of them to be burned. The countess of that town, corrupted by the great gifts of the Jews, had handed over to them a certain Christian whom they falsely designated a thief and a murderer. Moved by old hatred, the Jews led this Christian throughout the entire town, with his hands tied behind his back and crowned with thorns, beating him. Subsequently they hung him from a gibbet, although they had said at the time of the passion of the Lord: "We are not permitted to kill anyone."

❧

KING EDWARD I OF ENGLAND, 1278-79

BECAUSE OF THEIR INVOLVEMENT *with business and finance, the Jews of medieval western Christendom were often accused of tampering with currency. It was only, however, when governmental authorities supported such accusations that serious suffering resulted. During the late 1270s, the English monarchy became concerned with the problem of coin-clipping. In 1276, a series of trials took place, but they left no significant impression. Two years later, however, new judges were appointed and given responsibility for trying accused Jews and Christians, with death as the punishment for those found guilty. The result was a number of hangings of Jews and Christians, with the former predominating. Although the king soon mitigated the harshness of the campaign, the substantial loss of Jewish life and property provides once more an instance of governmental acceptance of popular stereotypes and of financial profit from anti-Jewish violence as well.*

WHEN THE SOLEMNITIES of Christmas had been completed, the lord king established provident and prudent men as justiciars of his kingdom to proceed to judgment with Jews and Christians concerning coin-clipping, so that the guilty might be punished and the innocent freed. They condemned to hanging an innumerable multitude of Jews whom they found guilty of clipping. They punished by similar hanging several Christian perpetrators of the same crime, as well as a few accomplices. When investigations had been made throughout the area, certain moneyers and other suspicious persons, freed of charges, evaded the danger of death—I know not whether justly or unjustly. Since the lord king had made a special designation because of the holiness of the period, the justiciars ceased from the aforesaid judicial clamor throughout all of Lent, resuming it strongly immediately after Easter and hanging an infinite multitude of Jews.

22 GOVERNMENTAL
EXPULSION OF THE JEWS

THE ABBOT OF SAINT EDMUND, 1190

THE CLEAREST INDEX *of the vulnerability of the Jewish position in medieval western Christendom is the widespread phenomenon of expulsion. Marginally accepted by their neighbors, the Jews could settle and flourish only with the active support of their overlords. When this protection was withdrawn, the Jews had no choice but to depart. Never could they claim any kind of inalienable rights of settlement, no matter how long they were residents of a given locale.*

Expulsions took place during the Middle Ages at a variety of levels. There are many local banishments recorded and many more which have been long forgotten. The accompanying selection shows one local expulsion from the late twelfth century. It is interesting that the chronicler sees the banishment as one of the major achievements of Abbot Samson. The basis for the edict is presented in political terms —"the Jews must either be Saint Edmund's men or be expelled from the town." Since these Jews were royal Jews, they were fortunate enough to have their property carefully protected. Such was rarely the case during the upheavals that accompanied banishment.

THE RECOVERY OF THE MANOR of Mildenhall for eleven hundred paltry marks of silver, and the expulsion of the Jews from the town of Saint Edmund, and the foundation of the new hospital of Babwell are all proofs of the abbot's excellence.

The lord abbot petitioned the king that he might have letters for the expulsion of the Jews from the town of Saint Edmund, alleging that everything that is in the town of Saint Edmund or within its liberties belongs of right to Saint Edmund. Therefore the Jews must either be Saint Edmund's men or be expelled from the town. Leave was therefore given him to expel them, but on this condition, that they should keep all their chattels and have the value of their houses and lands as well. And when they had been sent forth and conducted under armed escort to other towns, the abbot ordered that all those who from that time forth should receive Jews or harbor them in the town of Saint Edmund should be solemnly excommunicated in every church and at every altar. Nevertheless, afterward the king's justices ordained that, if Jews came to the abbot's great pleas [court sessions] to exact the money owed them from their debtors, they should under those circumstances have leave to be lodged in the town for two nights and two days, and on the third day should depart in freedom.

KING PHILIP AUGUSTUS OF FRANCE, 1182

FAR MORE DESTRUCTIVE *than the local banishment, from the Jewish point of view, were expulsions that involved significant principalities and large numbers of Jews. One of the earliest and most disturbing of these banishments was from the royal domain of France in 1182. King Philip Augustus was both young and insecure upon the throne. As noted already, he had amassed both wealth and popular commendation by confiscating Jewish wealth, by seizing 20 percent of all Jewish loans, and by annulling the remainder. In 1182, still badly pressed, he expelled the Jews from his domain. Again the young monarch gained direct revenue by retaining for his treasury all Jewish real estate, and at the same time he further ingratiated himself with the masses. Although Jews were allowed to sell their movable goods, these were clearly purchased at a much reduced price—a benefit to the Christian buyers. Jewish synagogues were converted into churches, a move aimed at winning ecclesiastical approbation. The king's success in the latter effort is reflected in the enthusiastic narrative of his clerical biographer.*

IN THE YEAR OF OUR LORD'S INCARNATION 1182, in the month of April, which is called by the Jews Nisan, an edict went forth from the most serene king, Philip Augustus, that all the Jews of his kingdom should be prepared to go forth by the coming Feast of Saint John the Baptist [June 24]. And then the king gave them leave to sell each his movable goods before the time fixed, that is, the Feast of Saint John the Baptist. But their real estate, that is, houses, fields, vineyards, barns, winepresses, and such like, he reserved for himself and his successors, the kings of the French.

When the faithless Jews heard this edict, some of them were born again of water and the Holy Spirit and converted to the Lord, remaining steadfast in the faith of our Lord Jesus Christ. To them the king, out of regard for the Christian religion, restored all their possessions in their entirety and gave them perpetual liberty.

Others were blinded by their ancient error and persisted in their perfidy. They sought to win with gifts and golden promises the great of the land, counts, barons, archbishops, bishops, that through their influence and advice and through the promise of infinite wealth, they might turn the king's mind from his firm intention. But the merciful and compassionate God, Who does not forsake those who put their hope in Him and Who humbles those who glory in their strength . . . so fortified the illustrious king that he could not be moved by prayers nor promises of temporal things . . .

The infidel Jews, perceiving that the great of the land, through whom they had been accustomed easily to bend the king's predecessors to their will, had suffered repulse, and astonished and stupefied by the strength of mind of Philip the king and his constancy in the Lord, exclaimed "Shema Yisrael!" and prepared to sell all their household goods. The time was now at hand when the king had ordered them to leave France altogether, and it could not be in any way prolonged. Then did the Jews sell all their movable possessions in great haste, while their landed property reverted to the crown. Thus the Jews, having sold their goods and taken the price for the expenses of their journey, departed with their wives and children and all their households in the aforesaid year of the Lord 1182, in the month of July, which is called by the Jews Tamuz, in the third year of the reign of King Philip Augustus, and in the seventeenth year of his life . . . So the seventeenth year of the king's life was completed in the month following the expulsion of the Jews, namely in August. For they left in the month of July, as has been said; there thus remained three weeks or twenty-one days to the completion of his seventeenth year.

When the expulsion of the infidel Jews and their dispersal throughout the entire world had been completed, King Philip Augustus, aware of their deeds, in 1183 A.D., at the beginning of the eighteenth year of his life, through the grace of God, finished auspiciously the effort so auspiciously begun. For all the synagogues of the Jews, which are called schools by them and where the Jews, in the name of a false faith, convene daily for the sake of feigned prayer, he ordered cleansed. Against the will of all the princes, he caused those synagogues to be dedicated to God as churches, and he ordered altars to be consecrated in these synagogues in honor of our Lord Jesus Christ and of the blessed Mother of God, Virgin Mary. Indeed he believed piously and properly that where the name of Jesus Christ of Nazareth used to be blasphemed daily, as indicated by Jerome in his commentary on Isaiah, the Lord, Who alone accomplishes great miracles, should be praised by the clergy and by the entire Christian populace.

DUKE JOHN OF BRITTANY, 1239

IN 1236, *there was an extensive popular uprising against the Jews of Brittany, associated with preparations for a new crusading effort. A few years later, the duke of Brittany ordered all the Jews to leave his principality. In this instance, the profit motive does not appear significant. Rather the duke seems to have bowed to popular pressure, particularly directed against Jewish moneylending. He indicates in the edict of expulsion that no Christians are to be prosecuted on charges stemming from the recent attacks on the Jews. All debts owed to the Jews are to be annulled. This expulsion seems the work of a ruler who shared widespread feelings of resentment against the Jews or who exploited these feelings in order to win popular favor.*

TO ALL who may read these letters, John, duke of Brittany, count of Richmont sends greetings:

Know that, at the petition of the bishops, abbots, barons, and vassals of Brittany, and having in mind the good of all of Brittany, we expel all the Jews from Brittany. Neither we nor our heirs shall have them in Brittany at any time in the future, nor shall we tolerate that any of our subjects have them in their lands which are in Brittany. Moreover, all debts due the said Jews from any who live in Brittany, in whatsoever manner and form these are due them, we completely remit and nullify. Lands pledged to the said Jews and all other pledges of movable or real properly shall revert to the debtors or their heirs, except for lands and other pledges which have already been sold to Christians by the judgment of our court. Moreover, no one shall in any manner be accused or summoned for the death of a Jew who has been killed. Moreover, in good faith and as much as in our power lies, we shall ask and urge the lord king of France by his letters to agree to and confirm this order and decree. Moreover, we promise for ourselves and for our father, that no debts at one time contracted in Brittany shall be paid to Jews who live in the lands of our father.

This edict thus decreed we swear to observe in good faith forever. If it ever happens that we act contrary to this decree, the bishops of Brittany may individually and collectively excommunicate us and place under the interdict our lands in their dioceses, notwithstanding any privilege to the contrary obtained or to be obtained. Furthermore, we grant and concede that our heirs, whenever they succeed us, shall, after coming of age, take an oath faithfully to observe this decree as above ordained. The said barons and vassals and whoever else owes fealty to the count of Brittany shall not swear fealty nor do homage to these our heirs until they shall have been properly asked by at least two bishops, or at least two barons in the name of the others, that they should swear to observe it faithfully. When the oath shall have been taken by these heirs, the barons and the others who owe fealty to the count of Brittany shall then swear fealty and do homage to the said heirs, just as they are supposed to do and without delay. Moreover, the bishops, barons, and vassals have sworn and granted that at no time will they hold or permit the holding of Jews in their lands in Brittany.

COUNT CHARLES OF ANJOU AND MAINE, 1289

BY THE END OF THE THIRTEENTH CENTURY, *the Jewish position in western Christendom had become increasingly precarious. Popular resentment had deepened, ecclesiastical animus had intensified, and the Jews themselves were playing a less significant role in the economy. In the last decades of the thirteenth century a number of expulsions occurred as the ruling class either bowed to anti-Jewish pressures or exploited those pressures.*

An important example is provided by the expulsion from Anjou and Maine. The order of expulsion is unusually full and explicit. The count begins by citing evidence of Jewish misdeeds—subversion of Christian faith, voracious moneylending, and seduction of Christian maidens. He concludes that the Jews must be expelled from the two counties. Jews are to leave and are prohibited from returning. Comital officials are ordered to expel any Jews they might find; barons are granted the right to despoil Jews they might chance upon and to drive them out; even commoners are encouraged to seize Jews, despoil them, and bring them before the authorities for expulsion. Emphasizing the losses which he would suffer as a result of this pious action, the count then indicates that the leading men of the county had agreed that he be compensated by a set of taxes. It seems quite probable that the income to be derived from this tax was the critical factor in motivating the count to undertake a program of banishment. Pious rhetoric notwithstanding, this seems another instance of substantive gain derived from expelling the Jews. The technique of an "expulsion tax" levied upon the Christian populace is relatively new; the motive of profit is not.

CHARLES II, by the grace of God king of Jerusalem, prince of Sicily and of Apulia and of Capua, count of Achea and Anjou and Forcalquier: We give notice to all by the contents of the present letter that we have considered the fine words of sacred authority, in which it is warned that a mouse or a viper or a serpent in the lap or a fire in the bosom tend to confer unjust retribution on their hosts. When careful investigation had been made, we readily recognized the condition and situation of the counties of Anjou and Maine, which by divine will are subject to our authority. We have ascertained the state of the aforesaid land and have found that it is subject to many enormities and crimes odious to God and abhorrent to the Christian faith. In many locales of that land, numerous Jews, enemies of the life-giving Cross and of all Christianity, dwelling randomly and publicly among Christians and deviating from the way of truth, subvert perfidiously many of both sexes who are considered adherents of the Christian faith. They seem to subvert all whom they can. They despoil these Christians of their movable and immovable goods by their devious deceits and by the endless abyss of usury, and thus they wickedly force these Christians to beg for alms. What is most horrible to consider, they evilly cohabit with many Christian maidens.

Since it is our responsibility to purge the territories subjected to us of evil men, we, pierced by the arrow of compassion, have consulted about these matters with the reverend father the bishop and with many clerics and with our faithful barons and nobles and with others deserving of trust, sometimes directly and sometimes through our faithful deputies, so that we might have the strength to overcome powerful maladies and to uproot totally the above-examined frauds from those places. Indeed it pleases our majesty, we believe with the assent of God, that we should provide for our aforesaid counties and for those living within the confines of those counties by an expulsion of the aforesaid Jews and of their descendants.

Although we enjoy much temporal profit from the aforesaid Jews, we prefer to provide for the peace of our subjects rather than to fill our coffers with the mammon of iniquity, especially since by the loss of temporal goods spiritual gains are achieved. Therefore, exhibiting zeal for the life-giving Cross, we have, for the honor of God and the peace of the aforesaid areas, expelled and ordered expelled from our aforesaid counties of Anjou and Maine all Jews, male and female, adults and young people, children and infants, of whatever sex or condition they might have been born and raised. We have expelled them from all areas of these counties not only for the present but for all times, both for our time as well as that of our successors upon whom the said counties may happen to devolve.

Thus they are prohibited from residing or living henceforth in the aforesaid places, both those already alive and those yet to be born . . . We shall hold contracts, if they make them, null. Insofar as it pertains to us and relates to our jurisdiction, they shall be prohibited from entering the aforesaid areas or crossing through them. We order all our bailiffs and vicars and officials by the firmest adjuration and under threat of the loss of our grace that, after this letter has been seen, should they find any Jew in any of the aforesaid places, they must seize him and expel him immediately. We grant and extend irrevocable authority to all our barons, knights, judges, and others exercising high and low jurisdiction in the aforesaid counties that, if, after this, they find any remnant of the Jewish sect, of whatever sex or condition, in any areas of the aforesaid counties subject to them, they shall seize him or her or them, shall despoil them utterly, and shall drive them out. We wish and demand, insofar as it pertains to us and to our jurisdiction, that their contracts, drawn up in the said places, shall not henceforth be executed. If a common man or a rustic finds a Jew or a Jewess dwelling in the aforementioned places and lacks jurisdiction or authority, we wish and grant and extend nonetheless authority for seizing the aforesaid Jews at any time in the future, for despoiling them, and for bringing them along with their goods before the local judge. He shall immediately expel these Jews from the said counties, properly beaten without the inflicting of wounds, and shall order and dispose of the said goods with the advice of our official.

In order that the sincerity of our intention show forth more openly and more clearly and lest fraud wickedly be perpetrated on our munificence, we decree and order that the aforesaid expulsion be extended to all Lombards, Cahorsins, and other foreigners who engage in public usury without public contracts and who are properly considered usurers. We expel from the aforesaid places now and forever those persons, both those already living as well as those to be born subsequently. We order that they be expelled in the future both by our successors and by all barons, knights, and nobles of the aforesaid counties, with no other permission required of us or of our heirs. Their goods shall be turned over to the lords of those places. If the lords of those places prove negligent or remiss in this regard, we reserve the confiscation of goods to our authority.

Since, according to the prophetic gift of the Holy Spirit, all, from the most significant to the most important, pursue desire, we fear lest— Holy Spirit forbid!—any of our successors be moved to recall the aforesaid persons because of the lure of wicked mammon. We wish and oblige ourselves and all our successors in those places not to recall any of the aforesaid persons and not to allow the dwelling or settling or advent of the aforesaid Jews, as has been stipulated above in regard to these Jews.

With the assent of our reverend fathers in Christ, Nicholas, bishop of Angers and Durrand, bishop of Nantes, of the chapters of these places, of the chapters of LeMans and Poitiers and Saint Martin of Tours, and of the abbots, Hospitaliers [a crusading order], Templars [also a crusading order], barons, counts, knights, and others worthy of trust who live and dwell within the confines of those counties, it has been conceded to us freely and without duress that we ought to receive from each hearth three shillings once only and from each wage earner six pence once only, as some recompense for the profit which we lose through the aforesaid expulsions. This has been granted according to agreements made between them and our faithful Maurice, lord of Craon, our seneschal and vicar in the aforesaid counties. We note that they do this freely and without duress. We wish that, by this act, no prejudice be generated against them, even if they are commoners, and that no other right be acquired thereby by us or our successors of further seeking or levying hearth taxes beyond those taxes and dues which we have and should have according to the custom of the aforesaid counties.

We oblige ourselves, our heirs, and our successors to return to the bishops, chapters, abbots, Hospitaliers, Templars, their subjects, and our subjects, whoever they might be, all the money which we have from the aforesaid hearth tax and wage-earners tax, if it happen that—God forbid!—we or our successors recall any Jew or Jewess to any of the aforesaid places or consent to the recall, settling, or advent of any of these, whether he engages in usury or not, or consent to the recall, settling, or advent of the Lombards, Cahorsins, or other foreigners, when it is clear to us or our successors that they publicly engage in usury . . . We wish that we and our successors be compelled to observe all this by our superiors, even by financial loss. We agree that, if it should happen that these stipulations be broken by us or our successors, by instituting a recall of the aforesaid persons to any of the aforesaid places, which are all part of our domain, when we or our heirs or our successors or the other aforesaid persons had first been sufficiently warned and reproached, then—God forbid!—the prelates of the area shall burden all our domain with an ecclesiastical interdict and they shall continue with that interdict until proper satisfaction has been made. We agree that none of our superiors shall hear us or our successors or our officials as claimants, so long as the aforesaid persons shall remain in the aforesaid places.

In testimony of this matter we have ordered the present letter to be drawn up and to be strengthened by the appended seal of our majesty.

Given at Angers, 1289 A.D., December 8, in the third indiction, in the fifth year of our reign.

KING EDWARD I OF ENGLAND, 1290

ENGLISH JEWRY *was a late-developing community which always led an unusually tenuous existence. Highly specialized economically, the Jews of England had, for a time, contributed notably to the development of royal power and had enjoyed effective royal protection. By the thirteenth century, this had begun to change.*

Popular clamor grew, and exploitation by a series of revenue-hungry monarchs stripped English Jewry of its economic strength. In 1288, King Edward I expelled the Jews from his continental possessions, profiting handsomely in the process. Two years later, the Jews of England became the first to suffer total expulsion from a kingdom. Once more the motivation was primarily fiscal, although phrased in the rhetoric of pious rationalization. The accompanying edict was enacted following the expulsion. In it, the king explains his banishment of the Jews, noting that all efforts to outlaw usury have failed and that his only recourse is to drive the Jews from the land. This new edict, however, is concerned primarily with the royal revenue to be realized from the expulsion. The debts owed to the departed Jews were taken over by the royal government. While stipulating that no usury is to be collected, the king proclaims firmly that the principal owed to Jews is to be assiduously sought. It is likely that once more the profit motive was uppermost in the royal mind as banishment was contemplated.

❧◆❧

EDWARD, etc., to the treasurer and barons of the Exchequer, greetings: Whereas in our parliament held at Westminster on the quindene of Saint Michael in the third year of our reign [October 13, 1275], we, moved by solicitude for the honor of God and the well-being of the people of our realm, did ordain and decree that no Jew should thenceforth lend to any Christian at usury upon security of lands, rents, or aught else, but that they should live by their own commerce and labor; and whereas the said Jews did thereafter wickedly conspire and contrive a new species of usury more pernicious than the old, which contrivance they have termed *curialitas* [ostensibly a gift but actually a subterfuge for usury], and made use of the specious device to the abasement of our said people on every side, thereby making their last offense twice as heinous as the first; therefore we, in requital of their crimes and for the honor of the Crucified, have banished them from our realm as traitors. We, being minded in nowise to swerve from our former intent, but rather to follow it, do hereby make totally null and void all penalties and usuries and whatsoever else in those kinds may be claimed on account of the Jewry by actions at what time soever arising against any subjects of our realm. Being minded that nothing may in any wise be claimed from the said

Christians on account of the said debts except only the principal sums which they have received from the said Jews, we decree that the said Christians do verify the amount before you by the oath of three true and lawful men, by whom the truth of the matter may the better be known, and thereafter pay the amount to us at such convenient times as may be determined by you. And to that intent we command you that you cause this our grace so benevolently granted to be read, and to be enrolled in the said Exchequer, and to be strictly observed, according to the form above indicated.

Witness myself at King's Clipstone, 5 November, in the 18th year of our reign [1290].

KING FERDINAND AND
QUEEN ISABELLA OF SPAIN, 1492

IT SEEMS FITTING *to conclude this volume with the expulsion of the Jews from Spain, the most stunning of the banishments of the Middle Ages. Although this expulsion occurred late in the Middle Ages when European Jewry had become accustomed to such decrees, it had a startling impact, for it affected the largest, most powerful, and most secure of western Christendom's Jewish communities. While Jewish settlement in England, France, and areas of Germany was prohibited, Spanish Jewry had remained confident of its future, certain that its size, economic diversity, and political power would protect it from the fate of its northern sister communities. The decision to expel the Jews from Spain appalled not only those immediately affected, but Jewry worldwide.*

The accompanying contemporary account emphasizes the grandeur of fifteenth-century Spanish Jewry, its numbers, distinguished academic centers, and powerful political leaders. It indicates intensive Jewish efforts to rescind the decree, the failure of these efforts, and the resultant need for a hurried exodus. In the summer of 1492, a great Jewish center was disbanded and its members spread to the winds, finding refuge in Portugal, North Africa, Italy, and Turkey. If a major theme of this volume has been the fragility of Jewish life in western Christendom, the closing selection highlights that precariousness by depicting the dissolution of medieval Europe's most firmly rooted Jewish community.

AND IN THE YEAR 5252 [1492] the Lord visited the remnant of His people a second time and exiled them in the days of King Ferdinand. After the king had captured the city of Granada from the Ishmaelites, and it had surrendered to him on the 8th of January of the year just mentioned, he ordered the expulsion of all the Jews in all parts of his kingdom —in the kingdoms of Castile, Catalonia, Aragon, Galicia, Majorca, Minorca, the Basque provinces, the islands of Sardinia and Sicily, and the kingdom of Valencia. Even before that the queen had expelled them from the kingdom of Andalusia. The king gave them three months' time to leave. It was announced in public in every city on the first of May, which happened to be the 19th day of the Omer, and the term ended on the day before the 9th of Ab. The number of the exiled was not counted, but, after many inquiries, I found that the most generally accepted estimate is fifty thousand families, or, as others say, fifty-three thousand. They had houses, fields, vineyards, and cattle, and most of them were artisans. At that time there existed many academies in Spain and at the head of the greatest of them were R. Isaac Aboab in Guadalaxara, R. Isaac Bezodo in Leon, R. Jacob Habib in Salamanca. In the last-named city there was a great expert in mathematics, and whenever there was any doubt on mathematical questions in the Christian academy of that city they referred them to him. His name was Abraham Zacuto. At the head of the other academies were R. Isaac Alfrandji in Valladolid, R. Jacob Canisal in Avila di Campos, R. Isaac Giakon in Toledo, after the death of R. Isaac of Leon, who was mourned in all parts of Spain, and his antagonist, R. Isaac Ziyyat—they disagreed on ritual questions —R. Samuel Franco in Fromista, R. Isaac Uziel in Alkendi, R. Simon Sarsa in Segovia, R. Samuel Zarfati in . . .

In the course of the three months' respite granted them, they endeavored to effect an arrangement permitting them to stay on in the country, and they felt confident of success. Their representatives were the rabbi, Don Abraham Senior, the leader of the Spanish congregations, who was attended by a retinue on thirty mules, and R. Meir, the secretary to the king, and Don Isaac Abarbanel, who had fled to Castile from the king of Portugal and then occupied an equally prominent position at the Spanish royal court, the very one who was expelled, went to Naples, and was highly esteemed by the king of Naples. The aforementioned great rabbi, R. Isaac of Leon, used to call this Don Abraham Senior, Sone Or [Hater of Light], because he was a heretic, and the end proved that he was right, as he was converted to Christianity at the age of eighty, he and all his family, and R. Meir with him. Don Abraham had arranged the nuptials between the king and the queen. The queen was the heiress to the throne, and the king one of the Spanish nobility. On account of this Don Abraham was appointed leader of the Jews, but not with their consent. The agreement permitting them to remain in the country on the payment of a large sum of money was almost completed when it was frustrated by the interference of an official, who referred to the story of the Cross. Then the queen gave an answer to the representatives of the Jews, similar to the saying of King Solomon: "The king's heart is in the hand of the Lord, as the rivers of water. He turneth it whithersoever He will." She said furthermore: "Do you believe that this comes upon you from us? The Lord hath put this thing into the heart of the king." Then they saw that there was evil determined against them by the king, and they gave up hope of remaining. But the time had become short, and they had to hasten their exodus from Spain. They sold their houses, their landed estates, and their cattle for very small prices, to save themselves. The king did not allow them to carry silver and gold out of his country, so that they were compelled to exchange their silver and gold for merchandise of cloths and skins and other things.

One hundred and twenty thousand of them went to Portugal, according to a compact which a prominent man, Don Vidal bar Benveniste del Cavalleria, had made with the king of Portugal. They paid one ducat for every soul and the fourth part of all the merchandise they had carried thither; and he allowed them to stay in his country six months. This king acted much worse toward them than the king of Spain. After the six months had elapsed he made slaves of all those that remained in his country and banished seven hundred children to a remote island to settle it. All of them died. Some say that there were double as many. Upon them the scriptural word was fulfilled: "Thy sons and thy daughters shall be given unto another people." He also ordered the congregation of Lisbon, his capital, not to raise their voice in their prayers, that the Lord might not hear their complaining about the violence that was done unto them.

Many of the exiled Spaniards went to Muhammadan countries, to Fez, Tlemcen, and the Berber provinces, under the king of Tunis. Most of the Muslims did not allow them into their cities, and many of them died in the fields from hunger, thirst, and lack of everything. The lions and bears, which are numerous in this country, killed some of them while they lay starving outside of the cities. A Jew in the kingdom of Tlemcen, named Abraham, the viceroy who ruled the kingdom, made part of them come to his kingdom, and he spent a large amount of money to help them. The Jews of northern Africa were very charitable toward them. A part of those went to northern Africa, as they found no rest and no place that would receive them, returned to Spain and became converts, and through them the prophecy of Jeremiah was fulfilled: "He hath spread a net for my feet, he hath turned me back." For, originally, they had all fled for the sake of the unity of God; only a very few had become converts throughout all the boundaries of Spain; they did not spare their fortunes, yea, parents escaped without having regard to their children.

When the edict of expulsion became known in the other countries, vessels came from Genoa to carry away the Jews. The crews of these vessels, too, acted maliciously and meanly toward the Jews, robbed them, and delivered some of them to the famous pirate of that time, who was called the Corsair of Genoa. To those who escaped and arrived at Genoa, the people of the city showed themselves merciless and oppressed and robbed them. The cruelty of their wicked hearts went so far that they took the infants from the mothers' breasts.

Many ships with Jews, especially from Sicily, went to the city of Naples on the coast. The king of this country was friendly to the Jews, received them all, and was merciful toward them, and helped them with money. The Jews that were at Naples supplied them with as much food as they could and sent around to other parts of Italy to collect money to sustain them. The Marranos in this city lent them money on pledges without interest; even the Dominican Brotherhood acted mercifully toward them. But all this was not enough to keep them alive. Some of them died by famine; others sold their children to Christians to sustain their life. Finally, a plague broke out among them and spread to Naples. Very many of them died, so that the living wearied of burying the dead.

Part of the exiled Spaniards went over the sea to Turkey. Some of them were thrown into the sea and drowned, but those who arrived there the king of Turkey received kindly, as they were artisans. He lent them money to settle many of them on an island and gave them fields and estates.

A few of the exiles were dispersed in the countries of Italy, in the city of Ferrara, in the counties of Romagna, le Marche, and Patrimonium, and in Rome.

SUGGESTIONS FOR FURTHER READING

BIBLIOGRAPHIC AIDS

Happily there are two excellent bibliographic essays now available for precisely the areas covered by this volume. These are: Kenneth Stow, "The Church and the Jews: From St. Paul to Paul IV," *Bibliographical Essays in Medieval Jewish Studies* (New York, 1977), pp. 107–65, and Ivan Marcus, "The Jews in Western Europe: Fourth to Sixteenth Century," *ibid.*, pp. 15–105.

Another useful bibliography is that appended by Guido Kisch to his *The Jews in Medieval Germany* (Chicago, 1949), pp. 567–605. This was updated in *idem*, "The Jews in Medieval Germany: A Bibliography of Publications on Their Legal and Social Status: 1949–1969," *Revue des études juives*, vol. CXXX (1970), pp. 271–94.

For the history of medieval English Jewry, the following works can be consulted: Cecil Roth, *Magna Bibliotheca Anglos-Judaica* (London, 1937); Ruth Lehmann, *Nova Bibliotheca Anglo-Judaica* (London, 1961); *idem, Anglo-Jewish Bibliography 1937–1970* (London, 1973).

For Spain see Robert Singerman, *The Jews in Spain and Portugal: A Bibliography* (New York, 1975).

Bibliographic suggestions on specific topics can be gleaned by consulting appropriate items in the *Encyclopedia Judaica*. Another rich source for bibliographic suggestions is the copious footnotes in Salo Baron, *A Social and Religious History of the Jews* (rev. ed.; 16 vols.; New York, 1952–76).

SOURCES

The only general source reader available is Jacob Marcus (ed.), *The Jew in the Medieval World* (Cincinnati, 1938).

A most useful collection of translated documents is provided by Solomon Grayzel, *The Church and the Jews in the XIIIth Century* (rev. ed.; New York, 1966).

A description of Christian polemical writings directed against the Jews is A. Lukyn Wiliams, *Adversus Judaeos* (Cambridge, 1935).

Christian and Jewish polemical texts are provided in Frank Talmage (ed.), *Disputation and Dialogue* (New York, 1975).

There are good sources available in translation for the history of medieval English Jewry. A general collection was compiled by Joseph Jacobs (ed.), *The Jews of Angevin England: Documents and Records* (London, 1893); this collection must, however, be utilized with caution. Better materials include: J. M. Rigg (ed.) *Select Pleas, Starrs, and Other Records from the Exchequer of the Jews, A. D. 1220–1284* (London, 1902); *idem et al.* (eds.), *Calendar of the Plea Rolls of the Exchequer of the Jews* (4 vols.; London, 1905-72); Israel Abrahams *et al.* (eds.), *Starrs and Jewish Charters Preserved in the British Museum* (3 vols.; Cambridge, 1930-2).

Anthologies of translated Jewish literary sources include: Benzion Halper (ed.), *Post-Biblical Hebrew Literature: An Anthology* (2 vols.; Philadelphia, 1921); Abraham Millgram (ed.), *An Anthology of Medieval Jewish Literature* (New York, 1935); Nahum Glatzer (ed.), *The Judaic Tradition* (Boston, 1969).

Translations of the Hebrew First and Second Crusade chronicles are available in Shlomo Eidelberg (trans.), *The Jews and the Crusaders* (Madison, 1977).

Rabbinic responsa are available in Irving Agus (ed.), *Urban Civilization in Pre-Crusade Europe* (2 vols.; New York, 1968). A register of responsa by the important thirteenth-century leader, R. Meir of Rothenberg, can be found in *idem, R. Meir of Rothenberg* (2 vols.; New York, 1947).

Jewish polemical sources are translated in Morris Braude (ed.), *Conscience on Trial* (New York, 1952) and O. R. Rankin (ed.), *Jewish Religious Polemics* (Edinburgh, 1956).

SURVEYS OF MEDIEVAL JEWISH HISTORY

General

The most valuable overview is provided by Salo Baron, *A Social and Religious History of the Jews.*

An important earlier statement by Baron can be found in his "The Jewish Factor in Medieval Civilization," *Proceedings of the American Academy for Jewish Research,* vol. XII (1941-2), pp. 1-48.

James Parkes, *The Jew in the Medieval Community* (London, 1938).

Useful is the section on the Middle Ages in Haim Hillel Ben-Sasson (ed.), *A History of the Jewish People* (Cambridge, Mass., 1976).

There are a number of worthwhile essays related to the Middle Ages in Haim Hillel Ben-Sasson and Samuel Ettinger (eds.), *Jewish Society through the Ages* (New York, 1971).

Again specific items in the *Encyclopedia Judaica* are most helpful.

The Early Period

James Parkes, *The Conflict of the Church and the Synagogue* (London, 1934).

Solomon Katz, *The Jews in the Visigothic and Frankish Kingdoms of Spain and Gaul* (Cambridge, Mass., 1937).

Cecil Roth (ed.), *The Dark Ages: Jews in Christian Europe 711–1096* (New Brunswick, 1966; *World History of the Jewish People*).

Irving Agus, *The Heroic Age of Franco-German Jewry* (New York, 1969).

Bernard Bachrach, *Early Medieval Jewish Policy in Western Europe* (Minneapolis, 1977).

Regional Studies

H.G. Richardson, *The English Jewry under Angevin Kings* (London, 1960).

Cecil Roth, *A History of the Jews in England* (3rd ed.; London, 1964).

Vivian Lipman, "The Anatomy of Medieval Anglo-Jewry," *The Jewish Historical Society of England. Transactions,* vol. XXI (1968), pp. 64–77.

Robert Chazan, *Medieval Jewry in Northern France* (Baltimore, 1973).

Guido Kisch, *The Jews in Medieval Germany.*

Abraham Neuman, *The Jews in Spain* (2 vols.; Philadelphia, 1942).

Yitzhak Baer, *A History of the Jews in Christian Spain,* trans. Louis Schoffman (2 vols.; Philadelphia, 1961–6).

Arthur Zuckerman, *A Jewish Princedom in Feudal France, 768–900* (New York, 1972).

Cecil Roth, *A History of the Jews in Italy* (Philadelphia, 1946).

Local Studies

Vivian Lipman, *The Jews of Medieval Norwich* (London, 1967).

Cecil Roth, *The Jews of Medieval Oxford* (Oxford, 1951).

Aron Freimann and Isidore Kracauer, *Frankfurt* (Philadelphia, 1929).

Max Grunwald, *Vienna* (Philadelphia, 1936).

Raphael Straus, *Regensburg and Augsburg* (Philadelphia, 1939).

Richard Emery, *The Jews of Perpignan in the Thirteenth Century* (New York, 1959).

Cecil Roth, *History of the Jews in Venice* (Philadelphia, 1930).

Hermann Vogelstein, *Rome* (Philadelphia, 1940).

ASPECTS OF MEDIEVAL JEWISH HISTORY

The Church and the Jews

Solomon Grayzel, *The Church and the Jews in the XIIIth Century* (rev. ed.; New York, 1966).

Edward Synan, *The Popes and the Jews in the Middle Ages* (New York, 1965).

Wolfgang Seiferth, *Synagogue and Church in the Middle Ages,* trans. Lee Chadeayne and Paul Gottwald (New York, 1970).

Hans Joachim Schoeps, *The Jewish-Christian Argument,* trans. David Green (New York, 1963).

Louis Newman, *Jewish Influence on Christian Reform Movements* (New York, 1925).

Solomon Grayzel, "The Papal Bull *Sicut Judaeis,*" *Studies and Essays in Honor of Abraham A. Neuman,* ed. Meir Ben-Horin *et al.* (Leiden, 1962), pp. 243–80.

Idem, "The Talmud and the Medieval Papacy," *Essays in Honor of Solomon B. Freehof,* ed. W. Jacob *et al.* (Pittsburgh, 1964), pp. 220–45.

Idem, "Jews and the Ecumenical Councils," *The Seventy-Fifth Anniversary Volume of the Jewish Quarterly Review,* ed. Abraham Neuman and Solomon Zeitlin (Philadelphia, 1967), pp. 283–311.

Solomon Katz, "Pope Gregory the Great and the Jews," *Jewish Quarterly Review* (n.s.), vol. XXIV (1933–4), pp. 113–36.

Hans Liebeschutz, "The Crusading Movement and Its Bearing on the Christian Attitude towards Jewry," *Journal of Jewish Studies,* vol. X (1959), pp. 97–111.

Amos Funkenstein, "Basic Types of Christian Anti-Jewish Polemics in the Later Middle Ages," *Viator,* vol. II (1971), pp. 373–82.

David Berger, "The Attitude of St. Bernard of Clairvaux toward the Jews," *Proceedings of the American Academy for Jewish Research,* vol. XL (1972), pp. 89–108.

Judah Rosenthal, "The Talmud on Trial," *Jewish Quarterly Review* (n.s.), vol. XLVII (1956–7), pp. 58–76 and 145–69.

Yosef Yerushalmi, "The Inquisition and the Jews of France in the Time of Bernard Gui," *Harvard Theological Review,* vol. LXIII (1970), pp. 317–76.

Siegfrid Stein, *Jewish-Christian Disputations in Thirteenth-Century Narbonne* (London, 1969).

Robert Chazan, "Confrontation in the Synagogue of Narbonne: A Christian Sermon and a Jewish Reply," *Harvard Theological Review,* vol. LXVII (1974), pp. 437–57.

Idem, "The Barcelona 'Disputation' of 1263," *Speculum,* vol. LII (1977), pp. 824–42.

The State and the Jews

Salo Baron, " 'Plentitude of Apostolic Power' and Medieval 'Jewish Serfdom,' " *Ancient and Medieval Jewish History,* ed. Leon Feldman (New Brunswick, 1972), pp. 284–307.

Idem, "Medieval Nationalism and Jewish Serfdom," *Studies and Essays in Honor of Abraham A. Neuman,* ed. Meir Ben-Horin *et al.* (Leiden, 1962), pp. 17–48.

Gavin Langmuir, " 'Judei Nostri' and the Beginning of Capetian Legislation," *Traditio,* vol. XVI (1960), pp. 203–69.

Idem, "The Jews and the Archives of Angevin England: Reflections on Medieval Anti-Semitism," *ibid.,* vol. XIX (1963), pp. 183–244.

Guido Kisch, *Jewry Law in Medieval Germany: Laws and Court Decisions concerning Jews* (New York, 1949).

Stephen Haliczer, "The Castilian Urban Patriciate and the Jewish Expulsions of 1480–92," *American Historical Review,* vol. LXXVIII (1973), pp. 35–58.

Anti-Jewish Animus

Léon Poliakov, *The History of Anti-Semitism,* trans. Richard Howard (3 vols.; New York, 1965–75).

Joshua Trachtenberg, *The Devil and the Jews* (New Haven, 1943).

Gavin Langmuir, "Prologomena to Any Present Analysis of Hostility against Jews," *Social Science Information,* vol. XV (1976), pp. 689–727.

Robert Chazan, "The Bray Incident of 1192: *Realpolitik* and Folk Slander," *Proceedings of the American Academy for Jewish Research,* vol. XXXVII (1969), pp. 1–18.

Cecil Roth, "The Medieval Conception of the Jew: A New Interpretation," *Essays and Studies in Memory of Linda R. Miller,* ed. Israel Davidson (New York, 1938), pp. 171–90.

Jewish Responses

Salo Baron, *The Jewish Community* (3 vols.; Philadelphia, 1942).

Louis Finkelstein, *Jewish Self-Government in the Middle Ages* (New York, 1924).

David Shohet, *The Jewish Court in the Middle Ages* (New York, 1931).

Robert Chazan, "The Blois Incident of 1171: A Study in Jewish Intercommunal Organization," *Proceedings of the American Academy for Jewish Research,* vol. XXXVI (1968), pp. 13–31.

Jacob Katz, *Exclusiveness and Tolerance* (Oxford, 1961).

Gerson Cohen, "Esau as Symbol in Early Medieval Thought," *Jewish Medieval and Renaissance Studies,* ed. Alexander Altmann (Cambridge, Mass., 1967), pp. 19–48.

Shalom Spiegel, *The Last Trial,* trans. Judah Goldin (Philadelphia, 1967).

Gerson Cohen, "Messianic Postures of Ashkenazim and Sephardim," *Studies of the Leo Baeck Institute,* ed. Max Kreutzberger (New York, 1967), pp. 115–56.

Cecil Roth, "The Ordinary Jew in the Middle Ages: A Contribution to His History," *Studies and Essays in Honor of Abraham A. Neuman,* ed. Meir Ben-Horin *et al.* (Leiden, 1962), pp. 424–37.

SOURCES

PART ONE: THE FORMAL POSITION OF THE CHURCH

1   The Teachings of Earlier Epochs: Gratian's Decretum

Emil Friedberg (ed.), *Corpus Iuris Canonis* (2 vols.; Leipzig, 1879–81). vol. I, pp. 160–1, 211–2, 489, 1087–9, 1392.

2   Codification of Papal Decrees: Raymond of Penaforte/The Decretales

Friedberg, *Corpus Iuris Canonis,* vol. II, pp. 771–8. The English translation of chapters V, IX, XIII–XVI, and XVIII–XIX is adapted from Solomon Grayzel, *The Church and the Jews in the XIIIth Century* (rev. ed.; New York, 1966), p. 297, #I; pp. 93–5, #5; pp. 115–7, #18; p. 135, #27; p. 309, #X; p. 311, #XI; pp. 191–3, #64; p. 217, #79.

*3   A Legal Synthesis: Raymond of Penaforte/*Summa de Poenitentia et Matrimonio

Raymond of Penaforte, *Summa de Poenitentia et Matrimonio* (Rome, 1603), pp. 32–8.

*4   A Theological Synthesis: Alexander of Hales/*Summa Theologica

Alexander of Hales, *Summa Theologica* (4 vols. in 5; Quaracchi, 1924–48), vol. III, pp. 729–32.

PART TWO: THE CHARTERS OF THE STATE

5   Local Charters

BISHOP RUDIGER OF SPEYER, 1084

The Latin Document: Alfred Hilgard (ed.), *Urkunden zur Geschichte der Stadt Speyer* (Strassburg, 1885), pp. 11–2, #11.

The Hebrew Report: Abraham Habermann (ed.), Sefer Gezerot Ashkenaz ve-Zarfat (Jerusalem, 1945), pp. 59–60.

EMPEROR HENRY IV, 1090

Hilgard, *Urkunden zur Geschichte,* pp. 12–14, #12.

EMPEROR FREDERICK I, 1157

Monumenta Germaniae Historica, Legum Sectio IV (9 vols. in 12; Hanover, 1893–1976), vol. I, pp. 227–9, #163.

KING RICHARD OF ENGLAND, 1190

>Thomas Rymer (ed.), *Foedera* (20 vols.; London, 1704–35), vol. I, p. 51.

KING ALFONSO I OF ARAGON, 1115

>Fritz Baer (ed.), *Die Juden im Christlichen Spanien* (2 vols.; Berlin, 1929–36), vol. I, pp. 920–1, #570.

COUNT RAYMOND BERENGUER IV OF BARCELONA, 1149

>*Ibid.*, pp. 16–7. #28.

KING SANCHO VI OF NAVARRE, 1170

>*Ibid.*, pp. 933–5, #578.

KING JAMES I OF ARAGON, 1239

>*Ibid.*, pp. 93–4, #91.

6   *General Charters*

KING JOHN OF ENGLAND, 1201

>Thomas Duffus Hardy (ed.), *Rotuli Chartarum in Turri Londinensis Asservati* (London, 1837), p. 93.

KING LOUIS X OF FRANCE, 1315

>Eusèbe de Laurière *et al.* (eds.), *Ordonnances des roys de la troisième race* (22 vols.; Paris, 1723–1849), vol. I, pp. 595–7.

DUKE FREDERICK OF AUSTRIA, 1244

>The English translation is taken from Jacob Marcus (ed.), *The Jew in the Medieval World* (Cincinnati, 1938), pp. 28–32.

DUKE BOLESLAV OF GREATER POLAND, 1264

>*Codex Diplomaticus Majoris Poloniae* (5 vols.; Posnan, 1877–1908), vol. I, pp. 563–6, #605.

PART THREE: PROTECTION OF THE JEWS

7   *Ecclesiastical Admonitions against Violence*

POPE ALEXANDER II, 1060S

>J. P. Migne (ed.), *Patrologiae cursus completus, series Latina* (217 vols.; Paris, 1844–55), vol. CXLVI, pp. 1386–7.

BERNARD OF CLAIRVAUX, 1146

>The English translation is taken from Bruno James (trans.), *The Letters of St. Bernard of Clairvaux* (London, 1953), pp. 460–2, #391.

BERNARD OF CLAIRVAUX, 1146

>*Ibid.*, pp. 465–6, #393.

BERNARD OF CLAIRVAUX, 1146

>*The Report of Otto of Freising:* The English translation is taken from Otto of Freising, *The Deeds of Frederick Barbarossa*, trans. Charles Mierow (New York, 1953), pp. 74–5.

>*The Report of Ephraim of Bonn:* Habermann, *Sefer Gezerot*, pp. 115–6.

POPE GREGORY IV, 1236

>*Letter to the bishops of Western France:* The English translation is taken from Grayzel, *The Church and the Jews*, pp. 227–9, #87.

>*Letter to the King of France: Ibid.*, pp. 229–31, #88.

8   Governmental Protection prior to the Outbreak of Violence

EMPEROR HENRY IV, 1096

Habermann, *Sefer Gezerot,* pp. 26–7.

KING LOUIS VII OF FRANCE AND COUNT HENRY II OF CHAMPAGNE, 1171

The Paris Letter: Ibid., p. 145.

The Troyes Letter: Ibid., p. 146.

The Letter of Nathan ben Rabbi Meshullam: Ibid., pp. 145–6.

EMPEROR FREDERICK I, 1188

Ibid., pp. 161–4.

KING JOHN OF ENGLAND, 1203

Thomas Duffus Hardy (ed.), *Rotuli litterarum patentium in Turri Londinensis asservati* (London, 1835), p. 33.

EMPEROR FREDERICK II, 1236

Monumenta Germaniae Historica, Legum Sectio IV, vol. II, pp. 274–5, #204.

KING JAMES II OF ARAGON, 1294

Baer, *Die Juden,* vol. I, pp. 153–4, #138.

KING PETER IV OF ARAGON, 1348-49

The First Letter: Ibid., pp. 324–5, #230.

The Second Letter: Ibid., pp. 327–8, #232.

The Third Letter: Ibid., pp. 333–4, #240.

9   Governmental Intervention during Periods of Violence

THE BISHOP OF SPEYER, 1096

Habermann, *Sefer Gezerot,* pp. 94–5.

THE BISHOP OF WORMS, 1096

Ibid., pp. 95–6.

THE BISHOP OF MAINZ, 1096

The Hebrew Report: Ibid., pp. 97–103.

The Latin Report: The English translation is taken from August Krey (ed.), The First Crusade (Gloucester, 1921), pp. 54–5.

THE SHERIFF OF NORFOLK, 1144

The English translation is taken from August Jessopp and Montague James (ed. and trans.), *The Life and Miracles of St. William of Norwich* (Cambridge, 1896), pp. 26–37.

A FRENCH BARON, 1147

Habermann, *Sefer Gezerot,* p. 121.

THE COUNT OF WINCHESTER, 1190

The English translation is taken from Richard of Devizes, *The Chronicle of Richard of Devizes,* ed. and trans. John Appleby (London, 1963), pp. 64–9.

THE BAILIFF OF GRENADE, 1320

The English translation is taken from Solomon Grayzel, "The Confession of a Medieval Jewish Convert," *Historia Judaica,* vol. XVII (1955), pp. 103–5.

10   *Governmental Reprisals in the Wake of Violence*

    KING STEPHEN OF ENGLAND, 1144

        The English translation is taken from Jessopp and James, *The Life and Miracles,* pp. 97–110.

    KING RICHARD OF ENGLAND, 1189

        The Report of William of Newburgh: The English translation is taken from William of Newburgh, "The History of William of Newburgh," *The Church Historians of England,* trans. Joseph Stevenson (5 vols. in 9; London, 1853–8), vol. IV, part 2, pp. 555–8.

        The Report of Ephraim of Bonn: Habermann, *Sefer Gezerot,* p. 127.

    THE DUKE OF AUSTRIA, 1196

        Ibid., p. 131.

    EMPEROR HENRY VI, 1196

        Ibid., p. 131–2.

    THE MUNICIPALITY OF BOURGES, 1251

        Adolphe Cheruel (ed.), *Normanniae nova chronica* (Caen, 1850), pp. 23–4.

PART FOUR: ECCLESIASTICAL LIMITATION

11   *Church Pressure*

    POPE INNOCENT III TO KING PHILIP AUGUSTUS OF FRANCE, 1205

        The English translation is taken from Grayzel, *The Church and the Jews,* pp. 105–9, #14.

    POPE INNOCENT III TO THE COUNT OF NEVERS, 1205

        Ibid., pp. 127–31, #24.

    POPE ALEXANDER IV TO THE DUKE OF BURGUNDY, 1257

        Isidore Loeb, "Bulles inédites des papes," *Revue des études juives,* vol. I (1880), pp. 116–7.

12   *Governmental Rejection of Church Pressure*

    KING FERDINAND III OF CASTILE, 1219

        The English translation is taken from Grayzel, *The Church and the Jews,* p. 151, #38.

    COUNTESS BLANCHE OF CHAMPAGNE, 1219

        Ibid., pp. 151–3, #39.

    KING PHILIP IV OF FRANCE, 1293

        Gustave Saige, *Les Juifs du Languedoc anterieurement au XIVe siecle* (Paris, 1881), pp. 233–4.

    KING PHILIP IV OF FRANCE, 1302

        De Laurière, *Ordonnances,* vol. I, p. 346.

13   *Governmental Acceptance of Church Initiatives*

    KING PHILIP III OF FRANCE, 1283

        Saige, *Les Juifs du Languedoc,* pp. 212–3.

    KING PHILIP IV OF FRANCE, 1299

        Ibid., pp. 235–6.

KING HENRY III OF ENGLAND, 1253

> The English translation is taken from J. M. Rigg (ed.), *Select Pleas, Starrs, and Other Records from the Exchequer of the Jews, A.D. 1220–1284* (London, 1902), p. xlix.

KING ALFONSO X OF CASTILE, 1260S

> The English translation is taken from Samuel Parsons Scott (trans.), *Las Siete Partidas* (Chicago, 1931), pp. 1433–7.

14 Jewish Usury: Ecclesiastical Views

FOURTH LATERAN COUNCIL, 1215

> The English translation is taken from Grayzel, *The Church and the Jews*, p. 307, #IX.

A JEWISH CRITIQUE, MID-1250S

> *Milḥemet Miẓvah*, ms. Parma 2749, folio 68.

THOMAS AQUINAS, MID-THIRTEENTH CENTURY

> The English translation is taken from J.G. Dawson and A.P. d'Entreves (eds.), *Aquinas, Selected Political Writings*, pp. 85-9.

THE ARCHBISHOP OF NARBONNE AND A JEWISH SPOKESMAN, MID-THIRTEENTH CENTURY

> *Milhemet Mizvah*, folios 32–5.

15 Jewish Usury: Governmental Reactions

KING PHILIP AUGUSTUS OF FRANCE AND COUNTESS BLANCHE OF CHAMPAGNE, 1206

> H.-Francois Delaborde (ed.), *Recueil des actes de Philippe Auguste* (3 vols.; Paris, 1916–66), vol. II, pp. 549–51, #955.

KING PHILIP AUGUSTUS OF FRANCE, 1206-19

> Edmond Martène and Ursin Durand (eds.), *Veterum scriptorum et monumentorum amplissima collectio* (9 vols.; Paris, 1724–33), vol. I, pp. 1181–2.

KING PHILIP AUGUSTUS OF FRANCE, 1219

> De Laurière, *Ordonnances*, vol. I, pp. 35–7.

KING LOUIS VII OF FRANCE, 1223

> Alexandre Teulet *et al.* (eds.) *Layettes du Trésor des Chartes* (5 vols.; Paris, 1863–1909), vol. II, p. 14, #1610.

KING LOUIS IX OF FRANCE, 1230

> *Ibid.*, pp. 192–3, #2083,

KING LOUIS IX OF FRANCE, 1235

> Léopold Delisle, "Recueil des jugements de l'Echiquier de Normandie," *Notices et extraits des manuscrits de la Bibliothèque nationale*, vol. XX, part 2, p. 370, #581.

KING LOUIS OF FRANCE, MID-THIRTEENTH CENTURY

> Martin Bouquet *et al.* (eds.), *Recueil des historiens des Gaules et de la France* (24 vols.; Paris, 1737–1904), vol. XX, p. 34.

A JEWISH COMPLAINT, MID-THIRTEENTH CENTURY

> *Milḥemet Miẓvah*, folios 64–6.

16 *The Attack on the Talmud*

POPE GREGORY IX, 1239

> *Letter to the Archbishops of France:* The English translation is taken from Grayzel, *The Church and the Jews*, p. 241, #96.
>
> *Letter to the King of France: Ibid.,* p. 243, #97.
>
> *Letter to the Dominicans and Franciscans of Paris: Ibid.,* #98.

NICHOLAS DONIN, 1240

> *A Hebrew Report: Vikuah R. Yehiel mi-Pariz* (Thorn, 1873), pp. 1–2.
>
> *A Latin Report:* Isidore Loeb, "La controverse de 1240 sur le Talmud," *Revue des études juives,* vol. III (1881), pp. 55–6.

A JEWISH LAMENT, 1242

> Habermann, *Sefer Gezerot,* pp. 183–5.

POPE INNOCENT IV, 1244

> The English translation is taken from Grayzel, *The Church and the Jews,* pp. 251–3,#104.

POPE INNOCENT IV, 1247

> *Ibid.,* pp. 275–81, #119.

THE PAPAL LEGATE IN FRANCE, 1247-48

> *Ibid.,* pp. 277–8.

THE PAPAL LEGAL IN FRANCE, 1248

> *Ibid.,* p. 279.

PART FIVE: MISSIONIZING AMONG THE JEWS

17 *Traditional Conversionary Literature*

PETER OF BLOIS, LATE TWELFTH CENTURY

> Migne, *Patrologia Latina,* vol. CCVII, pp. 825–35.

A JEWISH MANUAL, MID-THIRTEENTH CENTURY

> Judah Rosenthal (ed.), *Sefer Yosef ha-Mekane* (Jerusalem, 1970), pp. 15, 29, 31, 33, 44–5.

JOSEPH KIMHI, MID-TWELFTH CENTURY

> The English translation is taken from Joseph Kimhi, *The Book of the Covenant,* trans. Frank Talmage (Toronto, 1972), pp. 32–5.

18 *The Forced Sermon*

KING JAMES I OF ARAGON, 1242

> The English translation is taken from Grayzel, *The Church and the Jews,* pp. 255–7, #105.

A DOMINICAN FRIAR, MID-THIRTEENTH CENTURY, 1263

> *Milhemet Mizvah,* folios 17–9.

KING JAMES I OF ARAGON AND RAYMOND OF PENAFORTE

> Chaim Chavel (ed.), *Kitvei R. Moshe b. Nahman* (rev. ed.; 2 vols; Jerusalem, 1971), vol. I, pp. 319–20.

PAUL CHRISTIAN, 1269

> Bibliothèque nationale, fonds Dupuy, vol. DXXXII, folio 79.

PAUL CHRISTIAN, 1269

>A Latin Report: Léopold Delisle, "Notes sur quelques mss. du Musée brittanique," Mémoires de la Société de l'Histoire de Paris, vol. IV (1877), p. 189.

>A Hebrew Report: Adolf Neubauer, "Literary Gleanings VIII," Jewish Quarterly Review (o.s.), vol. V (1892-3), p. 714.

19 The Forced Disputation

PAUL CHRISTIAN, 1263

>A Latin Report: Yitzhak Baer, "The Disputation of R. Yechiel of Paris and of Nachmanides" (Hebrew), Tarbiz, vol. II (1931), pp. 185-7.

>A Hebrew Report: Chavel, Kitvei R. Moshe b. Nahman, vol. II, pp. 302-19.

PART SIX: GOVERNMENTAL PERSECUTION

20 Governmental Confiscation

KING LOUIS IX OF FRANCE, 1234

>De Laurière, Ordonnances, vol. I, pp. 54-5.

KING LOUIS IX OF FRANCE, 1237

>The English translation is taken from Grayzel, The Church and the Jews, pp. 233-5, #90.

KING LOUIS IX OF FRANCE, 1246

>Claude de Vic and Joseph Vaisette, Histoire générale de Languedoc (15 vols.; Toulouse, 1872-92), vol. VIII, p. 1191.

KING LOUIS IX OF FRANCE, 1257-58

>De Laurière, Ordonnances, vol. I, p. 85.

KING PHILIP AUGUSTUS OF FRANCE, 1180

>The English translation is taken from James Harvey Robinson (ed.), Readings in European History (2 vols.; New York, 1904-6), vol. I, pp. 426-7.

KING PHILIP IV OF FRANCE, 1306

>Siméon Luce, "Catalogue des documents du Trésor des Chartes relatifs aux Juifs sous le règne de Philippe le Bel," Revue des études juives, vol. II (1881), p. 42, #XLVI.

KING PHILIP IV OF FRANCE, 1309

>Arthur Beugnot (ed.), Les Olim ou registres des arrets (3 vols in 4; Paris, 1839-48), vol. II, pp. 506-7, #VI.

21 Governmental Attacks

KING ROBERT OF FRANCE, 1007

>Habermann, Sefer Gezerot, pp. 19-20.

COUNT HUGH III OF MAINE, 992

>Ibid., pp. 11-5.

COUNT THEOBALD OF BLOIS, 1171

>Ibid., pp. 142-4.

KING PHILIP AUGUSTUS OF FRANCE, 1192

> *The Report of Ephraim of Bonn: Ibid.,* p. 128.
>
> *The Report of Rigord:* H.-Francois Delaborde (ed.), *Oeuvres de Rigord et de Guillaume le Breton* (2 vols.; Paris, 1882-5), vol. I, pp. 118-9.

KING EDWARD I OF ENGLAND, 1278-79

> Henry Luard (ed.), *Annales Monastici* (5 vols.; London, 1864-9; *Rolls Series),* vol. III, p. 279.

22 *Governmental Expulsion of the Jews*

THE ABBOT OF SAINT EDMUND, 1190

> The English translation is taken from Jocelin of Brakelond, *The Chronicle of Jocelin of Brakelond,* trans. H. E. Butler (London, 1949), pp. 45-6.

KING PHILIP AUGUSTUS OF FRANCE, 1182

> The first part of the translation is taken from Robinson, *Readings in European History,* vol. I, pp. 427-8. The full Latin text can be found in Delaborde, *Oeuvres de Rigord,* vol. I, pp. 27-31.

DUKE JOHN OF BRITTANY, 1239

> The English translation is taken from Grayzel, *The Church and the Jews,* p. 345.

COUNT CHARLES OF ANJOU AND MAINE, 1289

> Pierre Rangeard, *Histoire de l'université d'Angers* (2 vols.; Angers, 1877), vol. II, pp. 183-7.

KING EDWARD I OF ENGLAND, 1290

> The English translation is taken from Rigg, *Select Pleas,* pp. xli-xlii.

KING FERDINAND AND QUEEN ISABELLA OF SPAIN, 1492

> The English translation is taken from Alexander Marx, "The Expulsion of the Jews from Spain," *Jewish Quarterly Review* (o.s.), vol. XX (1908), pp. 253-6.

INDEX

Abraham, viceroy of Tlemcen, 321
Abraham Senior, R., 320-321
Abraham Zacuto, 320
Acre, 119
Aelward Ded, 142-143
Agde, Council of, 24-25
Akiba, R., 270
Alexander of Hales, 43-51
Alexander II, pope, 99-100
Alexander III, pope, 30-31
Alexander IV, pope, 176-177
Alfonso I, king of Aragon, 69-70
Alfonso X, king of Castile, 190-195
Alkendi, 320
Amaury, count of Montfort, 214
Amaury, seneschal of Anjou, 212
Angouleme, bishop of, 109-110
Archembaud of Bourbon, 212, 215
Ashi, R., 270
Augustine, St., 47, 49
Auverne, Council of, 25
Auxerre, bishop of, 175
Avila di Campos, 320

B., abbot of Bonneval, 287
Baldwin, archbishop of Canterbury, 158
Barcelona, 128-131, 258-261, 265-276
Baruch b. David ha-Cohen, 302-303
Baruch b. Meir, 304
Baruch the German, 149-150
Benedict of York, 159
Bernard, 289
Bernard of Clairvaux, St., 100-108, 145
Bernard Saxerius, 149
Blanche, countess of Champagne, 180-181, 205-207
Blanche of Castile, regent of France, 166
Blois, 114, 296, 300-304
Blood Libel accusation, 93, 123-126
Boleslav, duke of Greater Poland, 88-93
Bonet of Agen, 150
Boppard, 163, 165
Bordeaux, archbishop of, 109-110
Bourges, 165-166
Brabant, duchess of, 199-200
Bragayrac, 149
Bray, 305-306
Bribery, 14, 114, 115-117, 118, 143, 164, 175, 299, 304, 311
Brittany, count of, 211
Burgundy, duchess of, 211
Burgundy, duke of, 176

Cagliari, 29
Calatayud, 127
Calixtus, pope, 31
Capestang, 202
Charles II, count of Anjou and Maine, 313-317
Clarebold, 141
Clement III, pope, 27, 31
Cologne, 106
Conversion of Christians to Judaism, 19, 191, 194
Conversion of Jews to Christianity, 7, 8, 19, 25, 30, 38-39, 48-51, 193-194, 256, 311

David b. Meshullam, 60
David of Troyes, 149
Deicide, 3, 123
Dominicans, 181-182, 223-224, 226, 256-257 259, 261-262, 266, 275, 322
Dreux of Mello, 212
Durrand, bishop of Nantes, 316

Eborard, bishop of Norwich, 156
Ecclesiastical vessels as pawns, 68, 78, 172 205-206, 209
Edessa, 100
Edward I, king of England, 306-307, 317-319
Ekron, 119
Elazar b. Judah of Mainz, R., 117-122
Elazar the Small, 120
Eleazar of Norwich, 142, 152-157
Eliezer of Ondes, 150
Emicho, count, 134, 137-141
Enguerrand of Coucy, 212, 215
Épernay, 116
Ephraim of Bonn, R., 107-108, 145-146, 161-165, 305-306
Eugenius III, pope, 31, 100
Expulsion of Jews, 12, 79, 216-217, 280, 290-292, 309-322

Ferdinand III, king of Castile, 179-180, 190
Ferdinand, king of Spain, 319-322
Ferrara, 322
First Crusade, 100, 104, 113-114, 133, 136, 141, 145, 300
Forced conversion, 20-21, 31, 38, 40, 49, 60, 61, 64, 110-111, 149-150, 159, 193, 293-294
Forced debate, 8, 243, 265-276
Forced sermons, 8, 243, 255-263
Franciscans, 181-182, 223-224, 256, 266, 275